Interactional Categorization and Gatekeeping

LANGUAGE, MOBILITY AND INSTITUTIONS

Series Editors: **Celia Roberts**, *King's College London, UK* and **Melissa Moyer**, *Universitat Autònoma de Barcelona, Spain*

This series focuses on language and new ways of looking at the challenges facing institutions as a result of the mobility and connectedness characteristic of present day society. The relevant settings and practices encompass multilingualism, bilingualism and varieties of the majority language and discourse used in institutional settings. The series takes a wide-ranging view of mobility and also adopts a broad understanding of institutions that incorporates less studied sites as well as the social processes connected to issues of power, control and authority in established institutions.

Full details of all the books in this series and of all our other publications can be found on http://www.multilingual-matters.com, or by writing to Multilingual Matters, St Nicholas House, 31-34 High Street, Bristol BS1 2AW, UK.

LANGUAGE, MOBILITY AND INSTITUTIONS: 4

Interactional Categorization and Gatekeeping

Institutional Encounters with Otherness

Louise Tranekjær

MULTILINGUAL MATTERS
Bristol • Buffalo • Toronto

Library of Congress Cataloging in Publication Data
A catalog record for this book is available from the Library of Congress.
Tranekjær, Louise.
Interactional Categorization and Gatekeeping: Institutional Encounters with Otherness/
Louise Tranekjær.
Language, Mobility and Institutions: 4
Includes bibliographical references and index.
1. Categorization (Linguistics) 2. Conversation analysis. 3. Sociolinguistics. 4. Language
acquisition. I. Title.
P128.C37T73 2015
401′.47–dc23 2014047899

British Library Cataloguing in Publication Data
A catalogue entry for this book is available from the British Library.

ISBN-13: 978-1-78309-367-0 (hbk)

Multilingual Matters
UK: St Nicholas House, 31-34 High Street, Bristol BS1 2AW, UK.
USA: UTP, 2250 Military Road, Tonawanda, NY 14150, USA.
Canada: UTP, 5201 Dufferin Street, North York, Ontario M3H 5T8, Canada.

Website: www.multilingual-matters.com
Twitter: Multi_Ling_Mat
Facebook: https://www.facebook.com/multilingualmatters
Blog: www.channelviewpublications.wordpress.com

Front cover: 'Just Noise' 2012 by Mads Gamdrup. Inkjet print mounted on diasec, 50×60cm. What happens if parameters of recognisability are suspended? How do relations between nearness and distance come into being under such condition? The Danish artist Mads Gamdrup explores these questions with the series 'Monochrome Colour Noise'. The colours are created by the same amount of light and graduation of transparency. With the technique 'colour noise' the artist works with a saturation of colour that is out of focus in order to create an intense physiological effect on the viewer. The relation of colours and organic basic forms invites to nearness and yet if approached the effect is dizziness. It is not possible for the eye to find rest on neither form nor colour. The artwork invites the viewer to become out of focus and explore another rhythm of nearness and distance than the one already known to him or her.

The policy of Multilingual Matters/Channel View Publications is to use papers that are natural, renewable and recyclable products, made from wood grown in sustainable forests. In the manufacturing process of our books, and to further support our policy, preference is given to printers that have FSC and PEFC Chain of Custody certification. The FSC and/or PEFC logos will appear on those books where full certification has been granted to the printer concerned.

Typeset by Deanta Global Publishing Services Limited.
Printed and bound in Great Britain by the CPI Group (UK Ltd), Croydon, CR0 4YY.

Contents

Acknowledgements

Many people have contributed to the completion of this book and thanks are due. First and foremost I would like to thank Melissa Moyer and Celia Roberts for their editorial guidance and also Katherine Kappa, whose reading helped me clarify my arguments and ideas in the final stages of the book. Especially thanks to you, Celia, for your support and friendship throughout this challenging and long process. I am sincerely grateful to you and also to Karen Risager for your encouragement with respect to my interdisciplinary and boundary-stretching endeavour, as well as your acknowledgement and appreciation of the project. Your individual capacities and perspectives inspired me to find my own theoretical and methodological bearings, and your guidance helped solidify and clarify my ideas. I would also like to express my gratitude to the research group behind the project Learning and Integration, who initially made all of this possible by securing funding from the Danish Research Council and thereby creating a forum for sharing ideas, views, problems and frustrations. Thank you to Karen Risager, Karen Lund, Michael Svendsen Pedersen, Johannes Wagner, Rineke Brouwer, Gitte Rasmussen, Kristian Mortensen and not least Kirsten Kolstrup for making the journey a social and interactional process of learning. Finally, I would like to thank the people close to me who have become involved and affected by this book and have been supportive and helpful along the way. But above all, thank you Martin for your encouragement, discussions and loving support. You, Alma, Oskar and Astrid continuously remind me of what matters most.

Introduction

Categories, Membership and Non-membership

This book is about the power of social categories in institutional interactions, which is to be understood in two different ways. First of all, the meaning of categories such as *migrant, woman, Dane* and *second-language speaker*, which is established in interaction, has the power to influence not only the interactional development but also the relation and organization of interactants. Secondly, such categories are inherently powerful because they carry with them a range of culturally sedimented expectations about the features, attributes, activities and behaviours of their members and non-members.

More specifically, the book is about how categorizations of migrants in work-related interactions such as internship interviews present a challenge for accessing the labour market and being acknowledged as legitimate and equal participants in work-related settings. This book examines the internship as a *gatekeeping encounter* where the participants negotiate and establish not only the future reality of the candidates but the membership categories that the internship candidates belong to.

Gatekeeping encounters were originally developed as a specific object of study by researchers within the field of interactional sociolinguistics, namely Erickson and Shultz, Gumperz and Roberts (Erickson & Shultz, 1982; Roberts *et al.*, 1992; Gumperz *et al.*, 1979). They used the term to describe institutional, asymmetric settings where differences in language, culture and ethnicity result in discriminatory evaluation processes because of the gatekeepers' implicit favouring of the communicative behaviour of majority rather than minority members. Following from this, most other studies of gatekeeping describe institutional processes of discrimination and exclusion as a result of differences in communicative competence and linguistic, cultural and discursive resources.

While the type of encounter studied in this book can be described as a gatekeeping encounter and the occurrence of gatekeeping processes is a central part of the argument presented, the analytical perspective offered is rather different, and yet it is in no way incompatible with these previous studies. Gatekeeping, in this book, is described as interactional processes in which people establish, negotiate and organize social categories as they make sense of themselves and others. In so doing, categorization processes reproduce particular structures of meaning and ideology that work to confirm unequal power relations and exclusionary practices.

As part of our everyday lives, we continuously meet and interact with people who can be described with a range of different categories such as old, young, attractive, man, executive, lecturer, immigrant, Japanese and so on. As formulated by many theorists within diverse theoretical fields such as Conversation Analysis (Schegloff, 2007), Cultural Studies (Hall, 1997a) and Discursive Psychology (Billig, 1996), social categories or social identities are 'contingent'. They are, in other words, readily available and possible but their meaning and relevance is not given but rather produced and achieved in interaction. Different social categories are thereby made relevant and oriented to as people engage in particular actions and contexts. This obviously does not imply that the meaning of categories is continuously established anew, out of nothing. If that were the case, any form of communication would be impossible. Rather, the establishment and negotiation of what a particular category means – who is considered to be a member and a non-member of that category and what activities, predicates and features of these members are expected and not expected – is made possible by shared structures of meaning and *common sense*, which are established, reproduced and negotiated in social interaction. The study of categorization processes thus reveals not only how people orient to, perform and produce particular categories in particular ways within particular contexts, but also how such particularity is rooted in structures of common sense that set the boundaries for what is recognizable, meaningful and allowed – and what is not. The establishment of categories and the association of oneself or others with categories within a specific context of interaction has potential consequences for how people act and are expected to act within this context. Furthermore, these actions and expectations contribute to the setting up of expectations about actions and behaviours in the future.

While the contingency of categories is a shared point of departure for research within Conversation Analysis, Discursive Psychology, Interactional Sociolinguistics and Cultural Studies, there is great difference in whether and how the contingency of categories as a driving force of interaction is addressed as an object of study in its own right, and the extent to which a more critical perspective on this process is applied or not. Very briefly put, the perspective on gatekeeping offered in this book can be characterized as follows.

On the one hand, it is critical, in the sense that it points to patterns of ideology, processes of exclusion and inclusion and power relations, which is a perspective inspired by Interactional Sociolinguistics, Cultural Studies, and not least by some earlier studies within Discursive Psychology. In other words, from a microanalytical point of departure I explore the patterns of meaning and ideology that are reflected in the categorization practices of sense-making individuals as they interpret, formulate and act within the broader legislative, administrative and organizational context of an internship interview. I argue that such ideologies inform and influence processes of meaning and social organization within and beyond the internship interviews and that they contribute to making the process of integration into the Danish labour market and Danish society as such more or less difficult. The examination of how broader structures of meaning and ideology manifest themselves in the discursive and social practice of an internship interview in this way raises some interesting questions about the problems and benefits of establishing specialized job-counselling programmes and internships for migrants. These questions will be ultimately addressed though not answered in this book.

On the other hand, the book is dedicated to illuminating the micro-dimension of categories and identities as they are made relevant and produced in interaction. This is inspired by Discursive Psychology and Conversation Analysis, and more specifically by a particular strand of research herein called Membership Categorization Analysis (MCA) which is rapidly increasing in strength and scope. Within the field of Conversation Analysis, the term Membership Categorization Analysis is used to describe the study of how people orient towards and establish various categories and the underlying and culturally specific apparatus or 'common-sense' that constitutes the premises of these processes. In other words MCA denotes the study of the interpretative apparatus that people use as a resource to organize and navigate in the interactions that constitute our social reality.

In this way, processes of membership categorization constitute a window to contextually specific understandings of how a given social reality is organized and to the way that this organization projects and prevents certain actions and behaviours. Membership categorization is thereby intimately tied to the processes in which normativities and deviances are established and reproduced. In relation to the pragmatics of language learning, the establishment and negotiation of normativity related to categories such as native versus non-native, second-language speaker versus first-language speaker, become of particular relevance and interest. By using MCA to illuminate processes of gatekeeping in institutional contexts the book not only highlights the potential of MCA for more critical types of research but also points to a new dimension of gatekeeping processes which in fact broadens the scope of the concept as such.

In defining and describing gatekeeping as processes of categorization which, fuelled by ideology and common sense, reveal and reproduce patterns of asymmetric power relations, I am not only illuminating gatekeeping related to differences in nationality, language and religion. I am also suggesting that gatekeeping processes can be considered a possible dimension of any type of interaction where politicized categories and differences of various kinds are oriented to and made relevant by participants. However, that being said, it is important to emphasize that institutional interactions like those traditionally studied as Gatekeeping Encounters, namely institutional interactions such as job interviews, service encounters, medical interactions and so on, are situations where categorization processes have potentially greater consequences than internship interviews for the individuals involved. This is to say that while the type of gatekeeping processes that are defined and illuminated in this book could have taken place in a different institutional or non-institutional context, they are reinforced by the institutionality of the setting and the distribution of roles and rights between the participants. To summarize, the research question that the book addresses is: how are categories, memberships and non-memberships related to nationality, language and religion negotiated in internship interviews with migrant candidates and how is this influenced by and influential to relations of power between the participants.

A Context of Migration, Employment and Diversity

Globalization has made migration a reality and raised issues of marginalization, exclusion, inclusion and integration worldwide. Debates about migration issues often focus on how and whether migrants constitute a burden or a benefit to society and the notion of *integration* is frequently mentioned as one of the main challenges and problems to be addressed.

While the issue of integration is not the subject of this book, it nevertheless presents itself in the data as a politicized and ideological notion that is relevant and salient to the participants and emerges from their words, actions and interpretations. The book shows that being a member of categories such as 'migrant' or 'second-language speaker' involves very specific expectations of particular practices and behaviours that are naturalized through ideologies related to nationality, language and religion. Furthermore, the book inevitably presents a contribution to political, public and academic debates about issues related to integration because it illuminates how employment processes are sites of gatekeeping where political and cultural ideologies play a central role. I will argue that while particular practices, behaviours and skills of migrant applicants may be the source of conflict or trouble in employment processes and the labour market in general, the implicit assumptions about migrants and about their differences related to nationality, language and religion become barriers in themselves. Employment processes are thereby highly driven by notions of not only the ideal employee but also the ideal citizen and the ideal migrant that determine the boundaries for and limits to diversity and difference, which is problematic. A central part of the barriers and obstacles that migrants encounter in the labour market can in this way be said to be the very ideas and expectations of difference between migrants and ethnic Danes.

The notion of integration has for many years now been the object of academic, political and public controversy. Nevertheless it is politically and legislatively established in Denmark that migrants should (and should want to) integrate with Danish culture and society and that employment is a central means to the achievement of this goal. One of the problems frequently discussed is the marginalization of migrants in the labour market and the problem of their dependency on the welfare system as a result thereof. For this reason, employment initiatives for migrants have been considered to not only lead to economic independence from the social security system but also to contribute to the establishment of social relations with the local community and thereby to social cohesion and stability.

In Denmark, employment is officially formulated as one of the three overall goals of Danish policy for the integration of migrants and refugees, along with the goal of education for bilingual children and a commonly shared set of democratic values.[1] It is implied that integration presupposes self-sustenance and an equal participation in and contribution to the Danish labour market. While the assumption that employment naturally leads to integration can certainly be discussed and contested, the overrepresentation of migrants and refugees in unemployment figures cannot. In 2007, nearly 47% of migrants from non-western countries were registered as unemployed compared to around 21% unemployment among people of Danish origin (Danmarks Statistik, 2007),[2] which is the biggest difference registered in Europe. A vast amount of research points to various factors behind this overrepresentation of migrants in unemployment statistics, such as language difficulties, lack of mobility, lack of social networks and institutional discrimination (Hjarnø, 1990; Rezaei, 2005; Schultz-Nielsen, 2002; Hummelgaard et al., 2002; Rosdahl, 2006; Rogstad, 2001; Nekby & Özcan, 2006; Sahin & Schröder, 2007). These studies suggest some of the specific challenges that may contribute to the marginalization of migrants in the labour market. While this book in no way claims to address, let alone explain, the high rate of unemployment among migrants, it provides a tiny piece in this puzzle by highlighting the linguistic and interactional challenges that migrants face in the labour market by representing 'the other' and having to convince employers, employees and job consultants of their ability to 'fit in'. The gatekeeping practices and processes described in this book are in other words related to ideas and ideologies of difference in relation to nationality, language and religion where practical and mundane negotiations about the ability to take on a particular job-function become tied in with negotiations about membership, non-membership and terms of 'fitting in' more generally speaking.

Internships as an Employment Strategy

With respect to the employment processes of migrants (or lack thereof), research has established that in Denmark most born-abroad migrants[3] find jobs through social networks or get jobs that require no formal application procedures (Hjarnø, 1990: 326) while only a few use common strategies of employment such as written applications and regular job interviews. Finally, many migrants use the strategy of becoming self-employed by starting up small businesses within the food or retail industry (Rezaei, 2005). Those that are unable to find employment on their own are placed in various job-counselling programmes by the municipality or the national job service, Arbejdsformidlingen, where they learn to write resumés, receive Danish lessons and professional training and are placed in internships. The internship is an employment strategy, which is legislatively and institutionally supported in the welfare system and the labour market. It is also particularly used to introduce people with particular occupational barriers to the labour market. In the case of migrants, it constitutes a central element of an overall integration strategy. The purpose of the internship is thus to bring the candidate one step closer to an 'ordinary job' related to either their skills, professional background or interest, and perhaps enable them to continue working in the company on regular terms after the internship.

The common internship procedure is that the candidate or the job consultant contacts an institution or a company and sets up an interview for the candidate and the job consultant. This book focuses on such internship interviews with migrant candidates that are carried out as part of the planning and evaluation of the internships and investigates the processes of meaning and social organization that they involve, with an emphasis on the interactional and linguistic mechanisms through which migrants are excluded or *othered*.[4]

In short, the internship interview may be characterized as a decision-making and assessment encounter between an employer, a job consultant and an internship candidate as well as, at times, an employee. During these interviews the participants present themselves and the workplace, and the conditions and tasks of the internships are decided and agreed upon. What is most interesting about these interviews in relation to other assessment interviews such as job interviews is that the candidates are in fact unlikely to fail since the candidates are unpaid 'free' labour for the employers. Furthermore, they are not competing with other candidates for the internships in question. They are in this sense gatekeeping encounters that seem less 'high-stakes' compared to the encounters traditionally described in studies on gatekeeping. And yet, the internship interview will be shown to involve processes of inclusion and exclusion that are in many ways similar to those occurring in high-stakes encounters. Ultimately what is at stake in the internship interview, as in many other interactions involving migrants, is the success or failure of the candidates in managing their visible otherness by minimizing their differences from the norm. From this perspective, the only difference between the internship interview and other interviews such as the job interview is that the consequences of a potential failure in this management are less clear to the candidate.

While internships are a possible point of entry into the labour market, they provide no guarantee of future employment or economic security. And yet for the migrant the internship presents an opportunity and a point of access and the stakes of 'passing' are therefore high. The intern can thereby gain professional experience and training, a network and insight into application and recruitment procedures. In this respect, the internship interview may be a rather important and consequential communicative event, at least for the candidate, and in this sense can be likened to the counsellor–student interactions that Erickson and Shultz describe as gatekeeping interactions.

Another factor that contributes to raising the stakes of the internship interview is the fact that in Denmark internships have increasingly become an obligatory element in the 'activity plan' for migrants. An 'activity plan', or *aktiveringsforløb* as it is called in Danish, is a programme designed individually by a social worker in cooperation with the unemployed. The aim is to qualify, prepare and aid the citizen in entering the labour market. Apart from an internship, the plan may include various courses such as computer, driving and hygiene courses, language training, job counselling and visits to different workplaces etc. This means that the internship and the internship interview, apart from being a possible step towards ordinary employment, is an obligatory part of an activity plan that the migrant is required to follow in order to receive welfare. In this way, the internship is a last resort and an alternative to the less favourable situation of getting no financial support or being forced to accept any job appointed by the municipality – a job that is not necessarily in any way related to the experience, qualifications and wishes of the migrant.

As will be shown in this book, the participants orient to and co-construct the internship interviews as real high-stakes interviews, and there is plenty of implicit and explicit assessment going on with respect to the experiences, knowledge and behaviour of the candidates. To the participants, they are in this sense very 'real' gatekeeping encounters. As will be shown and argued, this assessment involves categorizations related to nationality, language and religion that in themselves have immediate as well as more wide-ranging gatekeeping effects. Gatekeeping is in this sense redefined in this book as the implicit and explicit processes of inclusion and exclusion that are involved in the categorization of the candidates. While the candidates are unlikely to 'fail' the interviews in terms of not being chosen for the internship, the processes of categorization related to nationality, language and religion that they are involved in are very much matters of 'passing' and 'failing' in relation to living up to the normative expectations and demands of a Danish workplace and Danish society in general. The findings of this book in this sense acknowledge and confirm the findings of other gatekeeping studies – namely that inequalities related to cultural and linguistic differences are manifested and reproduced within a variety of institutional encounters. On the other hand, my definition and analysis of gatekeeping processes differs from other types of gatekeeping studies in that I focus on gatekeeping as a manifestation of ideologies of difference and processes of 'otherness' in the negotiation of identities, social categories and naturalized common-sense ideas.

The data which forms the basis of this book consists of 16 internship interviews audiorecorded in Copenhagen from 2004 to 2007. The internship candidates who participated in the interviews were involved in one of four different job-counselling programmes that were all aimed at unemployed adults that were born abroad and spoke Danish as a second language. The duration of the interviews varied approximately between 30 and 90 minutes and they took place at various workplaces where the internships were supposed to take place. The different workplaces were primarily residential homes and kindergartens but also included an orchard, a kitchen which prepares food for the homeless, a school and a company that offers home help services. Besides the internship candidate, other interview participants included an employer at the given workplace and a job consultant involved in the job programme or language programme of the internship candidate. During some interviews, there was also an employee present, who was responsible for the particular type of work that the internship candidate would be doing.

The Purpose and Structure of the Book

The book has three major purposes. First of all it aims to illuminate the challenges that migrants face in gaining access to the labour market and being acknowledged as legitimate and equal participants in work-related settings. Furthermore, it aims to raise critical awareness among academics and practitioners alike about how common-sense assumptions on nationality, language and religion are manifested in institutional encounters between migrants and representatives of a majority society. These then become barriers for communication and social relations.

Second, it provides a different perspective on the types of communicative settings in which diversity is brought into play and made relevant. Such encounters are often studied within the field of intercultural communication, where the emphasis tends to be on how interethnic/cultural differences are brought along and become a source of tension and misunderstanding rather than how differences are brought about and negotiated. This book highlights the latter rather than the former perspective and illuminates how interactants formulate, orient to and negotiate ideas on differences and how these work as resources as well as barriers in the achievement of actions and activities in an institutional speech situation. Many studies of intercultural communication focus on describing how differences in cultural, ethnic and language background lead to miscommunication that results in negative evaluations. Such studies seek to link ethnically determined differences in behavioural patterns with the inferences and, ultimately, evaluations made. This book emphasizes how participants manage to establish meaning and social organization despite linguistic and cultural differences. It shows how negotiations of the competences, experiences and qualifications of the candidates tie in with categorizations related to nationality, language and religion with gatekeeping effects.

More specifically, the book aims to provide insight into the role and effect of categorization practices in institutional encounters involving migrants with Danish as their second language. Institutional encounters such as internship interviews are windows of opportunity for migrants which may give access to material and cultural resources of their new country of residence. Categorization practices are a central part of the way in which we organize meaning and social relations when we interact and communicate with each other. They can be seen as a reflection of the culturally specific common sense that makes this process possible.

Finally, the book shows how the notion of gatekeeping can be introduced and redefined to describe the way that categorization processes involve a hierarchical organization of social categories and social relations in institutional settings, such as the internship interview which presents a barrier and problem for the migrant. A central argument made is that gatekeeping occurs in more settings than those traditionally studied as gatekeeping encounters. In relation to classic gatekeeping studies, the internship interview can be said to represent instances of 'false gatekeeping', since there is no actual selection process taking place but rather an evaluative encounter prior to a somewhat prearranged internship programme. However, as will be shown, there is plenty of gatekeeping going on in these and other institutional encounters, as processes of categorization, inclusion and exclusion tie in with processes of evaluation and unequal power relations. So the book presents an interdisciplinary way of working with the relation between language, culture and identity by combining perspectives from Discursive Psychology, Conversation Analysis, Interactional Sociolinguistics and not least Cultural Studies, which allows for a fuller picture of how local processes of categorization and social organization tie in with broader structures of meaning, ideology and power.

The book comprises eight chapters. Chapter 1 presents the interactional context of the internship interview by first providing a description of the broader context in which the internship interview is embedded and by second presenting an analysis of how the participants establish and orient to the internship interview as a particular communicative event. Chapter 2 introduces the notion of gatekeeping as central to describing the processes of inclusion and exclusion that extend and reinforce the asymmetries related to the particular communicative event. Chapter 3 presents the theoretical and methodological framework of the book, which comprises concepts and analytical perspectives from Discursive Psychology, Conversation Analysis, Interactional Sociolinguistics and Cultural Studies. Furthermore, it presents an analytical toolbox that will be applied in Chapters 4, 5 and 6, which provide an analysis of processes of exclusion and inclusion related to categorizations of nationality, language and religion respectively. Each of these chapters describes how negotiations of roles and rights related to the participation framework tie in with negotiations of broader membership categories and how this process is informed by patterns of meaning and ideology. The analytical findings are concluded in a summary at the end of each analytical chapter. Chapter 7 offers a concluding discussion of the analytical findings in relation to previous studies of gatekeeping and reflections on the analytical and methodological propositions made in the book. Chapter 8 is written primarily for practitioners who find themselves curious about how the results presented can be 'translated' into practical suggestions or a set of 'do's and don'ts'. While this chapter should in no way be read as an interactional recipe for successful communication, it can hopefully provide insights into how to improve interactional practices in institutional encounters involving migrants.

Notes

(1) These goals are formulated on the official website published by the Ministry of Refugees, Migrants and Integration: https://www.nyidanmark.dk/NR/rdonlyres/ 1B8DFA83-01D5-4C53-B800-08B35D149E1C/1625/ny_integrationspolitik.pdf.

(2) Danmarks Statistik (Statistics Denmark) define *migrants* as people who are born abroad and where neither of the parents are Danish citizens and born in Denmark. The figure presented refers to migrants from non-Western countries. *People of Danish origin* are defined regardless of place of birth by having at least one parent who is a Danish citizen and born in Denmark.

(3) I use the term 'born abroad' to signify migrants and refugees who are not born in Denmark but have come here during their adulthood. It is a term used by Roberts and Campbell (2006) in their study of job interviews in Britain.

(4) The research presented in this book was funded by the Danish Research Council for the Humanities (DRCH) as part of a larger research project on Learning and Integration. The overall focus of this project was to gather a large corpus of various forms of data that would illuminate different aspects of linguistic, cultural and social processes of learning among migrants and refugees in Denmark. Nine researchers are involved in this project: Karen Risager, Michael Svendsen Pedersen and Louise Tranekjær from University of Roskilde; Catherine E. Rineke Brouwer, Gitte Rasmussen, Johannes Wagner and Kristian Mortensen from University of Southern Denmark; and finally Karen Lund and Kirsten Lundgaard Kolstrup from University of Aarhus, School of Education. The project gathered audio and video recordings and participant observation data from various language training programmes in the cities of Copenhagen, Roskilde, Odense and Svendborg. Furthermore, a total of eight language learners were interviewed in Danish and in their mother tongue and some of these were equipped with hard-disk recorders that were used to record some of their daily interactions within and outside the language training facilities during the entire four-year period of the project. The researchers within the research project had different theoretical orientations, methodological approaches and positions and used different data. However, there was a shared interest within the group in illuminating processes of cultural and linguistic integration and learning as well as a shared understanding of culture and language as intimately linked with social practice and interaction. For further elaboration of the project see http://edu. au.dk/forskning/omraader/forskningsenheder/interkulturellelaeringsprocesser/ laeringogintegration/. See also Risager, 2008 and forthcoming; Wagner, 2006.

1 The Internship Interview – A Hybrid Communicative Event

The internship interview is a hybrid communicative event (Gumperz & Hymes, 1972; Hymes, 1972) that is shaped by the participants' knowledge and expectations of other similar and related events such as job interviews, counselling sessions and service encounters. It can then be said that the internship interview is not invented anew by the participants but is rather co-produced based on features of other speech situations that are familiar and recognizable within the particular linguistic, social and cultural context. As the participants engage with each other during the internship interview, they each contribute to negotiating and establishing the event, based on their previous knowledge, expectations and experiences with similar interactions or any kind of interactions in general. The internship interview should in this sense be understood as a product of the resources, actions and orientations of the interactants.

Levinson's (1992) notion of *activity type* is useful to highlight the way that the internship interview is continually *brought about* (Sarangi & Roberts, 1999), that is produced and negotiated interactionally as participants employ their individual resources in order to make sense of the event. Levinson establishes the structure of an activity type from within, so to speak, and uses the contextual knowledge which feeds and supports this structure as a background for understanding specific utterances, inferences and activities within the interaction. Characterizing an activity type is hereby not an end in itself, but rather a means to a better understanding of the dispositions and orientations of participants in interaction.

I take the notion of an activity type to refer to a fuzzy category whose focal members are goal-defined, socially constituted, bounded, events with *constraints* on participants, setting, and so on, but above all on the kinds of allowable contributions. Paradigm examples would be teaching, a job interview, a jural interrogation, a football game, a task in a workshop, a dinner party, and so on … It appeals to the intuition that social events come along a gradient formed by two polar types, the totally pre-packaged activity, on the one hand (e.g. Roman Mass) and the largely unscripted event on the other (e.g. a chance meeting on the street). (Levinson, 1992: 69)

The purpose in this chapter is to describe the structure of the internship interview as a communicative event, and the way this structure is shaped by the specific activity, the different episodes that constitute this activity and the specific goals and strategies of the participants in relation to this activity. If we are to make sense of the participants' actions, utterances and interpretations of one another, we need to first examine how the participants interpret and establish their goals and strategies regarding the internship and the internship interview.

The internship interview, as well as the participants' knowledge and past experiences, is fundamentally shaped by and embedded in a social, cultural and institutional context that must be considered if one is to understand what is locally achieved and negotiated (Roberts & Sarangi, 1999: 478). The purpose of such contextualization is to provide a necessary understanding of how a communicative event, such as the internship interview as it is realized and understood by the participants, is made possible by a complex meeting of, on the one hand, locally established meanings and actions and, on the other hand, a broader spectrum of ritualized linguistic, social and cultural practices. As Erickson and Shultz (1982) describe, interactions involve social and cultural organization which is at once ritualized and locally produced:

We have said that the social organisation and the cultural organisation of communication are jointly involved in the conduct of face-to-face interaction. This interaction can be said to be locally produced in the taking of practical action of the moment by the particular people who encounter each other in an immediately local face-to-face situation. It is through the local production that distinctive local nuances of meaning and impression arise. The production is orderly and institutionalized, yet also creative and spontaneous. We assume here that people apply cultural principles in their social operating face-to-face, but that the practical application of these normative standards is not done by people in mechanical ways. (8)

What Erickson and Shultz emphasize here is how people are neither free-floating agents that continually recreate and establish the world around them nor automatized puppets in a web of norms, conventions and ritualized practices. Instead, they are active users of available and established meanings and practices which they contribute to shaping and creating the communicative event. From this perspective, the internship interview is an interactional event which is achieved by reproduction, repetition and replication on the one hand and production, creation and constitution on the other hand. The resources used by the participants for this process of renewal and re-enactment are afforded simultaneously by the specificity of each interaction and the particularity of the internship interview as a certain type of encounter. The cultural and social organization in which the internship interview is embedded must, in other words, be established by looking at practices and meanings within the internship interview and comparing these with the meanings and practices of other similar or related interactions.

The Institutional Context – Employment Strategies and Government Initiatives

The internship interview is embedded in, and a result of, various legislative, structural and administrative matters related to immigration, the labour market, social policies and the political situation in Denmark. As such, it is part of an institutional order (Sarangi & Roberts, 1999: 3) which involves a web of social relations and shared habitual practices related to job counselling.

This web of relations constituting the institutional order may then be said to constitute one aspect of the broader context of the internship interview. Furthermore, it may potentially provide knowledge and awareness of practices for the members of the interaction and thereby potentially also influence the processes of meaning and social organization within the web of relations? Goodwin and Duranti (1994: 8; Sarangi & Roberts, 1999: 25) use the notion of *extrasituational context* to refer to the level of context that involves wider social, political and cultural institutions and discourses, which is the level of context described in this chapter.

The orientations and actions of the participants during the internship interview inevitably reflect this extrasituational context either implicitly or explicitly. However, in order to analyze the microdynamics of a particular interaction, the specialized background knowledge that the participants are in possession of needs to be uncovered. Sarangi and Roberts (1999: 21–23) describe the difference between the interactional and the extrasituational context as frontstage and backstage respectively and argue the need for analyzing both. Frontstage research is the type of research that deals with given institutional encounters in their own right and describes the actions and behaviours of the participants based on interactional analysis. Backstage research, on the other hand, is the type of research that deals with all the actions and meanings 'behind the scenes' before and after the institutional encounter studied. While this book emphasizes what is taking place frontstage, a glance into what goes on 'behind the scenes' of the internship interview is necessary in order to understand the 'dramas' that unfold in the actual 'performance'. In other words, the aim is to provide the reader with an idea of 'the language game' and the goals of 'the players' (Levinson, 1992) before showing sequences from 'the actual matches'.

The Internship – The Rules, the Goals and the Players

Internship, or *virksomhedspraktik* in Danish, has for many years existed in Denmark as an integrated element of various educational programmes that require some form of practical training and experience. As an example, nursing and pedagogy or professions such as chefs, electricians or bakers can be highlighted. However, with the Integration Act ('Integrationsloven') in 1998, *virksomhedspraktik* was introduced as an obligatory work placement for newly arrived migrants and refugees as part of The Introduction Programme ('Introduktionsforløbet'). The Introduction Programme is a three-year integration programme consisting of various forms of activation (*aktivering*) of the migrants or refugees, such as courses in Danish language and culture, specific educational programmes and internships.[1] The declared purpose of the introduction programme is to:

> … ensure that newly arrived migrants are granted the possibility to use their abilities and resources in the prospect of becoming participating and contributing citizens on equal terms with society's other citizens. (*Bekendtgørelse af lov om integration af udlændinge i Danmark (integrationsloven)*, 2006: Chapter 1, § 1, my translation).

A particular logic is implicitly at play behind this strategy of integration – namely that migrants are not currently able to use their abilities and resources and that this is preventing them from becoming equal citizens. The former at least is confirmed by unemployment figures and by research on migrants and the labour market in Denmark. As described by Rezaei (2005), the Danish labour market is increasingly developing into a dual labour market which is made up of a primary labour market, with well-paid, professional jobs carried out by Danish citizens of Danish descent, and a secondary labour market, with poorly paid jobs that require no formal education and carried out by migrants or refugees irrespective of their level of formal education.

The job training programmes constitute a strategy to counter or remedy both this marginalization of migrants in the labour market and not least the negative consequences that it is considered to have for the welfare state. The job training programmes often provide additional language training and thereby become a quicker way of getting migrants and refugees integrated into the secondary as well as the primary labour market. The rationale is that many migrants and refugees have education and experience which is wasted on low income jobs while there are many high income positions with a shortage of applicants.

Since the passing of the Integration Act, internships have become an increasingly common employment strategy for not only migrants but also unemployed citizens in general. The legislative framework around internships has since 1998 been developed and specified in the 2003 Act on Active Employment Measures (*Lov om en aktiv beskæftigelsesindsats*), where it is specified that a contact programme (*kontaktforløb*) should be established between the social worker/job consultant and the citizen. The programme entails individual meetings between the citizen and the social worker or job consultant at regular intervals, with a maximum interval of three months (*Lov om en aktiv beskæftigelsesindsats,* 2003: Section III, Chapter 7). Due to this, the job consultants and the internship candidates figuring in my data were already well acquainted with one another on a mandatory basis. The contact programme also involves deciding on a range of activities and goals for the citizen to undertake, and the meetings take place to ensure that these activities and goals are met. For this reason, it can be said that the role of the job consultant is to both supervise and assist the citizen in their employment pursuits.

Another important clarification in the Act on Active Employment Measures is the legislative framework around the internship, which had thus far only been mentioned in the Danish integration law. In the Integration Act from 1998, internships were formulated as part of the specific duties of foreigners in relation to the *activation* element of the Introduction Programme. In the Act on Active Employment Measures from 2003, however, the internships were then presented as an offer to all persons who either needed to clarify their occupational goals in general or who lacked professional, linguistic or social competences.[2]

What is important to emphasize in this context is that these internships and the internship interviews are not voluntary in the same way as other internships that are part of a career plan or an educational programme chosen by an individual. Even though migrants may have a strong interest in doing the internships and are included as well as consulted with in the planning and decision-making process around the internship interview, the internship itself constitutes an obligation to Danish society which is embedded in an institutional, legislative and administrative context. This creates a particular framework for these internships with regard to, for example, the content, timeframe and purpose, and it sets up particular relations and roles of the parties involved in the internship and the internship interview. The following three sections will illuminate this by describing the situation and position of the job consultants, the employers and the internship candidates respectively.

The job counsellors

The job counsellors figuring in my data are all, except for one, women between 30 and 50. In addition to this, aside from one counsellor who is from Iran, they are all of Danish origin and speak Danish as a mother tongue. The job counselling agencies or services that they worked for (UCI, Væksthuset, Kofoeds Skole and MHTConsult) represented the wide spectrum of public as well as private institutions and organizations that together form the totality of the job services offered in Denmark. Figure 1.1 represents the various job counselling actors, specific employment centres, individual projects and external consultants representing the job-seeking candidates in my data:

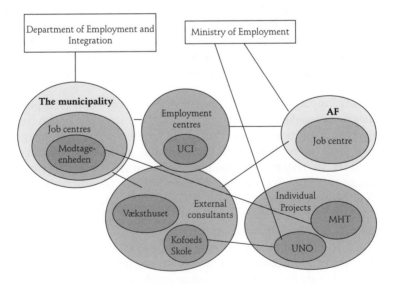

Figure 1.1 Various actors undertaking job counselling

All of the job counselling programmes represented in my study, except for Kofoeds Skole, specifically targeted migrants or 'people with language difficulties'. While these programmes were different in structure, focus and length, the functions of the job counsellors were quite similar. To a varying degree, they all involved: (1) having individual counselling sessions with the candidates, (2) teaching classes on various themes related to job application procedures, the labour market and workplace culture and (3) helping to establish an internship position for the candidate by contacting different employers, setting up an internship interview, taking part in the interview, writing up an internship contract and having a follow-up interview with the candidate and the employer where the internship is evaluated and any possibility for future employment is discussed.

The employers

Another central actor in the internship interview is the employer. On the one hand, the employer is embedded in the explicit and implicit laws and rules of the labour market and the specific workplace, while on the other hand, she or he has to comply with the legislative, administrative and structural requirements of the internship. The employers in my study represent very different types of companies – namely schools, kindergartens, cleaning companies, residential homes, an orchard and an organization for homeless people; some of these were public, while others were privately owned. The majority of the workplaces represented are, however, residential homes and kindergartens, since these areas suffer from a shortage of labour and require a relatively low level of professional training and experience. The specific employers figuring in my data are all, except for two, women between the ages of 40 and 50, and they are all of Danish origin and speak Danish as a mother tongue. In one of the interviews, an employer who participated was identifiable as a second-language speaker of Danish, but her background was not made relevant or clarified.

The employer's role and position is ambiguous with regard to the internship, the internship interview and the other participants. On the one hand, she or he is the person to decide whether to take the intern on, but on the other hand, she or he has none of the usual responsibilities and obligations that go with being an employer, because the intern is only there on a temporary basis. This means that they are not employers in the traditional sense, but rather, or perhaps equally so, benefactors who have agreed to do the intern and the job consultant a favour by agreeing to the internship arrangement. At the same time, however, they are very much taking on the role of employers during the internship interview since they ultimately have to accept the candidates and are to a great extent the ones orchestrating the communicative event.

One of the factors influencing the role of the employer is the legislative guidelines for the duration of an internship, which are outlined in *Bekendtgørelse af lov om en aktiv beskæftigelsesindsats* (Declaration of the Act on Active Employment Measures) (2008: Chapter 11). According to these the employers can have the intern working for them without any financial cost for a minimum of 4 weeks and a maximum of 26 weeks, depending on a variety of circumstances of the candidate's situation related to union membership, financial situation and their abilities and resources. (*Bekendtgørelse af lov om en aktiv beskæftigelsesindsats*, 2007: Chapter 11). The employer is often not aware of these specific rules and it is something which is discussed and clarified during the internship interview.

The internship candidates

The candidates figuring in the data used for this study are mostly Muslim women between the ages of 25 and 40, coming from a range of different non-Western countries with varying educational backgrounds. Aside from the overrepresentation of women in this study, they can be said to be a realistic representation of the demographic of unemployed migrants in Denmark at the time when the data was collected. While they could all be categorized as unemployed with specific challenges in the labour market, compared to the members of the Danish majority, their specific situations differed with respect to migrant status, financial support, length of their period of unemployment, physical and mental health, language skills etc., and their placement in the various job counselling programmes also varied accordingly. In this section, I will outline some of the factors which were influential in determining the situation of all of the candidates in order to provide an understanding of the status and importance of the internship and the internship interview for the internship candidates. First, for the sake of an overview of the migrants involved in my study, Table 1.1 may be useful.

Immigration status

The job counselling programmes that the candidates in this study participated in are all, except for one (Kofoeds Skole), specifically aimed at migrants and refugees. The immigration status of the migrants is, however, not the same among all the participants and the reasons for their referral to the various specific job counselling projects also vary. Some have been granted asylum and have the status of refugees, while others have been granted a temporary or permanent residence permit because they are married

Table 1.1 Overview of 16 candidates figuring in the data

Nr.	Job counselling	Gender	Age	Country of origin	Arrival	Internship area
1	MHT Consult	K	35	Colombia	2001	School
2	Kofoeds Skole	K	45	Bosnia	2000	Kindergarten
3	Jobvækst	M	40	Somalia	1997	Orchard
4	Jobvækst	K	35	Morocco	1989	NGO
5	Jobvækst	K	39	Iran	2000	Nursing home
6	Jobvækst	K	40	Afghanistan	1994	Home Help Company
7	Jobvækst	K	42	Iraq	2004	Kindergarten
8	UCI	K	30	Lebanon	1994	Nursing home
9	UCI	K	25	Turkey	2000	Nursing home
10	UCI	K	28	Bosnia	2000	Nursing home
11	UCI	K	25	Iran	2002	Nursing home
12	UCI	K	30	Turkey	1994	Nursing home
13	UCI	K	30	Somalia	1998	Nursing home
14	UCI	K	33	Somalia	1996	Nursing home
15	UCI	K	30	Iraq	1996	Nursing home
16	UCI	K	25	Bosnia	1999	Nursing home

or related to someone who is a Danish citizen, and some have simply been granted permission to stay (*Bekendtgørelse af lov om integration af udlændinge i Danmark (integrationsloven)*, 2007: Chapter 1, § 9). Ten of the participants have been in Denmark for more than four years and have finished the previously mentioned Introduction Programme. Six of the participants have been in Denmark from anywhere between one and four years at the time of the recording and have not yet finished their three-year Introduction Programme. Consequently, they have been referred to the job counselling programme and the internship as an integrated part of the Introduction Programme (*Bekendtgørelse af Udlændingeloven*, 2008: Chapter 1, § 11).

The immigration status of the participants contributes to raising the stakes of the internship and the internship interview. In order to elaborate on this, further legislative background information is necessary. Irrespective of whether one arrives in Denmark as a refugee or a migrant, it is possible to obtain either a permanent or a temporary residence permit. If one holds a temporary residence permit, a permanent residency can be applied for, provided that a number of conditions have been fulfilled. This is where the internship and job counselling become relevant. Normally, one can only obtain a permanent residence permit after seven years. However, a permanent residence permit can also be obtained after only five or even three years[3] (*Bekendtgørelse af Udlændingeloven*, 2008: Chapter 1, § 11, Stk. 3) which is made possible by getting a permanent job and going off financial support from the government. In any case, for all the participants, a permanent residence permit is conditioned by participating in the Introduction Programme and the Act on Active Employment Measures. On a practical level, this means, among other things, showing up for job counselling and doing an internship if that is part of the job counselling programme.[4]

Thus, the internship interview is not only an important means of access to the labour market: it is also an obligatory part of the Introduction Programme and a necessary step in the direction of obtaining a permanent residence permit. In this sense, the immigration status of the internship candidates is a factor that contributes to raising the stakes of the internship interview and can potentially influence the actions and behaviour of the participants.

Finally, the obligations related to the immigration status of the internship candidate involve language skills and language learning of the country of residence. In the same way that the internship can be a way of meeting the employment requirements, it can be a means for achieving a certain level of language proficiency. In this regard, the language skills of the candidate and the legislative requirements and obligations are, in other words, another factor that potentially contributes to making the internship important to the internship candidate and raises the stakes of the internship interview.

Language skills

According to the Integration Act, all migrants and refugees are required to take Danish lessons within approximately a month of arrival and for a period of no more than three years (*Bekendtgørelse af lov om integration af udlændinge i Danmark (integrationsloven)*, 2007: Chapter 4, § 16). In 2003, the Act on Danish Courses for Adult Aliens (*Lov om danskuddannelse til voksne udlændinge m.fl.*) was passed. As part of the legislation, Danish courses for adult migrants were divided into three separate programmes – Danish education (*Danskuddannelse*) 1, 2 and 3. *Danskuddannelse 1* (*DU1*) is aimed at people who are illiterate and have received little or no formal education; *DU2* is for people with some level of education; and *DU3* is for people with higher education (*Lov om danskuddannelse til voksne udlændinge m.fl.*, 2003: Chapter 2, § 3). The purpose of the Danish education is, first of all, legislatively stated, to contribute to foreigners' Danish language competences and their knowledge on Danish culture and society; second, to enable migrants to become familiar with, and integrate into, the Danish labour market and Danish society.[5] Apart from being an explicit and obligatory element of the Introduction Programme, the passing of Danish test 3 (*Dansk Prøve 3*) has recently become a requirement for being granted Danish citizenship (*Cirkulæreskrivelse om naturalisation*, 2006). In this light, Danish language skills are a principal issue for those internship candidates participating in the Introduction Programme as well as for those potentially aspiring to become Danish citizens. Furthermore, it is a relevant contextual factor for all of the participants to the extent that they have all, except the one who participated in the job counselling program at Kofoeds Skole, been placed in job counselling programmes specifically designed for people with problems beyond unemployment, such as language difficulties, for which doing an internship is a strategy used to overcome such problems. It should be noted, however, that the candidates in this study had all completed at least one year of language training, and many of them had passed either Danish test 2 or 3 or were at an advanced level in their Danish programmes. This raises some interesting questions about the process of referral to the specialized job counselling programmes and about notions of 'language difficulties' or 'problems besides unemployment'. Though the logic of placing people who have passed Danish test 2 and 3 in special job counselling programmes for people with language difficulties or other problems besides unemployment may be challenged, this does not change the fact that adequate language skills were a prevalent part of the broader context of the internship interviews and were continually made relevant by the participants in the actual interactions.

History of employment/unemployment

All of the participants in this study are involved in the various job programmes due to their status of being unemployed, and most of them receive some form of financial support from either the government or a union. Hence, they are complying with the Active Social Policy Act (*Lov om en aktiv socialpolitik*), which means that they are obliged to accept any activation offer from either the municipality, *AF* or the external job consultants in order to continue receiving the financial support (*Bekendtgørelse af lov om en aktiv socialpolitik*, 2005: Chapter 4, § 13). This is in itself a reason and a motivating factor for participating in the job programme and for accepting the internship offered by the job consultants. In addition, for those candidates who are not union members, there is also a financial incentive involved as the welfare benefits they receive are much lower than the amount offered to Danish citizens in comparable social situations. Only Danish citizens, or people who have resided in Denmark for at least seven years in total within the last eight years, qualify for full welfare benefits (*Bekendtgørelse af lov om en aktiv socialpolitik*, 2005: Chapter 4, § 11, stk. 3). Consequently, some of the participants receive a drastically smaller amount of money. The rationale behind this arrangement is that the reduced welfare benefits should increase the motivation for finding a regular job and achieving financial independence. The reduced welfare benefits have been strongly criticized for being inadequate, and critics argue that beneficiaries are unable to sustain a decent standard of living this way. Whether this is in fact conducive to getting a regular job and whether it is a justifiable means to this end is a question that will not be addressed nor answered here, but it is very likely that it increases the pressure on the internship candidates and raises the stakes of the internship interview.

Furthermore, it should be noted that people who are not Danish citizens, EU citizens or a family member of one or the other and who receive financial support for a period longer than six months may be deported unless they have lived here for more than seven years. This rule does not apply to refugees and others covered by the Integration Act, at least not until the three-year introduction period has ended (*Bekendtgørelse af lov om en aktiv socialpolitik*, 2005). After that period, however, the pressure to go off financial support by finding a regular job increases considerably. Hereby the stakes of the internship and the internship interview increase accordingly. Thus, the motivation of candidates for achieving ordinary employment and for doing the internship as a means to this end is possibly not only financial.

Regardless of whether the internship candidates are familiar with or affected by the rules and regulations about their financial situation and their status as unemployed migrants, it seems safe to assume that their situation and status can be associated with a great deal of pressure. In short, these factors may be viewed as an aggregate of motivating factors in relation to succeeding in the interview and getting the internship. This is reflected in the orientations of the candidates towards the interview as a high-stakes evaluative and gatekeeping encounter, which will be further explored and illustrated later in this chapter.

The Speech Situation – Interactionally Constituted and Manifested

The contextual outline provided so far allows us to now engage with a more fine-grained and detailed investigation of the moment-to-moment structuring and organization of the internship interview by the participants. The following investigation will explore how the context of the internship and the internship interview is manifested in the actions and orientations of the participants. In other words, we move from a backstage perspective to a frontstage perspective on the actual doings and sayings of the participants in which the extrasituational context is made relevant and used as a resource for the establishment of roles, categories and hierarchies.

First, I will show how the participants construct the *participation framework* (Goffman, 1981) of the interaction, i.e. how the participants orient to and establish the various participant roles in the interaction. These roles are defined dynamically according to the different forms, functions and stances of participation enacted by the interactants.

Second, I will describe the internship interview using Hymes's concept of the *speech situation*, which involves looking at the way the participants define and establish the setting of the various interviews through their orientations towards specific goals and strategies.

Finally, I will look at the various *speech events* that constitute the hybridity of the internship interview as a communicative event. This involves characterizing the interactions in relation to certain institutionalized and recognizable types of interactions or culturally familiar *institutional events*, the organizational traits of which can be seen to influence the structure and organization of the internship interview.

The participation framework

Erving Goffman employs the concept of *participation framework* (1981) to criticize and refine the notions of 'speaker' and 'hearer' as the participants in interaction that imply a one-directional and simplistic form of communication. Goffman argues that these notions are too unsophisticated to capture the various forms, functions and stances of interactional participation. He suggests that the participation status of any member of a social gathering should not be based on preconceived notions but should rather be established through empirically based analysis of specific utterances:

Finally, observe that if one starts with a particular individual in the act of speaking – a cross-sectional instantaneous view – one can describe the role or function of all the several members of the encompassing social gathering from this point of reference (whether they are ratified participants of the talk or not), couching the description in the concepts that have been reviewed. The relation of any one such member to this utterance can be called his 'participation status' relative to it, and that of all the persons in the gathering the 'participation framework' for that moment of speech. (1981: 137)

This notion of participation status and participation framework suggests an interactional context which is fluid and potentially changing with every utterance, leaving the mutual expectations of the other participants susceptible to challenge and redefinition. Goffman elaborates on the notion of participation framework and participation status by extending their application to the broader context of the situation as a whole:

> The same two terms can be employed when the point of reference is shifted from a given particular speaker to something wider: all the activity in the situation itself. The point of all this, of course, is that an utterance does not carve up the world beyond the speaker into precisely two parts, recipients and non-recipients, but rather opens up an array of structurally differentiated possibilities, establishing the participation framework in which the speaker will be guiding his delivery. (1981: 137)

This means that the participation status of the interlocutors in the internship interview can be established by simultaneously looking at, firstly, how specific utterances position the participants in specific ways and make various roles and statuses relevant and, secondly, by considering utterances in relation to the situation as a totality of various activities. In order to describe the participation framework of the internship interview, it is, in other words, not sufficient to merely list them according to specific etic social categories such as 'woman', 'man', 'migrant', or according to identifiers such as names, numbers, letters and so on, since none of these will tell us anything about the activities, roles or statuses at play. On the other hand, it would be equally inaccurate and insufficient to identify the participants by categories such as 'employer', 'intern', 'interviewer' etc., since this would potentially overemphasize and solidify the various functions, roles and statuses being established and negotiated with every turn and action. The participation framework of the internship interviews must thereby be determined through a shift in analytical gaze between the immediate utterances of the participants and the activity as a whole.

During the internship interviews in my data many different participant roles are constructed and oriented to by the participants, but the most central and recurrent ones are those linked to the central activity in the situation – namely, the interviewing of the internship candidate. While these roles are locally established, defined and challenged throughout the interviews, they can be said to be potentially established already as part of the arrangement and set-up of the interview, as well as via the expectations of the participants regarding the purpose of the interaction. In the very beginning of the interviews, there is, in other words, an initial and temporary establishment of the participants with an internship candidate, who is applying for an internship, an employer, who will potentially take on the candidate, and a job consultant, who is in charge of the job counselling programme that the candidate is partaking in. In some of the interviews, there is an additional participant, namely an employee, who works at the company or institution where the candidate has applied. Furthermore, there is a researcher present as an observer in all, except for one, of the interviews.

These roles are then, from the onset of the interview, negotiated, co-constructed and established alongside other categories, functions, roles and statuses in relation to specific utterances and the general activity of the situation. Although the roles and functions of the participants are, as Goffman points out, constantly changing according to the activities and actions of the participants, I have chosen to identify the participants in the transcript according to the initially established roles, namely Internship Candidate (IN), Employer (HO), Job Consultant (CO) and Employee (EM). However, this does not always represent the activities or categories that the participants themselves make relevant and orient to at any given time during the interaction. This may mislead the reader and conceal some of the complexities of the interactions, but unfortunately this is an inevitable side effect of representation. I have attempted to remedy the potential risk of simplification by investigating how the categories are established and given meaning by the participants, and how they are also challenged and substituted throughout the interaction by other categories and roles.

The central purpose of this section is to describe the establishment and organization of the participation framework in relation to the internship interviews. Consequently, the participant statuses and roles linked to the activities related to the actual internship interview will constitute the focal concern. One of the main arguments of this book is that the activities and participant roles related to the internship interview involve other participant categorizations, such as 'second-language speaker', 'Muslim', 'Colombian' etc. Such categories cannot be described as roles since they are broader in scope and cannot be pinned to a specific activity such as doing interviews or making a self-presentation. Rather they are categories that are made relevant in relation to a range of different activities and inform as well as influence the development of the interaction in more subtle ways. Within most academic disciplines that study groups or categories of individuals, such as anthropology, psychology and sociology, such categories are often referred to as identities or social identities, but in this book I employ the term membership categories or social categories instead in order to highlight their properties as interactional constructs and means. The theoretical discussion around them will be discussed further in Chapter 3 and examined analytically in Chapter 5.

A good place to begin an examination of the participation framework is the beginning of the interactions where the participants present themselves through which they construct their role in the interaction and orient to the purpose of the interaction as such. Extract 1 is an example of this:

Extract 1 Welcome

```
13   HO:    Nå men det var jo dejligt det kunne komme så hurtigt i stand
14          well it was great that it could be arranged so quickly
15
16   CO:    ja det gik stærkt lige pludselig
17          yes it went quickly all of a sudden
18
19   HO:    ja
20          yes
21
22   CO:    men sådan er det jo nogen gange
23          but that is the way it is sometimes
24
25   HO:    nå men velkommen til
26          well welcome
27
28   IN:    tak skal du have
29          thank you
30
31   CO:    tak ska du have
32          thank you
33
34   LO:    °tak°
35          °thanks°
36
37   HO:    åh hhh ja hhh jeg hedder Tina Skov og jeg ersekretariatsleder
38          herinde øøhm Paul?
39
40          and hhh yes hhh my name is Tina Skov and I am leader of secretariat
41          in here eehm Paul?
42   (2.1)
43   EM:    ja det er mig der (0.8) står for køkken og madlavning og
44          frivillige og ja den mobile cafe som sådan og alt det der
45          foregår der
46
47          yes it is me who (0.8) is in charge of kitchen and cooking and
48          volunteers and yes the mobile cafe as such and all that
49          goes on there
50          (0.5)
51
52   EM:    og det er jo så der hvor (0.4) du skal være
53          and that is then where (0.4) you will be
54
55   IN:    ja hehe
56          yes hehe
57
58   EM:    være med
59          be with
60
61   IN:    det håber jeg [he he he .hh
62          I hope so      [he he he .hh
63
64                        [ha ha ha .hh
65                        [ha ha ha .hh
66   HO:    Jeg vil lige starte med [at ]fortælle helt kort om Projekt Udenfor
67          I will just begin by    [telling very briefly about Projekt Udenfor
68
```

This extract is a clear example of how the employer (HO) typically takes the role of initiating the interaction by commenting on the circumstances of the arrangement of the interview, hereby the 'nå' (well) in line 13. The person who responds to HO's initial utterance about the interview is the job consultant (CO), who in line 16 recognizes that he is the one who has organized the arrangement. In line 22, he adds to this recognition with the statement *'men sådan er det jo nogen gange'* ('but that is the way it is sometimes'), which brings attention to the fact that this internship interview is not the first one he has arranged and this establishes his role and position as the job consultant. In line 25, HO once again marks the beginning of the interview by a *'nå'* ('well') and welcomes the participants, hereby orienting to and establishing her role as the host and the one in charge of the interview.

The order in which the other participants respond to this welcome indicates their different participatory status regarding the purpose of the interaction and the Employer. First, we have the response from the internship candidate (IN), who places herself as the main recipient of the welcome, followed by CO, who identifies himself as a secondary participant, and finally by LO (the researcher present), who displays a more marginal participatory status by giving a shorter and more quiet response. The employee (EM) does not respond at all, which shows that he does not consider himself to be a recipient of the welcome and aligns his role with that of HO, i.e. with her role as host.

At this early stage in this interaction, the typical distribution of roles found in the introductory interview has been established, namely that there are two people hosting the interaction, HO and EM, and three people there by invite, namely IN, CO and LO, where CO has contributed to organizing the arrangement and LO is merely there to record. In the utterance in line 37, these roles are further elaborated on and defined as HO presents her function as an employer as well as her status as a leader. She then gives the floor to EM by presenting him as a fellow host and simultaneously indicating his subordinate employment status. By doing this, she is once again demonstrating her right to determine the order of speaking.

EM acknowledges this right and responds to her invitation by presenting himself and his area of responsibility. He describes the work he administers and links this to the purpose of the interaction, i.e. the internship, by stating *'og det er jo så der hvor du skal være'* ('and that is where you will be') in line 52. With this he orients to the interaction as being about the future internship of IN, an orientation that is acknowledged and confirmed by IN in line 55, and he establishes his own role as a central participant in the interaction by claiming responsibility and knowledge about the area of work that IN will be doing.

This extract shows a typical participation framework of the introductory internship interviews characterized by the central and dominant role of the workplace representatives – that is, the employers and employees. We can see how HO and EM co-construct their roles as hosts of the interaction, their superior position at the workplace and the responsibility and/or privilege of being the decision-maker that comes with it.

Another central figure in the internship interviews, who also makes claims to the right to define and control the interaction, is the job consultant. Extract 2 is an example of this.

Extract 2 Talk about yourself

```
317   IN:   [(            -       )]
318   CO:   [Ka du ikke prøve] at fortælle lidt om dig selv Selma måske
319         [can you not t-y] to tell a little about yourself Se'ma maybe
320   (0.5)
321   CO:   °Hvad du har lavet før°
322         °what you have done before°
323
324   IN:   ja jeg har haft en øh øøh hvad hedder det jeg har haft eeh arbejde
325         på hotel (.) Merkur og (Hortsmund)
326
327         yes I have had a eh ehh what is i- called I have had eeh job
328         at hotel (.) Merkur and (Hortsmund)
329
330   HO:   ja
331         yes
332
333   IN:   Jeg starter som køkkenmedhjælp ( ) morgenmad fra klokken seks til
334         tolv
335
336         I begin as kitchen help ( ) break-ast from six o'clock to
337         twelve
338
339   HO:   okay
340         okay
```

This extract illustrates one of the common functions and roles of the job consultant, namely, to encourage the internship candidate to participate and contribute.

The job consultant takes the floor in line 318, overlapping with the internship candidate, and asks her to talk a little bit about herself. In line 321, he specifies that he is interested in her previous work experience. He thereby establishes his role as a consultant for IN as well his right as one of the people in control of the development and the content of the interaction. IN acknowledges and legitimizes this position by responding to his encouragement, and HO cooperates in securing the suggested development of the interaction by claiming recipiency to IN's response. In other words, HO acknowledges and displays understanding of the fact that CO is asking for information about IN on behalf of the other participants. In this manner, she has co-constructed his position as an advocate or consultant for IN and an assisting figure for HO and EM in the interaction and the process of getting to know the capabilities of IN and planning the internship.

As shown in this extract, the role of the job consultant is established on the one hand in relation to the employer and the employee, who otherwise construct themselves as the ones hosting and controlling the interaction, and on the other hand in relation to the internship candidate. The candidate is constructed as the other key participant and is, as illustrated above, generally encouraged by the job consultant to participate and contribute. This (Extract 2) and the previous extract (Extract 1) are illustrative examples of how the job consultants in my data establish their role as the representative and advocate of IN, as well as the assistant and support of EM and HO. This manifests itself in the activities and interactional functions that CO undertakes as well as in the distribution and organization of the right to speak. As is particularly evident in Extract 2, the internship interview demands a balancing act between the different responsibilities of the job consultant. On the one hand, job consultants have to stay in the background enough to allow for the interaction and participation of the other participants. On the other hand, they have to simultaneously encourage the internship candidate to contribute and demonstrate availability in relation to the employer and the employee with respect to arranging the internship.

Thus far, the investigation of the participation framework of the internship interview has focused primarily on the roles, positions and activities of the employer, the employee and not least the job consultant. A central element has been to examine the way they negotiate the right to talk, to invite others to talk and to control the topical development of the interaction. Though it would seem fair to presume that the internship candidate would be the most central participant in the internship interview, this is hardly ever the case. The internship candidate is in fact the main topic of discussion rather than the main discussant. As will be explored and shown in more detail later in the book, this distribution of roles has implications for categorization processes in which differences related to nationality, language and religion are produced and emphasized. In fact, they are a central aspect of the way in which the participation framework contributes to gatekeeping processes.

As has been evident in Extract 1 and Extract 2, the actual participation of the candidate is often quite limited in the internship interview as a whole, and in many cases the other participants take over by acting or speaking on the candidate's behalf. This confirms and supports the distribution of the right to speak and control the interaction. In many of the interviews in my data, there are long sequences of talk between the employer, the employee and the job consultant about the internship or the internship candidate during which the internship candidate is being addressed or engaging in the other participants' talk. This is also made possible by the fact that the internship interview is not a two-party but rather a multi-party interaction. This will necessarily change the turn-organization and allow for some of the participants, in this instance the internship candidate, to renounce recipiency. This will mean that some participants are at specific times included or excluded in a more or less explicit and intentional way.

Extract 3 is an example of one of the instances in which the employer and the job consultant interact on behalf of the internship candidate without including him/her.

Extract 3 Planning the internship

```
26
30   CO:    ... .hh øøh så det vil sige vi følger jo så praktikken og har
31          også lavet nogen redskaber som jeg vil vende tilbage til
32          .hh som jeg regner med i vil [prøve
33
34          ... .hh eeh so that means we then follow the
35          internship and have also made some tools that I will return to .hh
36          that I expect you to [try
37   HO:                        [hvilket tidsrum er praktikken
38                             [what timespan is the internship
39
40   CO:    den er tolv uger
41          it is twelve weeks
42  (0.7)
43   HO:    tolv uger tre måneder
44          twelve weeks three months
45  (0.3)
46   CO:    ja
47          yes
48
49   HO:    ja
50          yes
51  (0.5)
52   CO:    øøh
53          eeh
54
55   HO:    Med mulighed for forlængelse
56          with the possibility of extension
```

The first thirty seconds of this extract have been left out, but consisted of one long uninterrupted turn by the job consultant that finishes in line 30 of the extract. In this turn, the job consultant presents the job counselling project she is involved in.

As Extract 3 shows, CO is addressing HO, who acknowledges recipiency in line 37 by requesting additional information about the time span of the internship. Although the candidate could have presumably provided these answers just as easily, it is the job consultant who self-selects as the next speaker and answers. Once the duration of the internship has been settled, CO initiates another turn in line 52 but does not follow through. HO takes this as an opportunity to probe the possibility for extending the internship beyond the planned duration.

Extract 3 illustrates one of the many situations in which the internship candidate is not included or oriented to as the next relevant speaker by either the employer or the job consultant, who both co-construct themselves as the key participants and the ones in charge of planning and deciding the terms and organization of the internship. The sequence continues along very similar lines for approximately six minutes during which no introduction of, or conversation with, the internship candidate takes place. Here, CO and HO discuss the terms, obligations and possibilities of the internship with regard to the legislative and bureaucratic framework. There are only three times during this sequence in which the candidate is either addressed or selects herself as the next speaker. However, all three instances are very brief and merely serve the purpose of confirming what has already been stated or established by HO and CO previously. Extract 3 is in this way illustrative of a general tendency found not only in this interview but in the corpus as a whole. Namely, the internship candidate is granted (and accepts) a marginal role in the participation framework; the role of being the one talked about rather than the one doing the talking. This is not to say that the internship candidate does not negotiate her role and merely accepts being talked about, but generally she, and in fact most of the other internship candidates, can be said to both establish themselves and be established as having a less central participant status.

It is important to emphasize that although the participation framework of the internship interviews is generally characterized by the dominant roles of the job consultant, the employer and the employee as organizers of the internship interview, this does not mean that the more marginal role of the internship candidate does not add value to the interview at all. In fact, the candidates do, in most of the internship interviews, contribute with descriptions of their previous experience, their motivations for applying for the internship etc. However, their participation is almost always encouraged, invited and initiated by either the job consultant or the employer. In such cases, the job consultants often still manage to establish a space in which the primary participants are the internship candidate and the employer rather than the job consultant and the employer.

While some of the internship candidates participate and establish themselves as central parts of the participation framework, the extent and form of their participation is very much influenced by the ways in which the job consultant and the employer establish and manage their roles as organizers of the interaction and the internship. Similarly, the participation and roles of the job consultants and the employers are influenced and enabled by the participation (or lack of participation) of the internship candidates. The participation framework is in this way not dictated or controlled by any one of the participants, but is constituted through a complicated interplay of actions and opportunities for actions. And yet, when regarded as a whole, the internship interviews reveal certain limits in the extent to which the roles and rights of the participation framework can be negotiated and defined freely. From this perspective, the candidates are thus less in control of the interviews than the other participants.

To summarize this section, I have sought to describe and illustrate how the participation framework of the internship interview is dynamically co-constructed between the participants. The examples illustrate a certain pattern in the distribution of rights, actions and behaviour between the participants, and how this pattern is generated by the participants' repeated and mutual orientation towards the specific interactional context of the internship interview. Hence, the participants establish the participation framework through their orientations towards the speech situation and vice versa. Such interactions appear as culturally familiar events that the participants enact or carry out as part of their establishment of the speech situation.

The setting

The internship interview has thus far not been analytically described or characterized, compared to many other similar forms of communicative events and institutional forms of interactions, such as job interviews (Scheuer, 2001; Roberts & Campbell, 2006; Adelswärd, 1992; Auer, 1998; Akinnaso & Seabrook Ajirotutu, 1982), oral exams (Roberts & Sarangi, 1999), student counselling sessions (Erickson & Shultz, 1982) and report card meetings (Mazeland & Berenst, 2006). However, the internship interview as a communicative event can, to a large extent, also be described in relation to these other communicative events and to some of the features that have been described as characteristic to them.

Examining the structure of an internship interview involves not only looking at the participants and how they construct and organize their participant roles and functions, but also investigating how they construct and orient to the overall activity they participate in. Although this dimension is mentioned by Goffman in relation to his notion of participation framework, Hymes's notion of speech situation allows for a more concrete conceptualization of this level of organization. He describes how ongoing activities within a communicative event can be recognizable (at least for some of the participants) as a unit of various activities directed at a specific outcome, such as a fishing trip, lovemaking, hunting etc. Hymes defines speech situation in the following way:

> In a sociolinguistic description, then, it is necessary to deal with activities which are in some recognizable way bounded or integral. From the standpoint of general social description they may be registered as ceremonies, fishing trips, and the like; from particular standpoints they may be regarded as political, aesthetic, etc., situations, which serve as contexts for the manifestation of political, aesthetic, etc., activity. From the sociolinguistic standpoint they may be regarded as speech situations. (1974: 52)

By looking at the participants' structuring and organization of the internship interview, it is possible to describe how they construct the interaction as a specific speech situation and how they negotiate the common activity (activities) and overall goal(s) of the interaction. In this respect the notion of speech situation is very similar to Levinson's (1992) notion of *activity types*.

Hymes's notion of speech situation, however, has the advantage of highlighting how a given interaction is not just a range of separate activities. Rather, it is a situation as a whole, comprising various speech events in the way that a dinner party, for example, involves both verbal interaction, eating, playing games etc. Interactions are in this way considered culturally situated exchanges that are shaped by not only the activities of its participants but also the cultural and ideological properties that are linked to and created by these activities. In this respect, Hymes's notion allows for a description of the rules and restrictions as specific to the various speech events that a speech situation can comprise. However, in order to capture the dynamic process in which the rules of such events are generated, negotiated and challenged by the participants in relation to particular actions, the more interactional perspective of Levinson is necessary. In other words, the following description of the internship interview will maintain Hymes's distinction between speech situation and speech event, and Levinson's action-oriented perspective on how the participants orient to and co-construct different goals and activities within the interaction.

When describing the way in which the participants orient to and establish the goals of the internship interview, it is important to emphasize that, among the internship interviews I have collected, there are two types of interviews – the *introductory internship interview*, which amounts to a total of nine, and the *follow-up internship interview*, of which I have collected seven. The distinction between the two types of interactions is on the one hand formulated by the job consultants prior to the actual interview, and on the other established by the actions and orientations of the participants within the actual interviews.

Broadly speaking, the introductory internship interview was generally constructed and oriented to as a job interview situation, even though the position being applied for was not an ordinary job and the candidates were not competing with other candidates. In this way, there was very little, if any, chance of being rejected. These interviews consisted of the following elements, occurring in no specific order: the job consultants' presentation of the job counselling programme, the employers' and the employees' presentation of the workplace, questions about the applicants' interests in the workplace and motivation for wanting the job, descriptions of the relevant tasks and areas of work and, finally, practical information and planning of the internship with regard to the time period, work schedule, starting date etc. Since the point of these interviews was to establish a 'match' between the workplace and the candidate, the assessment of the candidate with respect to his/her experience, motivation and expectations played a central role. This assessment was different from that of a job interview since the candidates, as mentioned, were not likely to fail. Nevertheless, as will be shown, the participants orient towards the interaction as one in which implicit and explicit assessments were being made. Furthermore, as will be shown in Chapters 4, 5 and 6, these assessments involved categorizations, evaluations and prescriptions related to the nationality, language and religion of the candidates.

The follow-up internship interview was generally constructed and oriented to more as an evaluation encounter where the participants would discuss the tasks and work areas of the intern. This would also represent an opportunity to discuss any problems that might have presented themselves during the internship and, on such occasions, discussions about language problems would sometimes take place, involving categorizations related to nationality and language. The participants also used this interaction to plan the final part of the internship and discuss the intern's future plans and possibilities.

Due to the considerable differences between the two types of interviews, I will treat them as distinct categories in the ensuing description of the speech situations. In this book, I focus mainly on the introductory internship interviews, since these, as I will argue and illustrate, are situations in which the decision-making about the internship and the assessment of the candidate is mostly recurrent and predominant. The introductory interview in this way resembles the job-interview much more than the follow-up interview and the stakes for the candidate are similarly higher in these.

Although the follow-up interviews could potentially constitute an opportunity to discuss the prospects of a job based on the progress of the internship, the employers were in most cases unable to offer a regular job after the internship. Therefore, the follow-up internship interviews were in reality merely a summarizing description of the progress made during the internship and had no consequences for the employment future of the candidate.

The introductory internship interview

In the introductory internship interview, the participants orient towards the common overall goal of deciding on the possibilities of the future internship. As described previously, the responsibility for this decision-making, and thereby the role of controlling the interaction, is taken by and granted to the employer, who influences the distribution of talk between the participants. There are, however, marked differences in how this overall goal is realized and established and in the distribution of roles and responsibilities with respect to achieving this goal.

In some cases, the introductory internship interview is oriented to as if it was a decision-making process, similar to that of a job interview. Extract 4 provides a good example of this. Here, we see how the employers emphasize and orient to the internship as something that has not been decided and agreed upon yet.

Extract 4 **Now we will have to see**

```
59    HO:      Og Lizzie er
60             and Lizzie is
61    (0.6)
62    HO:      gruppeleder
63             head of division
64    (0.7)
65    HO:      i den
66             in the
67    (0.3)
68    HO:      gruppe
69             group
70    (0.3)
71    HO:      der er tale om du eventuelt skal i praktik
72             there is talk about you potentially will do an internship
73    |IN:     okay
74             okay
75    (0.3)
76    HO:      Ja
77             yes
78    (0.9)
79    HO:      ja
80             yes
81    (0.8)
82    HO:      Men tak for din ansøgning jeg har (fået/flot) .hh
83             But thank you for your application I have (received/great) .hh
84
85    IN:      .mlhh selv    [tak]
86             .mlhh you're [welcome]
87    HO:                   [såå]em
88                          [soo]em
89    (0.6)
90    HO:      Nu må vi jo- se
91             Now we will have to see
92    (0.6)
93    HO:      Ja
94             yes
```

In this extract, the employer expresses a reservation about the future reality of the internship in line 71 by the use of the word 'potentially' and in line 91 with the expression 'now we will have to see'. The employer is thereby setting the scene for the internship interview as a decision-making situation and highlights the uncertainty of whether the internship candidate will be accepted. By bringing up the application sent by the candidate, the employer further accentuates her framing of the setting as a job interview situation. The internship candidate aligns with this framing in line 73 and line 85.

In other instances, the participants orient to the speech situation as if it were a planning meeting where the goal was to arrange and describe the terms and tasks that the internship would involve. In these interviews, the future internship is oriented to as a given, which could be said to lower the tension and pressure on the candidate and the speech situation as a whole. This orientation is seen in Extract 5, where it is the employee who makes the future reality of the internship relevant.

Extract 5 And that is where you will be

```
43   EM:    ja det er mig der (0.8) står for køkken og madlavning og
44          frivillige og ja den mobile cafe som sådan og alt det der
45          foregår der
46
47          yes it is me who (0.8) is in charge of kitchen and cooking and
48          volunteers and yes the mobile cafe as such and all that
49          goes on there
50          (0.5)
51
52   EM:    og det er jo så der hvor (0.4) du skal være
53          and that is then where (0.4) you will be
54
55   IN:    ja hehe
56          yes hehe
57
58   EM:    være med
59          be with
60
61   IN:    det håber jeg [he he he .hh
62          I hope so     [he he he .hh
63
```

This extract is distinctly different from the previous, Extract 4, and the following, Extract 6. Here, there is no orientation towards the internship interview as a decision-making process; rather, it is oriented to as a planning situation and the internship agreement is constructed and talked about as an already established premise of the interaction rather than a goal of the interaction.

In line 52, the employee displays an understanding that the internship has already been agreed upon. From IN's uptake in line 55 we see how IN does not display shared knowledge of the internship as something which is already agreed on, but rather displays a continued orientation towards the internship interview as a decision-making process. She does not confirm the statement by EM, but rather, by expressing uncertainty and hope, calls this statement into question. This response can be said to be the result from the sequential context in which EM's request for confirmation occurs. EM is in the middle of a presentation of the workplace when he suddenly makes the declaration which suggests the future reality of the internship with this candidate. This latched-on formatting of the statement seems to take IN off guard, which explains the more reluctant reply and the laughter following it.

Thus far I have shown how in some of the introductory internship interviews the goal is established to be in the process of decision-making while in others it is merely about planning. If we consider these two types of introductory interviews as opposite poles on a continuum, the remaining introductory interviews fall in the middle. A third type of introductory interview is characterized by the participants being more ambiguous in their orientations towards the speech situation, their establishment of the goal of the interaction and the status of the internship. Furthermore, they are also distinct in that the needs, motivations, interests and competences of the internship candidate are addressed and constructed as a central factor in determining the future possibility of an internship.

The future reality of the internship is thus constructed as something that depends on the internship candidate, whereas in the previous examples this responsibility is to a large extent claimed by the employer. In some of these interviews, the internship is more or less laid out as an offer to the internship candidate, who is then, to a larger extent than in the other introductory internship interviews, given a more privileged right to define the terms and conditions of the following internship. In other interviews, the future internship is not so much presented as an offer but rather a potential possibility which depends on the interests and needs of the internship candidates as well as on their work history and skills. Extract 6 shows this most notably:

Extract 6 Start up cleaning

```
13
14   HO:    Ja .h (0.2) okay Zabia du kunne godt tænke dig at starte op på det
15          vi sådan snakkede om den dag,
16
17          yes .h (0.2) okay Zabia you would like to start up with what
18          we like talked about that day,
19   (.)
20   IN:    ˚ja˚
21          ˚yes˚
22
23   HO:    hvor du var inde hvor jeg sagde d- at det vi
24          where you were in where i said w- that what we
25   (0.6)
26   HO:    vi har her hos os det er at man gør rent
27          we have here with us that is that one cleans
28   (0.8)
29   HO:    i forskellige hjem.
30          in different homes.
31   (0.3)
32   (IN:)  ˚.hja˚
33          ˚.hyes˚
34
35          (.)
36   HO:    Ik'
37          right
38          (2.9)
39   CO:    Og der har du jo nogle erfaringer.
40          and there you have some experience.
41   (0.3)
42   CO:    tidligere fra
43          from earlier
44
45   HO:    JA [men det ø:hm: eh- Zabia du har aldrig prøvet at være ude
46          YES[but that e:hm: eh- Zabia you have never tried to be out
47
48   (IN):      [( )]
49   (0.9)   (sound of paper being moved)
50   HO:    hos kunder
51          with clients
```

In this extract, we can see how the internship candidate is explicitly addressed and included as a central participant by the employer in line 14, where she makes a request for confirmation of IN's interests in working as an intern. While IN responds to this in line 20 with a 'yes', uttered in low voice, the interaction is quickly turned into something that resembles the job interview framing, where the main activity taking place is the negotiation and assessment of the candidate's experience, motivation and qualifications in relation to a particular position and job description. After the first minimal response from the candidate, HO repeats what she has previously told IN about the workplace and the sort of work done there, which elicits another affirmative response from IN in line 32, also in low voice. This appears to be considered insufficient by HO who responds with 'right' in line 36 followed by a long pause, which can be understood as a request for a further response from IN. Since there is a lack of uptake from IN, CO takes the floor in line 39 and brings attention to the previous experience that IN has with the type of work described by HO.

In other words, CO interprets HO's description of the workplace and the type of work done here as an invitation for IN to describe her interest in, and previous experience with, cleaning, and since IN does not provide this, CO provides it on her behalf. This extract is a good example of the job consultant's role and right to speak on IN's behalf. Here it has the consequence of initiating a discussion of IN's previous experience rather than a planning of the future content of the internship.

What is particular about the introductory internship interviews found in my corpus is the lack of an immediate establishment of the purpose of the interaction as either 'decision-making' and 'assessment' or 'planning the details' of an already agreed upon internship. In these interviews, the internship candidate is addressed and included to a large extent in the decision-making process by the employer, who makes an opening statement requesting a confirmation of his or her interest in the internship from the internship candidate.

As we have seen, this does not necessarily imply that the internship candidate is hereby granted the right to decide and accept the internship. While in some cases the internship candidates' positive responses to the employers' request for confirmation makes the employers move right into planning the internship, Extracts 4 and 6 illustrate how the employer has the power to take the interaction in a different direction and postpone any certain indication that the internship was decided and a future reality.

As shown with the examples above, the introductory internship interview is an ambiguous speech situation in which the very reality or the specific terms of the future internship is an unsettled matter that has to be arranged, agreed on and discussed. This ambiguity does not disappear or diminish until the employer actually initiates the planning of the internship or describes the tasks and work that the internship candidate will be involved in. But even at that point, the overall goals of assessment and decision-making can still potentially influence the participants' actions and interpretations. Out of nine introductory internship interviews, there are only two in which the employers at an early stage in the interview explicitly express that they consider the internship as an established agreement and a future reality. In the other interviews, the decision of accepting the internship candidate is delayed for a certain amount of time, and the ambiguity of whether the employer has already made a decision is at times almost tangibly hanging in the air.

This can be said to influence the interaction on a general level in the sense that it creates an air of uncertainty and ambiguity that makes the situation more delicate and uncertain for the internship candidate. On a more concrete level, it can be said to possibly influence the interactional dynamics by causing the candidate to be more cautious and withhold their contributions and participation. In any case, the lack of explicitness and the ambiguity of whether the goal of the interaction is assessment and decision-making make the introductory internship interview resemble the gatekeeping interactions described by, among many others, Erickson and Shultz, Gumperz and Roberts (Roberts & Campbell, 2006; Roberts & Campbell, 2005; Erickson & Shultz, 1982; Gumperz et al., 1979). This will be elaborated on in Chapter 2.

The follow-up internship interview

In the follow-up internship interview, the central goal established by the participants is the evaluation of the internship and the performance of the internship candidate during the first part of the internship. Here, the responsibility and right to define the goal of the interaction is given to and claimed by the job consultant, whereas in the introductory interview the employer established him/herself as the one in control to a much larger extent.

In all, except for one, of the seven follow-up internship interviews that were recorded, the interactions were initiated either by the job consultant asking the intern about his/her experience so far, or by the employee eliciting an initiation from the job consultant by renouncing the floor and selecting the job consultant as the next speaker. It should be noted that the participation framework of the follow-up internship interview is also slightly different, since the employer is not present (except in one instance), as in the introductory internship interview, but only the employee who has worked most closely with the intern during the first part of the internship. Extract 7 is an example of a typical follow-up internship interview, which shows the distinction from the introductory interview outline clearly.

Extract 7 How it had been

```
11   CO:     så nu ville jeg bare høre hvordan
12           so now I just wanted to hear how
13   (0.6)
14   CO:     øøh
15           eeh
16   (0.3)
17   (   )   [( )]
18   CO:     [he he he]
19           (somebody enters the room, says goodbye and leaves)
20   CO:     hvordan det var gået siden sidst
21           how it had been since last
22   (1.5)
23   CO:     jeg ved ikke om: om du vil starte Nayab hvordan synes du det har
24           været den den sidste u:ge eller halvanden uge
25
26           I don't know if: if you will begin Nayab how you think it has
27           been the the last we:k or week and a half
28   (1.1)
29   IN:     det til mig det meget °godt°
30           it for me it very °gocd°
31
32   CO:     mm
33   (3.9)
34   CO:     kan du fortælle sådan lidt hva- hvad du har lavet
35           hvilke aktiviteter
36
37           can you tell like a little wha- what you have done
38           what activities
```

It shows the typical way in which the follow-up internship interview is established as an evaluative speech situation where the job consultant controls the structure and content of the interaction and distributes the rights to talk. It also shows a recurrent tendency for the job consultant to guide the contribution of the intern in the direction of a concrete description of the tasks he or she has undertaken and the specific content of the internship.

In lines 11–20, CO makes a general and very implicit inquiry about how the internship has been since the last time they met. This is followed by a noticeably absent uptake which makes CO reformulate her question, this time explicitly addressing the intern. In line 26, CO asks IN in general terms how the internship had been during the last week and a half, and after another long pause she gets a positive but very general response from IN in the following turn. In line 32, CO responds to this reply by shortly encouraging IN to elaborate but since this does not happen CO asks IN in line 34, after a 3.9 second pause, about the specific activities she has taken part in.

As Extract 7 shows, the follow-up internship interview is constructed as an evaluation in which the interns are expected to recount both their general feeling about the internship and the actual activities that they have taken part in. The job consultant is expected to orchestrate the interaction and support the contribution of the intern. This does not mean, however, that the employee is completely passive and does not have a role to play in the interaction. Often they are involved in the interaction at a later stage and contribute by giving their perspective on the internship and the performance of the intern. The employees are, in other words, oriented to and established as central figures in the evaluation of the internship. While the interns are often expected to provide descriptions of the activities they have taken part in, the employees orient to and are oriented to as the ones responsible for bringing up any problems that may have arisen during the internship.

The follow-up internship interview is only similar to the introductory internship interview in the sense that a central purpose and goal of the speech situation is the assessment of the internship candidate. The follow-up internship interview differs in its participation framework in the sense that it is the job consultant who is being oriented to and establishes herself as the one in control of the development, content and purpose of the interaction, and thereby also the right to define the speech situation. In the introductory internship interview, this role was mainly administered by the employer and the employee, whose participation and role in the follow-up internship interview is to a large extent defined and controlled by the job consultant.

The follow-up internship interview may be characterized as a speech situation in which the job consultant includes and invites the perspectives and experiences of the intern and the employer respectively. The job consultant thus invites them to co-construct an evaluation of the internship that forms the basis of a decision of the future plans for the intern. Sometimes the participants decide to extend the internship, often based on the argument that the language and communication skills need to be improved, and sometimes a plan is made for the specific skills that the intern needs to focus on during the remainder of the internship. The fact that the employee is often invited to describe their impressions of the intern and the internship progress, also that they often bring up any problems with the internship or the intern in response to the job consultant, shows a mutual orientation towards the goal of the internship as being the improvement of the interns' skills and future chances in the education system or the labour market. The specifics of this orientation will be elaborated on in Chapter 4, 5 and 6, where it will be argued that the formulation and topicalization of barriers, skills and knowledge are informed by particular understandings of nationality, language and religion and involve both processes of categorization and differentiation.

While the introductory internship interview and the follow-up internship interview may be characterized as decision-making and evaluative speech situations respectively, the extracts presented illustrate the complexity of the way in which the overall goals of the interactions and the roles of the participants are established and oriented to, and the way in which this influences the setting of the interaction. Both types of interactions in this way have moments where they resemble exam situations, counselling sessions, evaluation meetings or planning meetings. As the goals and orientations of the participants shifted within the introductory interviews and follow-up interviews, the roles and activities of the participants shifted as well. As I have already described, Goffman's notion of participation framework is useful to describe such flexibility in the distribution of roles between the participants. However, the various orientations towards the internship interview as a particular speech situation inform and shape the participation framework in a way which involves an asymmetric distribution of rights and roles. This distribution is not established from scratch but is modelled from the distribution of roles and rights found in other speech situations similar to the internship interview. The patterns found in organization of the speech situation, the participation framework and, not least, the asymmetry of this organization is, in other words, shaped by the routinized and recognizable institutionality of the speech situation and the speech events that it comprises. This will be illuminated in the ensuing section.

Institutional Hybridity

As previously mentioned, Hymes emphasizes that a speech situation is not organized and structured by a general set of rules and restrictions, since all speech situations, such as a fishing trip or a dinner party, comprise various different speech events such as, in the case of the given examples, having dinner, making small-talk etc. These events are individually structured and imbued with different rules and restrictions of speech and activities that make the event recognizable and understandable to the participants and which together form the overall situation. Dividing the speech situation into different speech events is useful when characterizing the internship interview because it is a speech situation that incorporates many different speech events that are recognizable and are found in other speech situations. Consequently, it is useful to organize and structure the previously mentioned activities and goals that the internship interview comprises and to relate them to culturally familiar events. Hymes defines a speech event in the following way:

The term speech event will be restricted to activities, or aspects of activities, that are directly governed by rules or norms for the use of speech. An event may consist of a single speech act, but will often comprise several ... Notice that the same type of speech act may recur in different types of speech event, and the same type of speech event in different contexts of situation. Thus, a joke (speech act) may be embedded in a private conversation, a lecture, a formal introduction. A private conversation may occur in the context of a party, a memorial service, a pause in changing sides in a tennis match. (1974: 52)

Although all verbal interaction, from an ethnomethodological or conversation analytical perspective, can be said to be rule-governed at the level of turn-taking and membership categorization, here, Hymes is talking about type of rules and norms associated with particular clusters of activities, found and recognized as units of actions within different speech situations.

This conceptualization of particular interactional and verbal events as specifically institutionalized and routinized resembles some of the characterizations of institutional interactions done within the field of Conversation Analysis (Drew & Heritage, 1992) and Interactional Sociolinguistics (Roberts & Sarangi, 1999). Here one finds similar ideas of verbal interactions being structured and organized by repeated and institutionalized speech events which entail a particular participation framework, organizational procedure and distribution of knowledge. Roberts and Sarangi, for example, describe how the oral examination interview is a blend of academic examination and selection interview (1999: 483), which are events that can also be identified and found in the internship interview. In this section, such characterizations will be used as a frame of reference in the identification of the various speech events that the internship interview comprises. The internship interview generally qualifies as an institutional speech situation, but it is more complex and heterogeneous than other institutional forms of interaction because the participants continually negotiate and redefine the main activities and goals of the interaction as well as the statuses and roles of the participants. The internship interview is therefore hardly definable as one type of institutional interaction but must rather be characterized as a hybrid of different and distinguishable types of speech events that are individually organized around particular goals and activities and structured by specific participation frameworks.

In *Talk at Work: Interaction in Institutional Settings*, Drew and Heritage (1992: 21–25) propose some overall distinctive features of institutional interactions in relation to ordinary talk that illuminate the rules and restrictions Hymes talks about regarding speech events. Firstly, the institutional interaction is characterized by at least one of the interlocutors orienting towards some overall goals or tasks in the interaction. Part of what characterizes the internship interview is that the participants are oriented towards many different goals and activities such as planning the internship, evaluating the internship, evaluating the candidate both before and after the internship, making a decision about and agreeing on the internship etc. Other institutional interactions have more clearly defined primary activities and goals, e.g. the job interview, where the main purpose and activity is the assessment of the candidates.

This is not to say that nothing besides an assessment is going on within a job interview or that the internship interview is the only institutional interaction comprising a complex interplay of activities, goals and agendas. In fact, in many institutional interactions the participants orient to one activity or goal as the primary one and other activities such as small-talk sequences, joking, self-presentations, storytelling and so on are secondary or supplementary to the main task at hand. Even though, as previous studies of job interviews show, these secondary activities are often central to the assessment of the candidates, they are oriented to as secondary in comparison with the primary goal of interviewing the candidate about their skills and qualifications. In the internship interview, on the other hand, the primary activity and purpose is, as shown previously, continually negotiated and changes from interview to interview, moment to moment and practically turn to turn, and the participants even seem to orient to the ongoing activity very differently at times.

The second defining characteristic of institutional interactions is, according to Drew and Heritage, the constraints that are imposed on the interlocutors in relation to the tasks or goals of the interaction. These may manifest themselves in certain conversational actions taking place and also in certain actions or topics being carefully avoided. Furthermore, the participants' mutual expectations of the institutionality of the interaction can influence the inferences, reasonings and implicatures of the interaction and make actions seem deviant in relation to the expectations. Actions that would normally be characterized as disaffiliative if they were to appear in ordinary conversation can be perfectly acceptable and unmarked in institutional interactions – for example long pauses or the absence of displays of empathy, enthusiasm, encouragement etc.

While the internship interview is clearly institutional according to these overall features described by Drew and Heritage, they do not suffice to account for or describe the various forms of institutionality that the internship interviews, individually and as a whole, encompass. One can say that the general category 'institutional interaction' does not express the way that institutionality is realized differently according to the specific speech situations and speech events that the participants orient to and establish. The particular institutionality of an interaction is closely related to the organization of the participation framework and the distribution of roles and rights to speak and act in specific ways and at specific times. The participants' orientation towards particular professional or institutional identities makes various tasks and actions relevant and this manifests itself in the character and outcome of the interaction in specific ways (Drew & Heritage, 1992: 4). They describe three ways in which the institutionality of an interaction manifests itself in the interactional organization, namely: (1) distribution of participation rights, (2) distribution of knowledge and rights to knowledge and (3) different access to organizational routines and procedures (1992: 49–53). In Table 1.2 I have summarized the ways in which the participants in the internship interview establish this organization.

Starting with the left column, the distribution of rights in the introductory internship interview is, as shown previously, predominantly established in a way that the employer is the one to take the first turn, select the next speaker and initiate or close topics.

This distribution of rights and turns is very similar to that in job interviews, which are described by various theorists as being interviewer-controlled and structured by the questioning of the candidate by the interviewer (Akinnaso & Seabrook Ajirotutu, 1982; Roberts & Campbell, 2006; Scheuer, 2001; Adelswärd, 1988). In the introductory internship interview, the employer and, to a lesser extent, the employee are the ones to ask the questions and select the next speaker, while the internship candidate, or the job consultant, is the one who answers.

In the follow-up internship interviews, on the other hand, the job consultant takes the role of interviewer and the employee and the intern take the role of interviewee. Although the two types of internship

Table 1.2 Manifestations of institutionality in internship interviews (based on Drew & Heritage, 1992)

Distribution of rights	Distribution of knowledge	Access to organizational procedure
• Turn distribution • Topic initiation and closing	• Orientation to HO, EM and CO as knowledge-able and IN as learner/ mentee	• Checklist topic organization • Case descriptions • Turn distribution an recipient design

interviews are similar to the job interview in the sense that they both have a central participant acting in the role of interviewer and controlling the interaction, they are not as neatly and tightly structured as the job interview, as described by Scheuer (2001) and Roberts and Campell (2006). In Scheuer's study of 41 interviews in Denmark with candidates of Danish ethnic background, he describes how these job interviews are 'structured in accordance with standard procedure' (2001: 225) and could be divided into five different phases – introduction, general information, asking questions, detailed information and ending. This structure, which is very similar to the structure found in other studies of job interviews by Adelswärd (1988) and Akinnaso and Seabrook (1982), is not found in either the introductory or the follow-up internship interviews.

In their study of 61 interviews in Britain, Roberts and Campbell (2006, 2005) describe how the interviews are either highly structured (2006: 70–71), where all questions are written down and read out and no follow-up questions or help is given by the interviewer, or semi-structured interviews (2006: 72). with a range of key questions and a varied range of follow-up questions.

The purpose of having this fixed or relatively fixed structure is to ensure a fair and equal treatment of all the candidates and to establish a common ground on which to base the assessment. This kind of purpose and goal is not in effect in the internship interviews since these interviews are from the onset part of an employment initiative specifically aimed at people with a different ethnic background than Danish. Although there are some questions and topics that repeatedly occur during the internship interviews, they are very different from the equal opportunities interviews that Roberts and Campbell describe, where all questions are written down and read out. Similarly, they also differ from the semi-structured interviews in that they are not organized around the same kind of key questions or as uniformly established as one type of speech situation.

Although the internship interviews contain many of the same elements and phases as described by Roberts, Scheuer, Akinnaso etc. and are generally similar enough to qualify as a specific type of speech situation, they are individually too different in the structuring and organization of these goals and elements to be neatly divided into phases. Part of the reason for this is that they are planned and orchestrated by different job consultants, represented by different job counselling projects, who each follow his or her own guidelines.

Another reason is that the internship interview is not, like the job interview, a well-known or recognizable type of speech situation and is therefore much more ambiguously and differently oriented to and established by the participants. Third, they are not, as in the job interviews described by Akinnaso and Seabrook Ajirotutu or by Peter Auer and his associates (Auer, 1998; Auer & Kern, 2001), staged or controlled by the researchers, which in Akinnaso and Seabrook Ajirotutu's study can be said to explain and enable the high degree of structure and homogeneity (1982: 132).

Although the activities, purposes and tangible outcomes of all verbal interactions are established in situ in negotiation between the participants, this establishment is often, in the case of institutional interactions, guided by the mutual expectations of the speech situation by the participants. In other words, each individual participant brings certain expectations about the speech situation to the table and they shape the development of the interaction individually by employing different strategies for dealing with limited or unexpected responses to such expectations.

In the case of the internship interview, and specifically the introductory internship interview, participants orient to the speech situation as if they do not know what to expect, or at least as if their expectations vary. Hence, the introductory internship interview is very much established and negotiated in situ and is, as mentioned, not merely oriented to as an evaluative and decision-making speech situation, but also as an informal planning situation in which the interests and needs of the internship candidate and the employer are to be established. This implies that in the introductory internship interview the employee and the job consultant also exercise the right to control the interaction and the distribution of turns, though to a lesser degree. Furthermore, although the intern generally orients to and aligns with the role of interviewee by answering in second turn, ending speech when interrupted and elaborating answers when probed (see for example Extract 1), the intern is also given the opportunity to initiate topics, raise areas of concern and voice specific needs or interests.

When looking at the function and goal of the questions themselves, some of them, like the questions in job interviews, encourage the candidate to present or introduce themselves. They are not however, as in the job interview, solely focused on the competences of the candidate in the sense that they do not probe or inquire into the exact span and content of these competences. Roberts and Campbell (2006) describe how, in their study of job interviews with migrant candidates, the interviewer would try to elicit a demonstration of specific skills and experience such as teamwork, self-organization, dealing with customers, making improvements etc. as well as descriptions of the candidates' motivations and previous work experience and routines. The interviewer would, apart from posing specific questions, ask the candidate to give an example from their previous work experience of a particular competence that they have. This way of asking questions by eliciting a narrative never occurred in the internship interviews I recorded. Although the employers or job consultants at times elicited narratives about the candidates' work history, the candidates usually answered questions about their competences, experiences and motivations by giving brief accounts that were often in a list format.

With respect to the middle column (Table 1.2), related to distribution of knowledge, the participants orient to the employer and the employee as professionally knowledgeable, and the intern as a learner or mentee. The employee makes elaborate presentations of the workplace, invites the intern to take part in the daily job routines and learn from future colleagues. The employer is often included in these claims to knowledge by being asked to elaborate on specific tasks and duties, and the job consultant contributes by making specific suggestions about skills that are relevant for the intern to acquire. The candidate orients to her institutional role of learner or mentee by expressing appreciation of the suggestions and offers made, and by displaying interest through asking clarificatory questions.

This particular distribution of knowledge between the participants and the institutionality of the introductory internship interview and the follow-up internship interview are similar to the institutionality of job interviews as described by Akinnaso and Seabrook Ajirotutu (1982), counselling sessions as described by Erickson and Shultz (1982), oral exams as described by Roberts and Sarangi (1999), and report card meetings as described by Mazeland and Berenst (2006). In these very different contexts, the distribution of knowledge is clearly defined and established by the participants in relation to a teacher–learner, or counsellor–learner relationship, which is also found in the introductory and follow-up internship interviews. The description by Akinnaso and Seabrook Ajirotutu of the job interview captures this more specifically:

> But perhaps the most pervasive structural feature of the job-interview is its fixed organisational structure and the strict allocation of rights and duties. Basically, the interviewer has power over the interviewee. S/he controls both the organisational structure of the interview and the mechanics of the interaction … S/he has the privilege of starting it, of introducing new topics or changing topic lines, and of terminating the conversation. (1982: 121)

Like these speech events, the internship interviews are characterized by a high degree of asymmetry in relation to distribution of knowledge, which is not only manifested in the orientations of the participants within the actual interactions but in the organization and structure of and around the job counselling projects. Furthermore, the internship interviews are, as will be shown in Chapter 5, characterized by an uneven distribution of knowledge of the Danish language, a matter which is made relevant in all of the interviews by the participants orienting to it either explicitly or implicitly.

In relation to the third column in Table 1.2, related to differential access to organizational routines and procedures, this aspect of the institutionality of the internship interview is most apparent in the actions of the job consultant. Given that the job consultant has many similar interactions with candidates with similar issues, concerns or goals, some of their actions in the interview are routinized and the client is at times treated as a case. The job consultant is responsible for helping many job candidates and during most of the interviews displays this by initiating topics in a checklist manner and by making 'case' descriptions of the internship procedure and the internship candidate. The internship agreement, which is a document that formalizes the timeframe and terms of the internship, is one example of a central and recurring element that the job consultant in the role of professional bureaucrat brings up in all of the introductory internship interviews and which entails an orientation towards the internship candidate as a case. The internship candidate's status as a 'case' is furthermore realized by the job consultant and the employer designing their turns in ways that exclude the intern as a recipient, which results in long sequences of interaction without the participation of the intern, which we saw in Extract 3 for example.

The orientation towards a difference in access to organizational procedures is a characteristic of all institutional interactions in which one of the participants is a candidate or a client and another is a representative of an institutional or bureaucratic system where certain procedures and regulations are followed systematically. In this sense, the institutionally defined relation between the job consultant and the candidate is similar to what is found in studies on medical interactions, job interviews, exam situations and so on, as already mentioned. Many of these studies describe how specific institutional routines and practices, such as grading or taking notes on papers, filling out forms, checking medical files on the computer etc., contribute to the establishment of the participation framework and the speech situation as a whole. Furthermore, they are practices which involve and accentuate the asymmetric distribution of roles and rights in the interaction.

As shown in this section, the comparison of the internship interview with the characterization of the general as well as the specific features of institutional interactions adds another layer to the understanding of the internship interview as a particular speech situation, and it illuminates how its specificity as an institutional encounter is characterized by being a hybrid communicative event, shaped by similar speech situations and speech events. Finally, it allows a further description of how the institutionality of the internship interview entails a certain distribution of rights, knowledge and access to organizational procedures, which make the very onset of the relation between the participants asymmetric. What has not been of central concern in this section, or in the entire chapter for that matter, are the implications of the fact that the candidates in these internship interviews are migrants who speak Danish as a second language while the employers and job consultants speak Danish as a mother tongue. The consequences of institutional asymmetry in this type of encounter have been the central concern in a number of studies within Interactional Sociolinguistics that deal with the phenomenon of gatekeeping. This phenomenon is, as I have already highlighted, central to the argument of this book and will be described and discussed in more detail in the following chapter.

Notes

(1) For the original as well as the translated versions of the actual legislative extracts please see Appendix 1.
(2) See Legal Extract 2, Appendix 1.
(3) See Legal Extract 3, Appendix 1.
(4) See Legal Extract 4, Appendix 1.
(5) See Legal Extract 5, Appendix 1.

2 Gatekeeping – An Interactional and Ideological Process

Characterizing the internship interview as a communicative event allows for revealing any asymmetries that may be taking place there on an institutional level. However, in this book I argue that not all forms of asymmetry established within the internship interview can be described through reference to the institutionality of an interaction. This is to say that institutional and interactional forms of asymmetry can also be interrelated with other forms of asymmetry related to the establishment and negotiation of membership categories that are associated with culturally and socially established meanings and hierarchies. Interactions can be influenced by asymmetries on not only an interactional and social level, but also on a cultural level.

Although the participants establish the internship interview as institutional through their orientations to a particular distribution of rights and knowledge, it is not only the membership categories of employer, internship candidate, job consultant and employee, or even interviewer, interviewee and administrator, that are made relevant. Participants in interaction have access to a range of cultural, linguistic and social membership knowledge that can be used as a resource to interpret not only the speech situation but also the social identities, roles and statuses of the participants. Gumperz describes the process in which statuses and roles are established in the following way:

> Communication is not governed by fixed social rules; it is a two-step process in which the speaker first takes in stimuli from the outside environment, evaluating and selecting from among them in the light of his own cultural background, personal history, and what he knows about his interlocutors. He then decides on the norms that apply to the situation at hand. These norms determine the speaker's selection from among the communicative options available for encoding his intent. (1972: 15)

This means that the participation framework and the speech situation are not only shaped by the institutionality of the interaction. They are also shaped by the participants' cultural, linguistic and social resources, as well as the knowledge available to them in a given context. This knowledge is used by interactants to interpret, categorize and evaluate one another. Such interpretations are fundamentally influenced by the normative expectations about identities, or membership categories, and the behaviours or actions associated with these. In the analytical chapters, 4, 5 and 6, I will show how the orientation towards membership categories related to nationality, language and religion reveals the manifestation of the normative expectations from the candidates.

This chapter will focus on discussing the notion of *gatekeeping*, which was first defined by Erickson and Shultz (1982), Gumperz and Roberts (Gumperz *et al.*, 1979; Campbell & Roberts, 2007; Roberts *et al.*, 1992; Roberts *et al.*, 2003; Roberts & Campbell, 2006; Roberts & Sarangi, 1999; Roberts & Campbell, 2005). The original studies of gatekeeping described situations where an institutional asymmetry enabled the sanctioning of or discrimination against individuals whose behaviour was found to not live up to the normative expectations within the given context due to differences in background and linguistic/cultural resources. In this chapter I aim to present the alternate approach to gatekeeping I have proposed in this book by presenting and discussing a wide range of studies that deal with gatekeeping implicitly or explicitly. While many other gatekeeping studies consider gatekeeping an institutional phenomenon where institutional asymmetries and processes of evaluation/selection coincide with cultural/linguistic differences between the participants, I will argue that gatekeeping is found in any process of categorization that involves the establishment of an asymmetric and hierarchical relation between categories and thereby between the members of such categories. While institutional asymmetries and selection processes naturally reinforce such processes and make them manifest in discriminatory and unequal practices, the notion of gatekeeping should not be limited to describe the aspect of discrimination related to differential treatment and unequal evaluation in institutional processes. Rather the notion of gatekeeping should be broadened to define processes of categorization that involve the establishment of an unequal power relation between individuals on the basis of majority defined expectations for categories and behaviours. While the consequences of gatekeeping in light of institutional discrimination may appear more substantial and tangible, the effect of gatekeeping in the sense of categorical hierarchization is even more powerful since it forms the basis of implicit processes of power as well as oppression, not only in institutional interactions but also potentially in any kind of interaction. The redefinition and broadening of the notion of gatekeeping that I propose here is naturally highly inspired and fuelled by previous gatekeeping studies but instead my emphasis is on the very concrete consequences of processes of categorization, interpretation and evaluation where differences in category membership, behaviour and common-sense knowledge are involved. I have opted for this approach as most of these studies tend to speak of asymmetry only in relation to the institutionally defined distribution of power between participants and in relation to the inequality produced through gatekeeping processes. I find it useful, on the other hand, to begin, and end, the discussion of gatekeeping by distinguishing between an institutional form of asymmetry and the form of asymmetry that I find even more central to gatekeeping processes – namely the culturally established asymmetry between broader social categories that are linked to but not defined by an institutional order.

The Construction and Negotiation of Asymmetries

The notion of asymmetry has been used in relation to talk-in-interaction and more specifically institutional interaction (Drew & Heritage, 1992; Sundberg, 2004). It is used to refer to an asymmetry in the contributions of various participants in such interactions. A specific interaction or form of interaction is considered as 'the whole' and the contributions of different participants are 'the constituent parts' that are measured or analyzed in relation to each other. This way of perceiving an interaction makes sense in light of the argumentative and dialogic nature of interaction as organized by the turn-taking system (see Chapter 3). However, it does not solve the problem of how to measure and compare the different contributions.

Asymmetry and symmetry exist on various levels of verbal interaction, and one may in fact question whether an interaction is ever symmetric on any level. Whether comparing the amount of turns and words or the actions made by various participants in interaction, the general picture would most likely not be symmetric. The use of the term 'asymmetry' is to be understood as an uneven distribution of rights and possibilities on various levels between participants in interaction. It should be noted however that using 'asymmetry' to describe some of the features of the internship interview does not suggest that some interactions are fundamentally symmetric or that the notion of asymmetry is in itself a meaningful criterion of analysis in interactional research. Rather, I use 'asymmetry' to describe patterns of actions and rights that manifest themselves in the internship interview at various levels and that can be said to, when oriented to and established, influence the interactional development and the process of meaning-making.

Asymmetry is not to be understood as something fixed or stable or as something predictable and unchallengeable. Rather, it is, like the notion of speech situation and participation framework, something which is continually established and negotiated between participants in interaction. It is something that may be reproduced, reified and institutionalized to form patterns that potentially influence actions, situations and processes of meaning-making as it is associated with specific speech situations, participant roles and social categories. Asymmetry is thus both an interactional achievement and a contextual basis for this achievement.

As illustrated in Chapter 1, where I argued for the nature of the internship interview as a communicative event, there are asymmetries in the analyzed internship interviews that are closely related to the establishment of the participation framework and speech situation. On an interactional level, one example of such asymmetry is the right to control the development of the interaction and the actions and purposes of the interactions; on a social level, it is the ability to limit, enable and dictate the future behaviour and possibilities of the participants. However, besides orienting towards these institutionally defined identities and the asymmetric distribution of rights related to them, the participants in the internship interview orient to membership categories other than those immediately related to the speech situation and the participation framework. The establishment of these other categories involves the establishment of asymmetries that are not related to the institutionality of this speech situation but to broader structures of meaning and power. Throughout these internship interviews, membership categories such as 'Danish', 'second-language speaker', 'Muslim' and 'Colombian', to name a few, were established and made relevant, but also associated with a distribution of rights that can be said to establish and reproduce asymmetries on a broader cultural level. Culture here refers to a shared community of meaning that encompasses processes of membership categorization as well as a range of shared structures of meaning, common sense and ideology that intertwines with such processes (Hastrup, 2004; Tranekjær, 2014).[1]

The effects of these asymmetries did not manifest themselves separate from the institutional asymmetry and distribution of rights in the internship interviews, but interplayed with these in complex and consequential ways. The complexity of this will be examined and illustrated further in Chapters 4, 5 and 6 but here the purpose is to argue that there are different levels of asymmetry at play within the internship interviews, one of which is related to the establishment of membership categories that are broader in scope and often referred to as social categories or social identities. This observation is of course not new. Previous research on institutional native/ non-native interaction (Bremer et al., 1996; Jupp et al., 1982; Sundberg, 2004) describes these as characterized by an interactionally achieved asymmetry.[2] Jupp et al. describe how linguistic interaction can either reinforce or alleviate distance, difference and stereotypes, and Svennevig (2004, 2005) describes how, in institutional interactions between clerks and non-native clients, the repetitions made by the native-speaking clerks show an orientation towards the linguistic asymmetry between the participants.

Thus, asymmetry can be described as an unequal distribution of rights and actions which is interactionally established and manifested and can be described with reference to three different levels: an interactional level, a social level and a cultural/ideological level. The interactional and social levels, as I have argued, can be examined through a characterization of the internship interview as a communicative event and is closely related to the membership categories established in relation to the participation framework and the speech situation. The latter level, on the other hand, is not directly linked to the context of the speech situation but rather to the internship interview's embeddedness in a broader cultural context of meaning. Furthermore, the cultural/ideological level manifests in relation to the participants' orientation towards membership categories that are not uniquely related to the context of the speech situation. This form of asymmetry is produced and reproduced in the orientation towards boundaries of normativity and deviance related to such categories. Putting it this way, gatekeeping is not limited to an interviewer–interviewee relation. Instead, gatekeeping also defines categorization processes that reproduce categories and the relation between them in a hierarchical way and thereby position its members in an asymmetric power relation. This broadens the definition of gatekeeping so that it refers not only to something which occurs at the threshold of some institutional gate, or even within these gates (Holmes, 2007). Rather it refers also to a phenomenon that can occur in any interaction, namely that interactants are placed in a subordinate position in relation to other interactants through being associated with categories, actions and features that are either culturally stigmatized or interactionally established as problematic or controversial.

Asymmetry on different levels

The three levels of asymmetry can be illuminated further by returning to Zimmerman's (1998) distinction between discourse identities, situational identities and transportable identities, where the first can be said to relate to the interactional level, the second to the social level and the third to the cultural level.

Zimmerman describes how *situational identities*, along with the institutional context, project a certain future development or overall structure of an interaction such as interrogation, interview and medical examination. These identities remain constant throughout the entire interaction once they are established. In emergency calls, for example, the situational identities are caller and call-taker. Situational identities do not, however, control the actual development and structure of an interaction – this depends on the actual actions and orientations of the participants and the way they project and infer what the participants are doing. Situational identities are, in Zimmerman's words, bound up with and related to the various *discourse identities* that the interlocutors enact in relation to their interactional goals (1998: 94). Examples of discourse identities are questioner, hearer, accuser, defender, joker, inviter etc. These identities change throughout interactions and are not specifically bound to given situational identities. However, discourse identities are not entirely independent of situational identities either since the latter make some actions more likely and to be expected than others. In a formal interview situation, for example, the context and situational identities prescribe that primarily one person will ask the questions and the other is to respond, while discourse identities are useful for distinguishing the very momentary and brief acts of identification with a particular role and position such as questioner, listener etc.

While Zimmerman is quite clear in his definition and illustration of how participants make certain discourse identities and situational identities relevant, he is less specific in his definition of transportable identities and he does not address the role they (potentially) play in interaction. As shown by the many gatekeeping studies reviewed in this chapter as well as the study of internship interviews presented in this book, such transportable identities are often made highly relevant for the interpretations, categorizations and evaluations of interactants.

In Extract 8 it is clear how situational identities can be said to interrelate with the discourse identities in a way which produces an asymmetric relation between the employer/employee and the candidate. Furthermore, the extract shows how the orientation towards *transportable identities* establishes asymmetry between the participants, which is on the one hand made possible by the rights of the employer to control topics, but is on the other hand resulting from the hierarchical organization of categories, which is rooted in and transported from the broader cultural context of ideology and common sense.

Extract 8 So you both have to learn Danish?

```
12
13   *EM:    Er din mand også fra I:ran, (very thouroughly pronounced)
14           Is your husband also from I:ran
15
16   *IN:    ·a
17           yes
18
19   |*EM:   ·a
20           yes
21
22   *IN:    ·a=
23           yes=
24
25   *EM:    =[.tsk]  •
26           =[.tsk]
27
28   ( )      [.hja]
29           [.hjyeah]
30
31   *EM:    Så skal I begge  [to lære £dansk£? =
32           So you both have [to learn £Danish£?=
33
34   *IN:                     [han kommer (ja/her)= •
35                            [he comes (yes/here)=
36
37   *EM:    =[sk.ha]   [( )]=
38           =[sk.ha]   [( )]=
39
40   *IN:    =[ja] ha ha [ha ]=
41           =[yes]ha ha [ha ]=
42
43   *CO:    =[Nej han har ]boet her i mange år. •
44           =[no he has  ] lived here for many years
45
46   *IN:    =[ja::      ]
47           =[ye::s
48
49   *EM:    Nå han har [boet her i mange år okay]
50           oh he has  [lived here for many years okay]
51
52   (CO/IN:)            [ja (            ) også] boet [her]
53                       [yes(           ) also] lived [here]
54
```

This extract will be analyzed in greater detail in Chapter 5, but here I want to point out the fact that EM uses the previously established situational identity of interviewer to claim the discourse identity of questioner and to make the transportable identity of Iranian relevant. Hereby she simultaneously makes the category Danish relevant, and in line 31 she uses her transportable identity of Danish and native Danish speaker to normatively prescribe a certain behaviour on IN's behalf. Hence, the asymmetry invoked through the orientation towards the transportable identities of Iranian, Danish, native speaker and second-language speaker is established on the grounds of privileges and rights associated with the situational identity of interviewer and made possible through the discourse identity of questioner.

Zimmerman describes how the initial actions of the interlocutors in, for example, emergency calls establish a set of mutually oriented-to identities which project the future development of the call. Drawing on Goffmann's work, he refers to these initial actions as establishing the 'footing' for the rest of the interaction (Zimmerman, 1998: 98). In Extract 8, the shift to an inquiry about the personal life of the candidate and her husband represents a change of footing in the interaction from a formal to a small-talk format. This right and ability to change the footing of the interaction enables the categorization of IN as an Iranian second-language learner who is expected to learn Danish by speaking it at home. The fact that EM changes to a more informal format does not make the interaction less asymmetric or make the participants equal. While the momentary backgrounding of the situational identity of candidate through the small-talk format can be said to mitigate the asymmetry imposed by the institutionality of the interaction, the foregrounding of a transportable identity which highlights a lack in competence reiterates the asymmetry. Now, if the employer had not picked up on the topicalization of Danish skills and the transportable identity of second-language speaker but continued the friendly small talk instead, the development in this interaction might have been different. Instead, EM takes the floor and poses a rather normative first-pair part and an authoritative follow-up response, which displays the abandonment of the friendly, conversational 'footing' and claims the discourse identity of accuser. Asymmetry cannot therefore be said to be merely related to situational identities and institutional interactions as such, but also to the way these situational identities and institutional settings are managed turn-by-turn. Furthermore, asymmetry is related to the transportable identities that are made relevant during the interaction which can make other situational and discourse identities less relevant. This is, in other words, an excellent example of the interrelatedness of interactional, social and cultural/ideological levels of asymmetry in gatekeeping encounters, as well as how the various levels of participant roles and identities relate to different levels of actions.

From the analysis of Extract 8 it may appear as if asymmetry, whether institutional or non-institutional, is something which is imposed by the employer and the employee on the internship candidate, but from an interactional perspective, this is only part of the story. All meanings, actions, identities, as well as the overall footing and context of the interaction, meaning a/symmetries, mis/alignments, dis/affiliations, are co-constructed and negotiated between the participants. When asymmetry is established from the start, the actions of all participants, both in direct and indirect ways, continue to contribute to the asymmetry. Again, in Extract 8, IN contributed to the establishment of interactional and social asymmetry by, through her actions and orientations, establishing the situational identity of interviewee. She also contributed to the cultural and ideological form of asymmetry by aligning with and answering the questions regarding her husband, their nationality and her language abilities and practices. The job consultant, however, did the opposite of EM. CO confronted the implications of EM's questions, disaffiliating with EM's line of argument (lines 43 and 52) and thereby challenging the assumptions and the asymmetry previously established by EM, but also re-negotiating CO's own discourse identity of questioner. I will not go further into the role of the job consultant here since it will be elaborated on in later analysis. However, I wish to highlight this extract as an example of how various levels of asymmetry are co-constructed and can therefore also be negotiated and confronted at each turn. Extract 9 shows an example of how the internship candidate was also able to confront the cultural and ideological asymmetry associated with the orientation towards the category of second-language speaker. This extract will be more thoroughly examined in Chapter 5.

Extract 9 Do you understand what I'm saying?

```
63    (.)
64    *HO:    .hh [nej] .hh er det svært f- øh kan du forstå
65            .hh [no]  .hh is it difficult f- eh can you understand
66
67    *IN:    ['kay]
68            [right]
69
70    *HO:    hvad jeg siger •
71            what I am saying
72
73    *IN:    £JAAA£↑ •
74            £YEES£↑
75
76    *HO:    >£Det godt£<
77            >£That's good£<
78
79    *IN:    h[hundrede procent heh. heh. he. jah.][heh. heh. .hhhh] •
80            h[hundred percent  heh. heh. he. jah. ][heh. heh. .hhhh]
81
82    *HO:    [heh. heh. he. he. he.                ]
83            [heh. heh. he. he. he.                ]
84
```

In line 64, HO makes the category of second-language speaker relevant by questioning IN's understanding of his previous turns. IN rejects this implication in line 73 in a way that can be said to be orienting to the asymmetry that this entails. By using emphasis and loud voice she is being assertive, rather than merely responsive. With that, her utterance works as a criticism of the implications of the preceding question and projects that some sort of excuse, account or explanation for HO's question is to follow. At the same time, IN expresses her assertiveness in a smile voice which mitigates the implied criticism and rejection. Although HO does not explicitly respond by giving an excuse or account, he orients to the assertiveness and the rejection by giving a quick, satisfied third-turn response in line 76, also in smile voice. In this manner, he immediately diminishes the negative impression of his previous question and closes the topic on a positive note. Although HO has thus signalled that he will not pursue the topic further, IN continues and upgrades her rejection of HO's question in line 79 by saying 'a hundred per cent', which is a contemporary, vernacular way of saying 'completely'. Hereby she demonstrates familiarity with formulaic phrases used by native speakers of Danish. So by combining prosodic features such as emphasis, loud voice, smile voice and laughter with a formulaic phrase, IN manages to confront the projected asymmetry.

Whether IN manages to confront asymmetry on all levels – interactional, social and cultural/ideological – or only the asymmetry established on an interactional level is debatable. By constructing a defence against her assumed linguistic incompetence, she is not in any way challenging the social asymmetry associated with the employer's rights to accept and define the internship. With respect to the asymmetry at play on a cultural/ideological level her defence potentially confronts the association EM makes between the membership category of 'foreigner' and a lack of proficiency. More broadly speaking, her actions can be seen to potentially challenge, although not change, established structures of meaning around foreigners and second-language speakers in Denmark. In Bakhtin's terms (1981: 270–272; see also Fairclough, 1995), her utterance can be said to work with the centrifugal forces of language rather than the centripetal, in the sense that she challenges established patterns of meaning by countering EM's assumptions and preconceived notions of her.

What is proposed in this book is that the root of gatekeeping processes is the cultural/ideological form of asymmetry, which is manifested in a hierarchical organization of established social categories or transportable identities. While this form of asymmetry is produced and reproduced in any social interaction, including institutional ones, it is facilitated and reinforced by the social and interactional forms of asymmetry that characterize the relation between situational identities in institutional encounters.

While previous studies of gatekeeping have been central in illuminating the discriminatory practices which are enabled by the institutionally defined power of the gatekeeper, they have only implicitly addressed the different forms of asymmetry involved in gatekeeping processes. They, in this way, emphasize how the social or situational level of asymmetry leads to the systematic (re)production of inequality between social groups (majority, minority, born abroad, native, British, ethnic, men, women). They do not, however, illuminate the manifestation of cultural/ideological asymmetries in the categorization processes involved in the orientation towards the transportable identities which interactants make relevant. The following review of previous gatekeeping studies will further clarify how the particular contribution of the present book is its emphasis on exactly this central dimension of gatekeeping processes.

The Notion of Gatekeeping

Gatekeeping as a theoretical term was first used and defined by anthropologists Frederick Erickson and Jeffrey Shultz in 1982 in the following way:

> brief encounters in which two persons meet, usually as strangers, with one of them having authority to make decisions that affect the other's future. (1982: xi)

This definition, which reveals a strong emphasis on the social and interactional form of asymmetry, can be used to categorize a range of different institutional encounters as gatekeeping encounters, such as job interviews (Jupp et al., 1982; Scheuer, 2001; Auer, 1998; Roberts & Campbell, 2006; Adelswärd, 1988), counsellor interactions (Erickson & Shultz, 1982), appraisal interviews (Trads, 2000), report card meetings (Mazeland & Berenst, 2006) and public service consultations (Svennevig, 2001). These are all interactions where one of the participants has the right, authority and obligation to make decisions about another participant, and where the outcome of this has direct and concrete consequences for the other person. The internship interview can also be described as a gatekeeping encounter, but as described in Chapter 1, the goals and participant statuses of the participants are not as clearly defined as in other gatekeeping encounters. Having said that, including the internship interview in this category calls for further justification and explanation.

First of all, the internship interview is not an event in which, for example, the guilt or innocence, the academic passing or failing, the health care provision or neglect, the welfare provision or refusal, or the employment of an individual is decided. As I explained in Chapter 1, the decision to accept an intern was already made by the employers prior to meeting the candidate. Consequently, the interviews were not decision-making events as such, but rather an opportunity to get acquainted and approve the candidate in question. Although the employers were perfectly entitled to retract the internship offer after having met the candidate, none of the internship candidates were rejected on the basis of the interview. Nevertheless, the participants oriented to and established decision-making as one of the purposes and activities of the internship interview. Furthermore, they oriented to the employer as having the authority and power to make this decision. In this respect, the internship interview can be categorized as a gatekeeping encounter.

There is a second problem with describing the internship interview as a gatekeeping encounter, as defined by Erickson and Shultz (1982). Namely, the effect of the decision made by the employer, prior to or during the interview, is not as straightforward and concrete as is the case in the counsellor sessions which Erickson and Shultz describe. In the case of a job interview as described by Roberts (Roberts & Campbell, 2006) or the counsellor meetings described by Erickson and Shultz, the decision-making and evaluative practices are clearly and substantially influential in determining the candidates' or the students' future. In the case of the internship interview, however, the decision-making does not have as much of an impact on the future of the candidate, since what is being offered is not a regular job but a temporary, unpaid internship that will not necessarily ensure a job with a monthly salary and a way out of the welfare system. The fact that the stakes are, in this respect, not as high as in other gatekeeping encounters so far researched can potentially change the power relation between the internship interview participants in a way that diminishes the authority and power of the employer and makes the internship candidate less dependent and victimized.

However, as I have illustrated with the extracts in this chapter, this was not the case. The participants, including the internship candidates, oriented to the internship and the internship interview as important and influential in relation to their future employment possibilities, professional development and language acquisition. Extract 5 (already discussed briefly in Chapter 1) is an example of how some of the candidates displayed an orientation towards the interaction as important and consequential, and towards the employer and the employee as decision-makers and gatekeepers.

Extract 5 And that is where you will be (repeated extract)

```
12   *EM:   ja det er mig der (0.8) står for køkken og
13          madlavning og frivilligeog ja den mobile cafe som sådan og alt det
14          der foregår der
15
16          yes it is me who (0.8) is in charge of the kithcen and
17          cooking and volunteers and yes the mobile cafe as such and all that
18          goes on there
19          (0.5)
20   *EM:   og det er jo så der hvor (0.4) du skal være
21          and this is then there where (0.4) you will be
22
23   *IN:   ja hehe
24          yes hehe
25
26   *EM:   være med
27          be with
28
29   *IN:   det håber jeg [he he he .hh
30          I hope so      [he he he .hh
31
```

Even though the internship interviews may not lead to paid jobs, the extract above illustrates how the interviews may well be considered gatekeeping encounters in the way that Erickson and Shultz define them. Even though the internship agreement has already been established and agreed upon prior to the actual interview, the candidates, and sometimes also the employers, orient towards the interview as an evaluative and selective encounter, while the candidates orient towards the employer as having the authority and power to grant the internship candidate access to the labour market, professional development and the possibility to improve one's language skills.

The problem with the definition offered by Erickson and Shultz is, however, that it primarily serves a descriptive purpose in that it may be used to determine whether a given interaction is a gatekeeping encounter or not. Although the term is useful in pointing to the power dimension of interaction and bringing attention to the fact that some interactions are central to assuring or preventing an even distribution of rights, the term itself does not reveal much about the actual processes in which this occurs. The perspective on gatekeeping proposed in this book and described in this chapter provides a more fine-grained illumination of the actual processes of categorization and sense-making in which inequality is produced. The remaining part of this chapter will unfold this perspective and this involves a closer review of some of the previous studies of gatekeeping.

In Erickson and Shultz's study of gatekeeping in student counselling sessions, they showed that the amount and type of information given to college students depended on whether or not moments of asynchrony occurred during the interaction, which again was found to correlate with the ethnicity of the students and the ability of the participants to find a common frame of reference and experience (Gumperz, 1982: 142; Erickson & Shultz, 1982). Thus, their study illuminates how the establishment of co-membership and interpersonal solidarity is influential to the development of an interaction and that such establishment is dependent on the normative social identity of the participant (i.e. ethnicity, race), the performed social identity (i.e. locally established) and the cultural communication style of the participants (Erickson & Shultz, 1982: 179).

In a much more recent yet similar study by Kerekes (2007) her analysis of job interviews shows how the success or failure of a job candidate is co-constructed by the interlocutors. But most importantly, she argues how candidates who do not have built-in means of establishing co-membership with their interviewers, whether it be due to differences in gender, education, career or socioeconomic status, are less likely to succeed in the gatekeeping encounter (2007: 1970). It is these interlocutors' background that determines their communicative style, and also how they interpret and respond to each other's utterances. In case of a lack of co-membership, the participants are unlikely to co-construct a positive rapport through their verbal interaction (2007: 1943) or to gain the trust of the interviewer (2006). Kerekes shows that it is the communicative style determined by the social background of candidates that impacts how they are perceived and accepted or rejected for the position.

The definition of gatekeeping offered in these studies points to a specific type of interaction where the decision-making of one person influences the future of another. However, the studies actually reveal an understanding of gatekeeping encounters as interactions in which an implicit process of inclusion and exclusion occurs. This process is conceptualized and described as related to the establishment of co-membership and interpersonal solidarity, which is closely related to interpretative and constructive processes of identity. In the early gatekeeping study by Erickson and Shultz, as well as in the study by Kerekes, a pattern is established in the relation between, on the one hand, the relative success and failure of the candidates and, on the other, the communicative behaviour and background of the candidates. However, while this analytical approach reveals the categorization processes of the analyst based on linguistic analysis of the communicative behaviour of the candidates and interviews with employers, it does not illuminate the categorization processes within the actual interviews, where the participants themselves negotiate the relevance and meaning of categories.

The point I wish to make is that the notion of gatekeeping holds the potential to encompass both a type of encounter in which selection, exclusion and inclusion takes place and the actual processes in which this occurs.

Another central figure in studies of gatekeeping encounters is the anthropologist John Gumperz, who spent 10 years doing field studies on communication in India, Europe and the USA. Moreover, he has used linguistic studies of Hindi/Urdu as the backdrop for interactional studies of simulated job interviews in Britain between English speakers from different cultural backgrounds using different language varieties and accents (Gumperz, 1982; Gumperz et al., 1979). His central argument is that there is a linguistic dimension to discrimination in the sense that people with a different language and cultural background from the majority are disadvantaged in encounters with members of the majority, since their culturally specific communicative styles and interpretative assumptions potentially hinder successful communication. Hence, Gumperz highlights how processes of interpretation and inference are influenced by cultural norms and assumptions that participants bring into an interaction (Roberts *et al.*, 1992: 88–89). The gatekeeping aspect of such processes was considered to be the way that differences in cultural norms and assumptions implicitly influenced the decision-making process of the interviewers.

The studies by Gumperz, focusing on intercultural differences between applicants, by Erickson and Shultz, focusing on interethnic differences between black, white, Hispanic, Italian etc., and by Kerekes, focusing on social differences, all emphasize how the establishment of rapport, 'interpersonal solidarity' or 'co-membership' is influential to the decision-making process and influenced by differences of interpretation and communicative style.

Gumperz also supervised a study carried out by Akinnaso and Seabrook Ajirotutu (1982) of simulated interethnic job interviews at a job training centre in Oakland, California in 1978. Much like Gumperz's work, their study focused on the way differences in interpretative framework and communicative norms influenced the performance and judgement of ethnic minority candidates. Akinnaso and Seabrook Ajirotutu found that the ethnic background and the communicative history of the candidates caused mismatches between the conversational mode expected by the interviewer and the ones used by the candidates. Furthermore, they argued that culturally specific discourse features related to narrative structure influenced the assessment of the candidates negatively (1982: 135).

Although the studies performed and supervised by Gumperz focused on misunderstandings and mismatches rather than the establishment of solidarity and co-membership, they adapted the approach to gatekeeping as found in the study of Erickson and Shultz. Namely, gatekeeping is understood as an implicit process of inclusion and exclusion related to processes of interpretation and the establishment and negotiation of participants' social identities. While Gumperz's goal was very similar to the goal of the present book, I find that the notion of gatekeeping can be explored further and redefined in a way that allows it to encompass and describe the membership categorization processes that manifest in the microdynamics of the interpretative process. When gatekeeping is defined as an outcome of an interpretative process rather than an aspect of it, such as in Gumperz's and Erickson and Shultz's studies, the process itself can be revealed by combining interactional analysis with a quantitative analysis of the relation between ethnic identity and a specific interactional outcome. It can also be revealed by combining the interactional analysis of processes of decision-making and assessment with interviews about such processes. In the former case, which is the methodology of Erickson and Shultz, the correlation between specific interactional findings and a specific interactional outcome is used to infer a discriminative interpretative practice. In the latter case, which represents the methodology of Gumperz, discrimination in job interviews is based on a correlation between interactional findings, an interactional outcome and the participants' stated impressions, interpretations and understandings of the interviews and candidates. In both cases, gatekeeping is emphasized as an interpretative and cognitive phenomenon triggered by cultural and ethnic differences in communicative style and interpretative frameworks which have consequences for interactional processes of sense-making.

This approach to gatekeeping was valid and possible since the data being studied were 'real' gatekeeping encounters – that is, encounters where candidates or clients are either granted or denied a particular position, benefit or service. The results generated by Erickson and Shultz's study as well as the studies by Gumperz were important, persuasive and groundbreaking in revealing processes of discrimination and gatekeeping in particular institutional interactions where discrimination and inequality were possible to measure. However, as I have argued previously in this chapter, and will show in later analysis, gatekeeping occurs in other types of encounters as well, and in other forms than actual processes of discrimination. The notion of gatekeeping holds the potential to encompass the more subtle and implicit processes of inclusion and exclusion that are not necessarily related to explicit processes of selection but rather to processes of membership categorization in general.

I argue that by redefining gatekeeping as an aspect of membership categorization processes, it is possible to describe gatekeeping as an aspect of the interpretative process through microanalysis, which is especially useful in cases where the comparison of 'outcomes' and feedback interviews are not possible. In short, processes of membership categorization are windows to interpretative and gatekeeping processes which can be described through patterns in the way participants orient towards one another and deal interactionally with chosen orientations. For the moment, however, a deeper insight into the findings of previous gatekeeping studies, and how this book's research focus differs from them, is in order.

Studies of Differences in Assumptions and Resources

Gumperz's work on job interviews and Erickson and Shultz's study of counselling interviews laid the ground for an entire field of research in gatekeeping interactions under the headings of Microethnography and Interactional Sociolinguistics, which represent a kind of bridge between the microanalysis of Conversation Analysis and the contextually informed perspective of Ethnography (Roberts & Sarangi, 1999: 13). A range of studies on gatekeeping interactions have been undertaken since the work of Gumperz, mainly by theorists such as Srikant Sarangi, and not least Celia Roberts who has carried on Gumperz's work on various forms of intercultural gatekeeping interactions, inspired by Conversation Analysis, Ethnography and Critical Discourse Analysis (Roberts & Campbell, 2006; Roberts *et al.*, 1992; Roberts *et al.*, 2003; Roberts & Sarangi, 1999; Jupp *et al.*, 1982; Roberts *et al.*, 2005; Roberts & Sarangi, 2005; Roberts & Moss, 2004).

During the 1970s and 1980s, Roberts and a team of other researchers were involved in a study on *Communication in Multiethnic Workplaces* in collaboration with Industrial Language Training Service (ILT) in the UK (Roberts *et al.*, 1992; Jupp *et al.*, 1982), which Gumperz also became involved in (Gumperz *et al.*, 1979). This Language Training Service, which essentially held English language training and cross-cultural training at workplaces, was a response to a need for ethnic minority workers to improve their language skills under conditions that were compatible with their often long workdays and odd schedules. During the 15 years in which this service existed, it was the site of much educational research and practice as well as the source of some important insights about interethnic communication in workplace settings, institutional discrimination and gatekeeping (Roberts *et al.*, 1992). The researchers worked with simulated job interviews and used the findings from these as a basis for developing practice-oriented language training methods. The findings included problems with the expectations and inferences of the participants, a lack of knowledge of the interviewing structure among the candidates and a lack of awareness of these problems among the interviewers (Jupp *et al.*, 1982).

In 1999, Roberts and Sarangi published a study on oral examinations for general practitioners with the aim of finding out whether the oral exam as such was in subtle ways disadvantaging ethnic minority candidates, who had been documented to have relatively little success (Roberts & Sarangi, 1999: 477). They discovered that in order to display the values and attitudes required by the examiners, the candidates had to use and integrate three different modes of talk: a professional, an institutional and a personal mode. The failure of candidates to present themselves in an appropriate way was related to mismatches between the discourses elicited by the examiners and the ones used by candidates, and difficulties in blending these different modes of talk in the right way. What is highlighted by this study is the way that moment-by-moment interpretations and actions during an interaction are influenced by ideological assumptions and expectations about the participants in the interaction, as well as the interaction as a social activity as such (Roberts & Sarangi, 1999: 479). The fact that gatekeeping interactions are not only explicit sites of assessment but implicit sites of negotiation on the basis of this assessment potentially makes it more difficult for candidates who have different institutional, professional and cultural experiences from the majority group, not to mention a different first language.

The relation between ideological expectations and gatekeeping has also very recently been researched by Kirilova (2012) in her study of job interviews with second-language speakers of Danish as part of a government-funded project that aimed to integrate foreigners and introduce them better to the Danish labour market. She focused on the linguistic and cultural fluency of the candidates by defining fluency as an interactional effort in which interlocutors understand each other comfortably. With the added insight from feedback interviews, Kirilova concluded that cultural fluency, which involved candidates linking to egalitarian and institutional discourses prevalent in Denmark, had a more positive impact than linguistic fluency in the case of successful candidates. Thus, candidates that the interviewers felt culturally most aligned with were chosen. This was considered problematic, however, as the programme was established to aid those who were precisely not yet culturally fluent in the 'Danish cultural norms'. This study points to the nature of ideologies as taken-for-granted common sense among interviewers in high-stakes gatekeeping encounters which has the continued effect of excluding and marginalizing individuals and groups, as long as interviewers continue to assess and evaluate candidates from the perspective of ethnocentric cultural practices (Kirilova, 2012: 221). While Kirilova's study resembles other gatekeeping studies like those by Erickson and Shultz and Kerekes in its comparative focus on linguistic performance and the relative success/failure of candidates, it differs in its emphasis on the role played by the ideologies and common-sense knowledge of interviewers. As I have very similarly argued elsewhere (Tranekjær, 2011, 2014; forthcoming b), and will argue and show in this book as well, ideology and common sense are fundamental to processes of categorization. The point I wish to make is that while other gatekeeping studies, including the one by Kirilova, illuminate the factors that contribute to patterns of exclusion, they fail to illuminate the micro-dimension of participants' orientations and interpretations of each other's utterances, actions and category memberships – that is, the categorization processes in which the power of established categories, common-sense knowledge and ideology manifests itself.

Returning to Roberts et al. (2005, 2003; Roberts & Moss, 2004; Roberts & Sarangi, 2005), another larger project was carried out on interactions between Patients with Limited English and Doctors in General Practice (PLEDGE) in Southern London. This study did not explicitly focus on processes of gatekeeping or discrimination, but aimed at identifying barriers for equal access to a specific social service, namely medical services, and the resources that were or could be used to overcome such barriers. The study highlighted how deviations from a given institutionalized interactional order and behaviour create interactional problems that require extra interactional work, which presents a barrier for equal access to medical services. The conclusion to be drawn from this in relation to gatekeeping is paradoxical. Namely, that the equal treatment of patients regardless of linguistic or cultural background will result in the disadvantage of those patients that have a different communicative style than the majority. Thus, gatekeeping is highlighted as a potential outcome of processes of differentiation as well as processes of unification, where everyone is treated in the same way without consideration for potential differences.

The most recent study of gatekeeping by Roberts and Campbell was a study on British job interviews for low-income and manual jobs (Campbell & Roberts, 2007; Roberts & Campbell, 2006; Roberts & Campbell, 2005). This study was the biggest and most elaborate made on naturally occurring job interviews, and the findings and arguments supplement and substantiate those from the 1999 study on oral exams. The purpose of the study was to compare the achievement of British candidates with British-born ethnic minority candidates and born-abroad (BA) ethnic minority candidates to see whether indirect or direct discrimination between the three groups took place.

What they found was that although no overt discrimination of candidates with ethnic minority backgrounds took place, the BA candidates suffered a 'linguistic penalty' in relation to the British-born ethnic minority candidates and the British candidates. They describe this penalty as related to two factors: competence frameworks and equal opportunities frameworks. Competence frameworks force the candidates to present themselves in accordance with certain institutional, occupational and personal discourses that are not necessarily familiar to born-abroad candidates. Equal opportunities frameworks, while developed to ensure the equality of the various candidates through the interviewing process, impose demands on candidates to present themselves in ways that are less conversational, since they do not allow for interviewers to respond to or aid the performance of the candidates. While this type of assessment may be equal it is not fair since it disadvantages candidates who are less familiar with formal and institutional vocabulary and discourse.

Roberts and Campbell's study, like the study by Kirilova, offers a valuable critique of the assumption that linguistic ability is the central cause of misunderstandings and communicative problems. They argue that linguistic ability should not be seen as something fixed which can be unproblematically measured or evaluated by interviewers but is rather shifting and interactionally produced. Inspired by Bourdieu, they argue that interactions such as the job interview require linguistic capital which the born-abroad candidates are not always in possession of. They suggest that the linguistic capital needed in the job interviews studied is first of all the ability to produce responses with an appropriate mix of personal, institutional and occupational discourse, and second the ability to produce coherent, consistent and credible talk. The problems of misalignments, reformulations and misunderstandings that Roberts and Campbell find in higher proportion in the interviews with BA candidates are in this way explained as a result of a lack of shared assumptions and knowledge about the demands of the interview and the indirect way that the interviewers indicated their intentions.

The study by Roberts and Campbell, and Kirilova as well, brings attention to the potential importance of the different cultural, linguistic and social resources that the individual imports into an interaction. Through repeated practices and interaction in different contexts and communities of practice, individuals gain access to a range of interpretative resources, some of which are shared with others but the totality of which is always unique. The notion of shared assumptions is a useful way of describing the contextually specific co-constructions of meaning that individuals manage to establish by means of the interpretative resources that they each have at their disposal and that are made available and relevant within a given context. It is important though to be cautious about mistakenly considering the notion of shared assumptions as fixed entities that one either has or has not, and which either enable or prevent communication. Shared assumptions are always brought about as much as they are brought along and they are never unambiguous and absolute but open to negotiation and challenge.

Roberts and Campbell's descriptions of how born-abroad candidates had consistently more difficulty with establishing sharedness can, as is shown, be explained not only by differences in levels of sharedness of interpretative resources and knowledge but also by differences in the extent to which the participants were able or willing to establish a shared common sense. Meaning is established between people of different experiences and even different languages every day, just like breakdowns in communication and the creation of meaning occur every day between people who share the same language and background and have been close for many years. What Roberts and Campbell's study shows is that patterns that emphasize differences in interpretative resources and differences in the level of sharedness cannot be assumed but must be established through microanalysis. While Roberts and Campbell's study emphasizes patterns of differences and sharedness in the participants' knowledge of relevant discourses and ability to combine these appropriately, this book emphasizes patterns in the way that participants establish *ideas* of sharedness and difference. Such patterns can be identified through Membership Categorization Analysis and it is an important dimension of sense-making processes since it influences the expectations and interpretations that each participant makes of other participants' actions, utterances and discourses. Similarly, the actions, utterances and discourses of each participant inform their interpretation and contribution to the negotiation of sharedness and difference.

What is central in this latest study by Roberts, compared to the previously mentioned studies by Gumperz, is that the resources for interpreting and producing meaningful actions applied by the participants are not considered properties of a specific national, linguistic or ethnic group. Rather they are considered as linguistic capital related to a specific speech situation, namely the job interview that a given individual may or may not have access to regardless of ethnic, linguistic or national group membership. Here, Kirilova's study adds another dimension by arguing that every linguistic act is also a cultural act (Kirilova, 2012: 114), thereby pointing to the necessity of candidates having cultural resources first and linguistic second in order to facilitate understanding in interaction. Thus, actions and interpretations should be determined by a specific speech situation and the context within which it occurs rather than by a particular social identity of the participants, contrary to what Kerekes (2007), for example, argues.

The gatekeeping studies within the field of Interactional Sociolinguistics highlight the importance of having access to appropriate and relevant social, cultural and linguistic knowledge to produce and interpret meaning in interaction, and they illustrate how some of the knowledge required is highly specific to the context of interaction. They also show how the contextualization cues supplied as to what knowledge is needed at various moments in interaction and what responses and actions are expected accordingly are often very indirect and non-transparent. In this respect, Roberts and Campbell argue that many of the 'discourse misalignments' that occurred during the job interviews were triggered by a lack of transparency in the interviewer's way of asking questions, in the sense that they would ask a question that seemed to invite a personally formatted type of answer while actually expecting a more analytical answer. Similarly, Akinnaso and Seabrook Ajirotutu highlight the indirectness of questions in job interviews and the culturally specific ways in which the intentions and expectations of interviewers are signalled as some of the central problems in interethnic gatekeeping encounters (Akinnaso & Seabrook Ajirotutu, 1982: 127).

Following the same line of argument, Baptiste and Seig (2007) did a much more recent study of naturalization interviews in the United States with the purpose of using these to train naturalization interviewers in order to make the interview format more explicit for the applicants. The interviewers were found to 'fly through' the routine of the interview without regard for how foreign the bureaucratic mode of communication may appear to outsiders, thereby lowering the chances for even competent applicants to succeed (Baptiste & Sieg, 2007: 1923). Baptiste and Seig's focus is on fair interviewing techniques, which for the interviewers would entail an awareness of linguistic tools that prevent or repair potential communication breakdowns. In essence, they shift their focus from the discussion on whether it is a lack of awareness of a particular communicative style on the applicants' side to putting the responsibility on interviewers to accommodate interviewees to a reasonable extent. In this sense, the success of naturalization interviews is illuminated to be a joint accomplishment with a central role played by the interviewer.

While the emphasis in Baptiste and Seig's study is on the problems caused by the interactional behaviour of the interviewer rather than the interviewee, the premise of the study is similar to most of the other studies mentioned – namely an emphasis on the link between the communicative and interpretative resources that the participants bring into play and the interactional behaviour of the participants in order to describe some of the problems that can arise in interethnic or intercultural communication. The purpose of much research within this area is to identify the strategies that are or could be successfully employed to overcome or solve some of these problems with a lack of sharedness.

From a conversation analytical point of view, there is reason to be cautious about explaining interactional misalignments, misunderstandings and breakdowns in communication with abstract notions such as discourse, shared assumptions and linguistic capital or ability. Part of the reason for this is related to the reservation in the field of Conversation Analysis (CA) about the way that interactional sociolinguists use ethnographic methods in order to reveal the intentions and expectations of the participants (Akinnaso & Seabrook Ajirotutu, 1982: 133), which is what enables them to relate the interactional context with the individual context of knowledge, ability and resources. On the other hand, it can be argued that CA does not manage to steer clear from abstract theoretical notions to explain and describe the systematics of talk either (Billig, 1999). With respect to the use of ethnography, many recent CA-based studies draw on ethnography in order to enrich or enable the microanalytical process in cases where the recorded data does not speak for itself or cannot be fully understood by itself. What is central, I would argue, is that patterns in the actions and orientations of interlocutors are established and documented primarily on the basis of microanalysis in order to ensure that the participant perspective is not overshadowed by the researcher's perspective. Such patterns can then be further illuminated or described by means of relevant concepts and alternative methodologies. A recent study on Oral Proficiency Interviews by Kasper and Ross provides an example of a gatekeeping study with a microanalytical perspective on the gatekeeping effects of differences in communicative behaviour. They show how the interviewers' style of questioning – that is their use of different multiple question strategies – has direct implications for the way in which candidates perform in their interviews. The differences in behaviour are however not, as in many other gatekeeping studies, explained with reference to differences in the background of interlocutors. Rather they are related to differences in the sequential environment of the ongoing interaction. The perspective on gatekeeping in this study bears resemblance to the one I am proposing, though they focus on patterns in use of questions rather than patterns in use of categories. In both cases, the establishment of difference (in multiple question strategies or in category membership) is considered an interactional phenomenon which can be illuminated in the microdynamics of interaction. While the production of difference can have implications for institutional processes of evaluation and selection, as Kasper and Ross show, the investigation of the relation between differences in communicative behaviour and the success/failure of candidates is not the main focus. Rather, the main focus is how gatekeeping occurs in the turn-by-turn production of difference which (re)produces an asymmetric relation between participants. This perspective is markedly different from those gatekeeping studies previously mentioned that illuminate communicative differences and relate these to differences in background or ethnicity. There is hardly any doubt that differences in background imply differences in linguistic and cultural resources. However, in some of the gatekeeping studies mentioned so far it is not always clearly stated or documented how and why the differences observed in the actual interactions are linked to the particular differences in background or category membership foregrounded by the analyst rather than to other category memberships that the participants themselves make relevant and orient to.

     Another problem that is particularly prevalent in some of the first studies of gatekeeping is that many of them are based on simulated interactional data (Akinnaso & Seabrook Ajirotutu, 1982; Auer, 1998; Gumperz *et al.*, 1979) which were staged and analyzed in ways which tried to control the speech situation in order to compare the performance of the candidates (Akinnaso & Seabrook Ajirotutu, 1982: 132). From an interactional perspective, this attempt to control and stage interactional behaviour is problematic as it does not offer enough insight into the instinctive and spontaneous actions and behaviour of candidates or interviewers.

A third objection, which can be made from a Conversation Analysis perspective, is the emphasis on partially preconceived levels of sharedness, or rather a lack of sharedness of interactional, social and cultural norms and conventions between the participants. While many of the earlier studies in interethnic gatekeeping encounters illustrate manifestations of lack of sharedness or at least differences in the interactional behaviour, such differences are attributed to certain group memberships and social categorizations of the participants without taking other alternative categories such as age, gender and class into account, which may also be potentially relevant.

The approach to gatekeeping used in this book thus differs from those gatekeeping studies that have used simulated data rather than natural data. Furthermore it differs from other gatekeeping studies in the way that no feedback interviews or ethnographic interviews are used as part of the analytical process. Rather I wanted to show how patterns of interpretation and processes of inclusion and exclusion can be identified through microanalysis of the membership categorization processes that take place within the interviews rather than after or before, though they obviously occur here as well. This further emphasizes the categories and orientations that participants themselves find relevant for the particular context in question rather than what I as an analyst might find relevant and interesting. In this sense, I seek to refrain from bringing something to the table analytically that has not already been addressed or produced by the participants themselves.

The central difference between this study of gatekeeping encounters and the original gatekeeping studies lies in the focus on describing the interactional production of social categories, their similarity and difference, rather than on explaining differences in behaviour and the evaluation of such on the basis of different variables such as language, ethnicity, occupation, education level etc. While such variables naturally influence the membership categorization processes described in this book, they are not the main object of interest here nor does the type of data studied allow for a comparison of how they relate to patterns in the outcome of the interactions. In other words, while the analysis in this book is more in line with the interactional as opposed to the ethnographic dimension of the above-mentioned studies on gatekeeping, the emphasis is on the relationship between what is produced in interaction.

Studies of Differences in Communicative Style

In order to offer an even deeper knowledge of gatekeeping studies, the research on gatekeeping mentioned above has also inspired studies of various forms of inter-group communication within Sociolinguistics and Conversation Analysis (CA). The theoretical and methodological position of these studies vary from CA, Discourse Analysis, Sociolinguistics and Ethnography, but they all focus on problems or differences in communication between different cultural, ethnic or social groups in institutional gatekeeping encounters.

Within the sociolinguistic field, Peter Auer's study (Auer, 1998; Auer & Kern, 2001) of the different communicative styles of East and West German job seekers in role-played job interviews should be mentioned as an example of a gatekeeping study that follows the emphasis on inter-group, rather than strictly individual, differences in communicative style. Auer describes how East German job seekers used a distinctly more formal and de-agentivized style, which he argues reveals the influence of the hegemonic presence of a Western communicative style. Auer's study is interesting and important as he highlights how a broader cultural, social and ideological context influences the actions and behaviour of the participants and affects processes of decision-making and evaluation. Although Auer reproduces the inter-group perspective on communication that is prevalent in studies of gatekeeping, he, like Roberts, introduces an ideological dimension. A more recent study, within discourse analysis, conducted by Sniad (2007) explores mock job interviews as part of a work-training programme aimed at preparing African American adults for jobs in the hospitality industry. While the study emphasizes how the teachers convey messages about recruiters as 'hostile gatekeepers' who only hire people who fit specific language values, appropriateness and expectations, the teachers' instructions speak volumes about the underlying values, ideologies and beliefs which the African American job seekers need to conform to in order to be successful in being accepted by the hospitality industry's 'gatekeepers' (2007: 1976). Further to this, Sniad points out how the trainees question whether speaking, acting and thinking in the ways that are expected of them would go against their own, as well as their community's, values (2007: 1979).

Although this book does not focus on the communicative style of the participants, as individuals or as a group, and how it affects processes of decision-making and evaluation, it concentrates on how ideology and structures of meaning influence and manifest themselves in processes of membership categorization.

Within a Scandinavian context, Jan Scheuer and Viveka Adelswärd have repeated Gumperz's and Auer's line of argument that communicative style is related to the success of candidates in job interviews (Scheuer, 2001), but contrary to Gumperz, Erickson and Shultz, Auer and Roberts, they focus on gender and class rather than ethnicity.

Scheuer's study is inspired by Ruth Wodak's discourse sociolinguistics and Viveka Adelswärd's quantitative studies, and he argues that a certain communicative style and discourse strategy, which he summarizes as an egalitarian, personalized performative style (Scheuer, 2001: 228), is more successful than others. Like some of the studies by Roberts, Scheuer's study emphasizes the appropriate and inappropriate use of discourses within a job interview setting and the incompatibility of certain discourses (2001: 233). The relative success of the candidates in integrating and using various discourses and styles is then related to the socialization and background of the candidates, and more specifically to the social parameter of class (Scheuer, 2001: 239). Scheuer concludes that: 'The job-interviews do not distinguish between individuals, but rather between types of communicative socialization' (2001: 240).

The studies by Auer, Sniad, Scheuer and Adelswärd, much like the recent studies by Roberts, Kirilova and Kerekes, show how differences in communicative styles and resources not only related to ethnicity influence the performance of candidates in relation to the norms and conventions of the job interview. However, in these studies there is more emphasis on how such differences manifest in a particular behaviour and style, not to mention the success of the candidates, than on how these differences of membership and belonging are established and oriented to between the participants.

In contrast to this, in this book, gatekeeping is identified in the processes where membership categories are made relevant and differences, or asymmetries, are established and (re)produced. From this perspective, social categories related to gender, class, ethnicity or nationality and the membership of such categories are not considered as explanations for actions, behaviours and interpretations but rather their products. This distinction calls for further elaboration.

The study of gatekeeping has since the early studies by Erickson and Shultz and Gumperz been focused on interactions between people belonging to different groups. When Roberts, Auer, Scheuer and Adelswärd all take their analytical point of departure in the grouping of the participants into social categories, namely male and female, East German and West German, and investigate the performance, behaviour and style associated with these categories, they are inspired by the early studies of gatekeeping and by predominant methods within Sociolinguistics, Interactional Sociolinguistics and Ethnography of Speaking. Ethnography of Speaking is an academic field or discipline. Sniad's study stands out here, as it does not concern itself with analyzing a particular style of communication but rather imposing a more preferred style of professional communication on a particular group of African Americans. While the various theorists carrying out these types of comparative studies, all consider and make reservations about the inherent reductionism of such categorizations: they share the goal of describing, or in the case of Sniad changing, the relation between the behaviour of individuals and the history of linguistic and cultural socialization and practice of these individuals as members of specific groups.

While many of these theorists deal with and acknowledge social and cultural categories as performed in interaction, they focus primarily on characterizing the culturally and socially routinized aspects of behaviour that are not necessarily oriented to explicitly by the participants but can nevertheless be identified as patterns of behaviour related to a particular group or category membership. The following quote by Auer demonstrates the predominant position and focus within the majority of studies on gatekeeping:

> It would clearly be inadequate to restrict the notion of interculturality to more or less explicit orientations towards cultural categories. In fact, the most prototypical cases of intercultural misunderstandings described in the linguistic and anthropological literature are based on the very opposite assumption, i.e., that speakers are unaware of the culturally constrained ways in which they speak, and that they may not orient themselves at all (and definitely not explicitly) to their co-participants' divergent cultural background ... Culturality can also be more implicitly produced on the level of the participants' diverging performances and their interlocutors' interpretations of them. (Auer & Kern, 2001: 97)

Overall, the original as well as the more recent gatekeeping studies have immensely contributed to illuminating implicit processes of exclusion and discrimination that follow from differences in the interpretative and communicative resources of various social and cultural groups. As a whole, the field of research on gatekeeping has illustrated how the phenomenon of interculturality involves the establishment of sharedness and difference related to a range of different social and cultural categories, and not least how this ties in with processes of inclusion and exclusion. There has been a tendency, however, within this field of research to focus on how differences in communicative style, misunderstandings and discursive mismatches lead to patterns in the outcome of interactions that systematically disadvantage some interactants in relation to others. While there are studies, such as the most recent study by Roberts, which describe how interactants orient to and deal with different cultural categories and the participants' membership of such categories, this dimension of interculturality is paradoxically underemphasized in gatekeeping studies as a whole.

The present book aims to remedy this by illuminating processes of categorization as a central element in gatekeeping encounters. Throughout this book, I will argue that interlocutors' orientations towards each other and their negotiations of sharedness and differences in themselves constitute an important aspect of the implicit processes of inclusion and exclusion described by previous gatekeeping studies.

Conversation Analytical Approaches to Gatekeeping Encounters

In recent years, another type of gatekeeping study has begun to appear, such as the one by Kasper and Ross already mentioned. These take an analytical point of departure which is inspired by the microanalytical perspective of conversation analysis and thus focuses less on communicative problems and discriminatory selection processes and more on particular interactional resources that interactants apply as they negotiate meaning, action and social organization. In such studies, the cultural, ethnic or social group membership of the participants is not the object of research as in the previously described studies of gatekeeping. Furthermore, although the speech situations studied can be described and categorized as gatekeeping encounters, gatekeeping as a phenomenon is not the primary focus. And yet the contexts studied can be defined as gatekeeping encounters and their findings contribute to our understanding of gatekeeping processes. The approach to gatekeeping presented in this book can in many ways be said to fall into this category of gatekeeping studies, although I address the concept and the process of gatekeeping explicitly rather than implicitly.

Jan Svennevig's (2004, 2005) study of repetition and reformulation as strategies of understanding in interactions between native-speaking social workers and non-native speaking clients is an example of this alternative approach to gatekeeping encounters. He is less interested in illuminating and explaining misunderstandings on the basis of cultural, ethnic and other group memberships and more focused on describing strategies of understanding and constructions of meaning between native speakers and non-native speakers (see also Sundberg, 2004; Fosgerau, 2007). Although Svennevig in this study orients to, and to some extent focuses on, the group membership of the participants and aspects such as asymmetry and processes of exclusion (2005: 52), this focus is much less pronounced. Instead, he displays a general interest in strategies for the interactional co-construction of meaning. In this sense, Svennevig's study is in line with other Conversation Analysis studies of interactions involving non-native, lingua franca or foreign language speakers (see Gardner & Wagner, 2004; Mondada, 2004). Such studies seek to avoid the categorization and labelling of the participants' cultural, ethnic, social or linguistic group membership and focus on describing how understanding and meaning is achieved. Rather than trying to answer the question of how linguistic and cultural difference influence interactions, they explore, for example, how the normality and abnormality of language practices is produced (Firth, 1996), how 'being a plurilingual speaker' (Mondada, 2004) is achieved, how 'second-language talk' can be interactionally characterized and compared with ordinary talk (Gardner & Wagner, 2004), and how 'proficiency' is interactionally co-constructed (Brown, 2003). Ironically, though, in the attempt to challenge prevalent theories within the paradigm of Second Language Acquisition and Second Language Learning, such studies end up importing abstract, theoretical and highly contested terms such as native speaker or plurilingual speaker into a Conversation Analysis framework that seeks to avoid doing precisely that.

This approach to interactions between participants with different language or cultural backgrounds, including gatekeeping encounters, offers a way of describing the relation between interactional, linguistic behaviour and a broader cultural context in an ethnomethodological sense without allowing the analytical gaze to be clouded by preconceptions of pre-established assumptions about the influence of this context or the group membership of the participants. The ordinariness of a lot of the actions and orientations of non-native speakers or ethnic minority candidates, as well as the influence of general contextual factors rather than specific cultural factors, are allowed to have a much larger emphasis in these studies. The problem with most CA studies of interactions with non-native speakers is that they marginalize the issue of how social categories and the establishment of such categories intertwine with the actions, behaviours and interpretations of the participants. In the case of gatekeeping encounters, defined as interactions where one person has the authority to make decisions that affect another person's future, this marginalization implies that their research focus is isolated from how certain meanings produce and maintain processes of exclusion and inclusion.

The contribution of CA to the study of gatekeeping encounters is its emphasis on what is actually achieved and occurs in the local context of the interaction, which involves a temporary isolation of the membership categories and identities of the participants. The full potential of this perspective should be explored more by illuminating the way in which categorization practices tie in with broader structures of meaning and produce processes of exclusion and inclusion. This ideological contextualization of categorization processes would be similar to the way Auer, as mentioned previously, relates a particular linguistic and interactional behaviour to broader ideological transformations. While the emphasis on processes of categorization found in this book prevents a systematic account of patterns in communicative style and linguistic behaviour, it will be clear from later analysis that interactional and linguistic behaviour is intimately tied with processes of interpretation and categorization. As I will describe in Chapter 4, this is especially clear in relation to categorizations of language.

In short, the present approach to gatekeeping seeks to combine the insights generated by classic gatekeeping studies about processes of exclusion and inclusion related to structures of meaning and ideology with the interactional approach to social, cultural and linguistic membership categories as interactionally produced. The following, and final, part of this chapter will unfold this alternative approach to gatekeeping as an interactional process of categorization related to practices of decision-making and evaluation which are embedded in ideological processes and structures of meaning.

Gatekeeping as an Interactional and Ideological Process

Studies of gatekeeping have brought attention to the way processes of inclusion/exclusion and selection operate during institutional interactions in both explicit and implicit ways. As I have argued in this chapter, previous studies of gatekeeping tend to focus on implicit processes of differentiation between individuals and groups within explicit gatekeeping encounters – that is, encounters where the main purpose is the assessment and acceptance/rejection of a participant by another participant. As described above, these studies illuminate how institutional processes of evaluation can in some cases systematically sanction and discriminate against some individuals and groups on the basis of their failure to comply with the behaviour, communicative style and dominant discourses that are expected by the gatekeepers. However, the vast majority of these studies explore and document processes of differentiation, inclusion and exclusion by relating patterns in linguistic/interactional behaviour to patterns in interactional outcomes. This approach highlights which linguistic and interactional behaviours are expected and favoured by gatekeepers in various institutional contexts. It also, in some cases, showcases patterns in the relation between linguistic/interactional behaviour and certain groups or membership categories such as born abroad, British, manager and so forth.

While these studies emphasize gatekeepers' inferences and evaluations of linguistic and interactional behaviour of individuals 'standing at the gate', they do not reveal the actual processes in which participants (not only gatekeepers) make sense of the context, the interaction and the participants involved in the encounter. While linguistic and interactional behaviour plays an important role in such interpretative processes, I wish to stress that there are many other interpretative resources employed in processes of categorization and evaluation, and many more inferences are made about participants that are not solely derived from their linguistic behaviour or communicative style. This is where the importance of taking a membership categorization analysis approach comes in. The inferences that interactants make about one another are informed by their knowledge and expectations of a vast range of categories that they find potentially relevant in a given context and the actualization of particular categories in turn sets up particular expectations for the behaviour of others. Such a perspective points out how gatekeeping processes are not limited to explicit processes of selection and assessment. Instead, they can occur in any type of context, since gatekeeping is quite fundamentally an essential part of the cultural processes in which boundaries of normativity and deviance are established and maintained.

Holmes (2007) has already attempted to walk in this direction by not focusing on communicative styles related to a particular background but on how colleagues orient to organizational boundaries in subtle ways through their actions and behaviour during interactions among each other. In her analysis of workplace interactions, she looks at two overt cases of gatekeeping among managers and subordinates and shows how joining an established community of practice, such as a workplace team, requires that the newcomer acquire the distinctive interactional style of a workplace or team in order to 'get through the gate' and achieve integration (Holmes, 2007: 2011). Holmes' study supports the argument that I am making in this book, since it reveals how the core of gatekeeping processes is not the discriminatory treatment of individuals as such. Rather gatekeeping processes consist of subtle hierarchizations of categories, behaviours and individuals within a given cultural context of established meanings and ideologies. What Holmes does not address, however, are the actual ways in which interactants establish the meaning of a particular community of practice (a workplace), group (team) or category (manager) turn-by-turn and thereby manifest their culturally established rules which determine membership or non-membership within that community.

Central to the notion of gatekeeping proposed in this book, then, is a broader perspective on the processes of differentiation and hierarchization involved in membership categorization and how these are informed and enabled by culturally established ideologies. In this sense, I explore gatekeeping as a process of differentiation that involves a hierarchical organization of categories in relation to one another and an orientation towards difference as problematic. In order to understand why differences in communicative style and behaviour have negative consequences for 'those who differ', the answer is not only that it causes communicative problems and misunderstandings. What I mean to point out here is that there is a need to further investigate how members of the majority, or those in power, define the boundaries of norm and deviance while sanctioning those that fail to comply with the norms. In other words, in order to understand the prevalence of discriminatory evaluation practices it is necessary to look at the processes of categorization in interaction in which difference is established and valorized in particular ways. Such processes manifest the culturally established hierarchization of categories, individuals and behaviours that enable the implicit sanctioning of communicative difference. What I wish to address, in other words, is not how differences in linguistic behaviour are negatively evaluated and lead to discriminatory evaluation practices, but how it is the very establishment and negative valorization of difference through processes of membership categorization which constitutes the central barrier for participants who fall outside established boundaries of normativity. In this book I aim to show how differences in linguistic behaviour are merely one example of how an orientation towards transportable identities enables the production of difference. By focusing on categorization processes, in other words how interactants orient towards each other and make a range of categories relevant in these processes, what surfaces is the very core of gatekeeping processes which is the production of difference and the hierarchization of categories, individuals and behaviours that it entails. The negative evaluation of deviance from linguistic norms is, in this light, only a ripple on the surface of the ocean of gatekeeping processes.

As highlighted by many different studies of gatekeeping, negotiations of social categories and category memberships are informed and enabled by interpretative frameworks or the interpretative resources supplied by the common sense of a given time and place. However, as I have argued, specific interpretative frameworks cannot necessarily be assumed to belong to and be constituted by specific social, national or linguistic groups and determine the behaviour and interpretations of its members. Rather, specific interpretative frameworks, or repertoires, are made relevant and applied by the participants in relation to specific actions and categorization practices within a particular context of interaction. The interpretative apparatuses that enable processes of categorization and are central to gatekeeping can in this way be identified as they manifest themselves in the orientation towards particular categories and the linking of these with particular actions, behaviours and attributes. This perspective on categorization processes involves a substantial difference in methodological approach from most of the gatekeeping studies discussed in this chapter.

In the majority of previous gatekeeping studies, except the ones that take a conversation analytical approach such as the aforementioned studies by Kasper and Ross (2007) and Svennevig (2005, 2004), for example, such interpretative processes have typically been illuminated through interview feedback sessions and ethnographic interviews with participants before and after the actual interaction. These interviews can certainly be useful in enriching the analytical results and are likely to provide findings that would not have been immediately apparent through interactional analysis alone. However, it can be argued that it is problematic to consider the reflections, experiences and opinions of the participants as accurate representations or recollections of what was 'really' going on. Ethnographic interviews and feedback sessions are speech situations in their own right that represent processes of argumentation and negotiations of meaning that are influenced by the participants' knowledge and interpretation of what is expected of them within that particular context. The opinions and reflections offered by the participants are in this way as much a reflection of the participants' understanding of the ethnographic interview or the feedback session as it is a point of access to the 'truth' or 'reality' of the interaction. This is not to say that such ethnographic interviews are futile, as they may in fact be useful in studies where one of the main interests is to analyze the implicit processes of selection and evaluation that lead to a particular position or service being granted. In such cases, the ethnographic interviews can be used to inquire about employers' reasons for making particular choices, choosing to ask specific questions, their opinions about particular answers received etc. Likewise, the data can be used to shed light on candidates' reasoning behind particular answers, their understanding of particular questions etc. However, when the main research focus is on processes of categorization, as it is in the present book, such ethnographic interviews would not be of much use for two reasons. First, they would mainly provide yet another interactional context in which to analyze processes of membership categorization that might show patterns similar or different to those found in the analysis of the actual internship interviews. In either case, such patterns would not substantiate or challenge the patterns found in the internship interviews since the given speech situation, participation framework and interpretative resources would be markedly different from the ethnographic interview. The two contexts cannot simply be compared or used to highlight findings from each when studying categorization practices. Second, the study of categorization processes makes little sense in relation to ethnographic interview data since the asymmetry of the participation framework and the ethnographic interview as a type of speech situation is more likely to influence which categories are made relevant in light of the original internship interview and how they are negotiated and established. While this process could be interesting in itself, it would reveal little about the processes of categorization and negotiations of common sense that take place during the internship interviews. Finally, there is no particular need to make use of ethnographic interviews and feedback sessions in order to understand how the participants orient towards each other and interpret each other's actions. Granted that there will always be understandings, interpretations and expectations that are not verbalized or made explicit – during the internship interview and the ethnographic interview alike – the interpretative framework and sense-making processes involved in the participants' orientations towards one another, and in their negotiations of the future internship, can just as well be brought forward through an analysis of the membership categorization practices and the patterns of assumptions that are formulated in relation to these.

To round up, in the analysis presented later in this book, the main object of investigation is processes of membership categorization which are involved in decision-making practices and negotiations about the future internship rather than communicative style or linguistic behaviour. Here, language is analyzed as one among other relevant categories that the participants orient to in their interpretations and categorizations of one another (see Chapter 5). I wish to argue that the systematic pattern in the foregrounding of language should be understood in relation to a broader cultural context of common sense and an established normativity related to these categories which make the candidates immediately interpretable as an 'other'. As I will show in the analytical chapters, 4, 5 and 6, the decision-making and assessment practices within the internship interview involve the orientation towards more social categories which are not related to language alone or which can be said to be made relevant exclusively by specific language behaviour. As will be illustrated, social categories related to nationality, language and religion are made relevant by the participants in relation to the negotiation of the future internship and the tasks, competences and situations this will involve. Most importantly, these processes of argumentation and categorization are influenced by ideology and structures of meaning and are thus central to gatekeeping practices.

With this in mind, and dissimilarly to previous approaches to gatekeeping, in this book, I consider gatekeeping to mean *processes of categorization that involve the establishment of a specific system of relations between categories and the systematic uneven attribution, by the participants, of rights, knowledge and status between the members of different categories.* This does not imply that all categorization processes are gatekeeping processes, since the notion of gatekeeping accentuates the establishment and effects of relations of power. While categorization processes do not necessarily produce or reflect relations of power, some categorization practices reflect and establish a system of relations between categories and the members of such categories that involve an uneven distribution of rights, knowledge and status.

As I have already argued, gatekeeping processes are in this light not limited to typical gatekeeping encounters, though their affects are reinforced and made explicit in these. In other words, gatekeeping is not solely a bureaucratic or institutional phenomenon but rather a general interactional and discursive phenomenon of categorization, category association and dissociation which produces and manifests relations of power between participants, and which in decision-making situations can have consequences for the person being evaluated and interviewed. In institutional encounters, such as the internship interview, processes of inclusion and exclusion, much as they take place in any kind of encounter, are influenced and reinforced by a particular distribution of power between participants. As highlighted by many different studies of gatekeeping, negotiations of social categories and category memberships are informed and enabled by interpretative frameworks or the interpretative resources supplied by the common sense of a given time and place. However, as I have argued, specific interpretative frameworks cannot necessarily be assumed to belong to and be constituted by specific social, national or linguistic groups and determine the behaviour and interpretations of its members. It is thus important to get an understanding of how specific interpretative frameworks, repertoires and ideologies are made relevant and applied by the participants in relation to specific actions and categorization practices within a particular context of interaction. In this way, gatekeeping does not reflect badly on the gatekeepers but on the institutional, social and cultural assumptions and expectations in which gatekeepers, and other participants, are embedded in and from which they draw their interpretative resources. Processes of gatekeeping can thus be said to reproduce common sense notions of categories and the ideological hierarchization of them which is culturally inscribed in the way they are organized in relation to one another. In other words, categorization involves the production, negotiation and reproduction of social categories and social organization, and this process is constitutive of and informed by patterns of assumptions and interpretative repertoires which reveal the embedding of local interactions in broader structures of ideology and common sense. This relation between categories, ideology and common sense will be described in the following chapter.

Notes

(1) It should be noted that the separation of these different levels is problematic in practice, not only in relation to asymmetry but also in general, as each level represents a dimension of social life that invariably involves or implies the others. The three levels described are in this way considered to be intimately related and mutually constitutive.

(2) There has been a vast amount of research on native/non-native interaction carried out within different research traditions, most of which focuses on second-language acquisition and processes of learning rather than processes of categorization and power. See for example Gardner and Wagner, 2004; Brouwer, 2003; Long, 1983.

3 Categories and Knowledge in Interaction

> *The terms and forms by which we achieve understanding of the world and ourselves are social artefacts, products of historically and culturally situated interchanges among people.* (Gergen, 1994: 49)

Social categories such as 'old', 'young', 'white' and 'migrant' are labels that interactants use as semantic tools to organize and interpret the social landscape that they navigate in and relate to as part of their daily lives. These categories are 'real' in the sense that they are made up of people who live, act, talk and think in particular ways at particular times. They are however 'constructed' in the sense that the collectives of people, traits, actions and behaviours that they refer to are fixing and shaping reality in a particular way rather than merely describing it. The use of specific categories works to momentarily collect, compare and pull together certain groups of individuals on the basis of particular traits, actions or behaviours that they share, thereby erasing or concealing the many differences within the group established as well as the features and properties that potentially challenge or even contradict the membership criteria. In this way, when we consider the complexity of the meaning of social categories such as 'migrant', 'white' and even 'woman' or 'child', no individual can ever be a full member of any given category just as no category will ever suffice in the description of an individual. We are, in other words, constantly faced with the need to interpret, negotiate and define the category memberships of ourselves and others as we act and interact.

The meaning and consequences of social categories, category memberships and processes of categorization has been a central topic of discussion within various different yet related academic fields such as anthropology, linguistics, sociology, cultural studies and psychology, and the perspective on social categories in this book represents a synthesis of lines of thinking coming particularly from ethnomethodology, discursive psychology, interactional sociolinguistics and cultural studies. Social categories are considered to be properties of socially generated and accumulated knowledge that have consequences for the way people act and think about themselves and others within a given context. This understanding challenges certain sociological (Miles, 1989) and psychological (Turner & Giles, 1981; Festinger, 1954; Tajfel, 1981) approaches to inter-group relations and conflict that consider social groups and social identities respectively as properties of macro-sociological or cognitive landscapes, constituted by economical or psychological dynamics (Wetherell & Potter, 1992: 72–79). Such approaches insert a division between the social and the individual realm and produce static and rigid conceptualizations of individuals and social life in which the individual is a slave of either cognitive functions or social and economic dynamics. As such they have been the object of criticism of ethnomethodologists (Garfinkel, 1967; Sacks, 1992a, 1992b; Heritage, 1984) and social psychologists (Potter & Wetherell, 1987; Wetherell & Potter, 1992), who in different ways and to different ends have advocated conceptualizations of social groups as products of social interaction and processes of meaning. Rather than considering social categories to be fixed entities that determine and fix people in a particular way within a particular social landscape, they can be thought of as products of the processes of meaning in which social reality is constructed and organized and whereby knowledge, thought and action can be considered communal constructs rather than individual properties (Gergen, 1994, 2001, 1991; Shotter & Gergen, 1989).

A Microanalysis of Patterns of Meaning and Ideology

The question of what social categories and memberships mean and imply is one that ties in with issues of identity, self-perception, social relations of power, discrimination and social marginalization just to name a few. The way we categorize ourselves and others and are attributed to or disaffiliated with particular categories is all an intrinsic part of the gigantic tapestry we call culture. Just as our actions as individuals through socialization crystallize into more or less routinized and recognizable patterns of behaviour, rituals, traditions and norms, our ways of categorizing ourselves and others become shaped, understandable and to some extent predictable through our familiarization and reproduction of already existing and newly developed categories. Our knowledge, understanding and expectations of social categories and their members are in this way intimately tied to our expectations of how people act, think and feel similarly or differently in various contexts. Furthermore, and equally important, individual contexts inhabited by different actors and members are woven together by individuals repeating, renegotiating and re-establishing their various category memberships and the attributed actions, roles and behaviours across different contexts. For example the meaning of the category 'mother' and the meaning of belonging to that category is familiar and recognizable to everyone but is nevertheless individually, or in fact relationally, shaped by the various contexts in which a given person bearing or having a child has encountered this category and other members of that category. What it means to be 'a mother' for any given person in any given context is in other words influenced by this person's experiences with other mothers, including their own, in various contexts of social life, such as kindergarten, workplace, family dinners, gym and so on. Thus, when two or more 'mothers' meet in a given context where this category membership is in the foreground of whatever activities they are engaging in, such as dropping off the kids at the kindergarten, their mutual negotiation of what it means to be 'a mother' individually and collectively is influenced by the interpretive resources they each bring to bear as part of their individual life trajectories. As is probably clear by now, from this perspective the notion of one singular meaning of the category 'mother', or any other social category for that matter, quickly becomes difficult if not impossible to sustain. This is not to say that we constantly have to establish the meaning of different categories and memberships from scratch, quite the contrary in fact. We all carry with us a range of ideas of the actions, activities, behaviours, norms and attributes of different categories and thereby a range of expectations of other people's actions and behaviours within different contexts, this is in fact the cultural tapestry that ties us together however loosely within any given cultural context. But the point is that within any given context, these culturally and individually shaped expectations, understandings and interpretations must be negotiated, co-constructed and potentially challenged in relation to the relevancies and the immediacy of that particular context. No categories or memberships are established from nothing and no categories or memberships can be completely predicted or assumed. This is what makes social life challenging and social research interesting.

The research perspective proposed in this book is a discursive and interactional approach to categories which involves the discursive tracing of understandings, expectations and interpretations about social categories and category 'members' as they are established, negotiated and reproduced across various interrelated contexts. Discourse is here to be understood as any type of language which has a particular meaning potential within a given context established and negotiated by those who produce and/or respond to it. The notion of *interdiscursivity* becomes immediately relevant when emphasizing the interest in the way discourses and ideas are carried across and transformed by interrelated contexts. Interdiscursivity is a notion coined by Bakhtin (Holquist, 1981) but adapted and applied widely within the field of critical discourse analysis (Fairclough, 1995; Blackledge, 2005) in the attempt to describe the heterogeneity of the broader structures of discourse that influence and transform discursive and social practice. Interdiscursivity highlights the heterogenic and contested nature of processes and the way that the establishment of meaning within any given context bears traces of and must be negotiated through meanings carried from other texts and contexts.

What this book offers is a discursive form of cultural analysis that investigates the boundaries of actions and representations of self and other, the belongings and non-belongings, the memberships and non-memberships within a culturally organized and partly routinized social landscape by drawing a conceptual map of the related contexts in which such boundaries are established and negotiated. It seeks to describe the system of meaning and knowledge that informs and influences the actions and interpretations of individuals within a given context. While inspired by John Gumperz's and Dell Hymes's characterizations of the contextual embedding of language use, the analysis presented in this book is very different from the type of work found within the field of *ethnography of speaking* (Hymes, 1972; Gumperz & Hymes, 1972). First of all, ethnography of speaking evolved as a partly anthropologically, partly linguistically descriptive endeavour where a particular cultural context would be studied with respect to the patterns and behaviours of speaking as an activity in its own right. The difference from the analytical perspective in this book is the markedly different emphasis on patterns of meaning and common sense as they manifest themselves in processes of categorization as well as the attention paid to not only the situational but the ideological embedding of such processes. As such, the study positions itself within the field of discourse analysis rather than linguistics and is closer to the field of cultural studies rather than anthropology, although the former two and the latter two are obviously related. The emphasis put on context in this way follows from a conceptualization of processes of meaning as fundamentally contingent and contextual, and the accentuation of the interrelation of contexts follows from the ambition to describe how meanings are negotiated, changed or reproduced through time and space and to illuminate the consequences of this for social action and interpretation.

The contexts investigated here are different internship interviews, tied together by the broader context of the unemployment initiatives that they were all part of with recognizable actors such as employers, job consultants and internship candidates, which contributed to generating similarity in the expectations of purpose and goal of the interaction, the roles and rights of the participants as well as the relevances and irrelevances with respect to topics and categories at play. While the goal of the present book is limited to illuminating processes of gatekeeping within the context of the internship interview, the findings presented point to the potential of a more extensive study of how the understandings and interpretations made within the context of the internship interview are interdiscursively tied to other related interactional contexts, such as workplace interactions involving the interns, visitation meetings between the job consultants, employee meetings involving the employers interviewing the candidates and so on. Such interactions would enable the weaving of a more complex and larger tapestry where not only the argumentative threads (Wetherell, 1998) but also the threads of categories and categorizations could be considered as part of a larger whole.

Interpretative repertoires, common sense and ideology

One of the central ideas behind the approach of this book is the conceptualization of social categories as something that cannot be defined internally or by reference to a specific essence or particular attributes or features but must rather be described as socially constituted in discourse, as part of interactional processes of meaning within and across various cultural contexts. The field that has contributed most to this idea and therefore deserves most attention here is Discursive Psychology (DP) (Potter, 2005; Hepburn & Wiggins, 2005; Potter & Wetherell, 1987). It is a field of study which was established through a theoretical and ontological opposition to central notions and conceptualizations within cognitive and social psychology, led by theorists such as Jonathan Potter, Margaret Wetherell, Kenneth Gergen, John Shotter, Derek Edwards, Charles Antaki and Michael Billig. In different ways these theorists contend the hegemony of 'individual minds' as the locus of explanation for 'psychological' constructs such as identity, emotions, attitudes and personality and for social issues such as racism, gender and inter-group relations. Such constructs and issues had previously been studied in relation to cognition, psychodynamics and inter-group dynamics. They argued that the traditional psychological objects of study, through structures of discourse and power, had gained an ontological status as phenomena that are separated from and determining of individual practice. DP seeks to redefine these phenomena within an interactional and social framework and advocates for understanding such 'individual' phenomena as products of social relations and interactions. Social categories are hereby linked to processes of language, discourse and ideology rather than cognitive processes and group dynamics. This 'discursive turn' within psychology was heavily inspired by the spread of social constructionist ideas (Shotter & Gergen, 1989; Gergen, 1991, 1994) and poststructuralist thinking

(Potter & Wetherell, 1987; Wetherell, 1998). Other influences fuelling the discursive turn include the discipline of rhetoric (Billig, 1996, 1991), Wittgenstein's ideas on language as action, Austin's speech act theory and not least the development of ethnomethodology and Conversation Analysis within sociology (Potter & Wetherell, 1987).

The importance of the development of DP is that identity and various social categories related to, for instance, gender, ethnicity and sexuality are now to an increasing extent being studied as phenomena which are produced and reproduced in social interactions and relations. DP has, in other words, moved the object of study from the psychic, cognitive realm to the social and discursive realm, which highlights the historical, linguistic, cultural and social context rather than the cognitive, psychodynamic and developmental context as the locus of individual as well as social processes of meaning. The discursive and cultural context is considered to be dynamic and constantly reconstructed and negotiated through interaction.[1] Three central notions have contributed greatly to developing the analytical perspective taken in this book and therefore deserve further attention, namely interpretative repertoires, common sense and ideology.

Interpretative repertoires

The notion of *interpretative repertoires* (Potter & Wetherell, 1987; Wetherell & Potter, 1988) is central because it illuminates the broader structures of meaning that contextualize and inform the microdynamics of interactional negotiation.

The term *repertoire* highlights the way that a specific collection of words, utterances and formulations are available as resources for the members of a given community. It first appears in the work of sociolinguists John Gumperz and Dell Hymes who use the term *linguistic repertoire* to explain the use of specific linguistic variables by members of a speech community. This use of the term has later been developed and employed by Jan Blommaert for his studies of the social and linguistic complexity afforded by globalization and hyperdiversity (Blommaert & Backus, 2013; Blommaert, 2013). The idea that a certain collection of discursive resources is available to and shared by the members of a given community and can be used in the explanation of people's language use is also central to, yet different from, the notion of *interpretative repertoires*. This idea is very similar to the concept mode of discourse or communicative style studied within interactional sociolinguistics, but the notion of interpretative repertoires focuses on patterns of meaning rather than patterns of linguistic behaviour. While these two dimensions of sense-making practices are, as mentioned, obviously related, the notion of interpretative repertoires is founded in poststructuralist approaches to semiotics, and linguistic behaviour is founded in sociolinguistics. Following a poststructuralist approach to sense-making practices, the exploration of patterns in language use can reveal repertoires that provide a discursive point of entry to the study of culture, when defining culture as communities of meaning. Here the notion of interpretative repertoire will be described as it is defined and used within DP, namely as an analytical unit that can be used to highlight the interpretative resources available within a particular discursive context and are used by interlocutors to construct meaning in interaction.

Within DP the notion of interpretative repertoire has been used and defined by Jonathan Potter and Margaret Wetherell as 'relatively internally consistent, bounded language units' (Wetherell & Potter, 1988: 172), which is inspired by Gilbert and Mulkay's study from 1984 of empiricist repertoires used by scientists as a means of representing their results as factual and objective. Repertoires are in this way defined as something that can be identified in language use and described as a unit. As is clear from the following definition, such units are however not straightforwardly and absolutely definable, since they constitute the sum of a range of different discursive tools such as tropes, imagery, words, expressions and so on. As Wetherell and Potter describe, they are 'summary units' that describe patterns of discourse and they are the 'building blocks' for establishing meaning in a particular way:

> In dealing with lay explanations the analyst often wishes to describe the explanatory resources to which speakers have access and to make interpretations about patterns in the content of the material. The interpretative repertoire is a summary unit at this level. Repertoires can be seen as the building blocks speakers use for constructing versions of actions, cognitive processes and other phenomena. Any particular repertoire is constituted out of a restricted range of terms used in a specific stylistic and grammatical fashion. Commonly these terms are derived from one or more key metaphors and the presence of a repertoire will often be signalled by certain tropes or figures of speech. (1988: 172)

In other words, interpretative repertoires are discursive registers of expressions, images, ways of speaking and concepts that the individual uses to construct versions of him/herself and reality (Wetherell & Potter, 1992; Potter & Wetherell, 1987). The identification of interpretative repertoires in this way involves the identification of patterns in one's ways of speaking, the use of particular expressions, words and formulaic phrases. Such patterns can be manifested at the level of content as well as the level of form, although the distinction between the two is hardly tenable. As Wetherell and Potter describe:

> Interpretative repertoires are pre-eminently a way of understanding the *content* of discourse and how that content is organized. Although stylistic and grammatical elements are sometimes closely associated with this organisation, our analytic focus is not a linguistic one; it is concerned with language use, what is achieved by that use and the nature of the interpretative resources that allow that achievement. (1992: 90–91; italics in original)

Interpretative repertoires are intimately linked with rhetoric and the argumentation for a specific opinion, position or version of reality in relation to a particular interactional context. Interpretative repertoires are used as part of the establishment and solidification of something as factual and 'real' and to define reality in a specific way. In Potter's words 'one of the features of any description is that it counters – actually or potentially – a range of competing alternative descriptions' (1996: 106). Thus, they are an integral part of any negotiation around meaning and not least processes of categorization. Furthermore, they illuminate broader social controversies and dilemmas of *common sense*.

Given the variation and complexity of their manifestation, interpretative repertoires are not easy to pin down and illustrate, nor are they easily exemplified as part of a theoretical outline such as the one presented in this chapter. For this reason, I will present a more concrete and elaborate description of interpretative repertoires in Chapter 4. However, to give a rough idea of what might be said to constitute an interpretative repertoire, the recent debate about the Danish cartoons depicting the religious prophet Muhammad provides an illustrative, although grossly simplified, example (Henkel, 2010). In this debate, two opposing positions may be identified: one in favour of the cartoons in the name of freedom of speech and another against the cartoons in the name of cultural and religious sensitivity. The arguments for these two positions would quite systematically evoke different interpretative repertoires regarding the Muslim population. Where the former would emphasize the problem of religious radicalism and fundamentalism that the cartoons were addressing by using imagery such as burning flags, guns, jihad and so on, the other would highlight the democratic, modern and moderate Muslims victimized by the cartoons by showing representatives of the Muslim community speaking publicly and eloquently against the printing of the cartoons or participating in official and orderly demonstrations.

While this example does not permit a more precise account of the patterns in wording, formulations, imagery etc. that reveal such repertoires, it illustrates the idea of how different clusters of meaning in relation to a specific issue or aspect of social reality can be evoked to represent this reality as factual in a specific way. It furthermore illustrates how specific words, expressions and imagery can be put together quite easily to produce meanings that are recognizable to an audience.

Similar to the notion of linguistic repertoires, interpretative repertoires constitute what is acceptable and recognizable within a given context and thus form a way to analyze what is considered culturally shared and familiar. However, as mentioned previously in relation to the notions of discourse modes and communicative style, the patterns found in wordings and formulations are related to patterns of meaning rather than patterns of linguistic behaviour. While patterns of linguistic behaviour can, as shown by Auer in his study of East/West German styles, very well reflect patterns of meaning and ideology, the central interest of Auers and other researchers within the field of interactional sociolinguistics is patterns of linguistic behaviour. Patterns of meaning in the form of discourses and ideologies are in these studies used to explain the demand for a particular linguistic behaviour within a given context. In this book these patterns of meaning are the central object of interest and the notion of interpretative repertoire is used to describe their manifestation as patterns of categorization practices. As Wetherell states:

> The term interpretative repertoire is an attempt to capture the 'doxic' (Barthes, 1977) nature of discourse. An interpretative repertoire is a culturally familiar and habitual line of argument comprised of recognizable themes, common places and tropes (doxa) ... These interpretative repertoires comprise members' methods for making sense in this context – they are the common-sense which organizes accountability and serves as a back-cloth for the realization of locally managed positions in actual interaction. (1998: 400–401)

The notion of interpretative repertoires is in other words an attempt to establish a link between the activities and actions of individuals in interaction and broader structures of meaning or discourses that, as formulated by Foucault, provide the resources for such activities and actions and define a range of possibilities for our understanding and formulation of reality (Foucault, 1978, 1980). Such discourses are not only manifested in our language and our interpretations, but also influence and determine our economic, political and societal organization (Foucault, 1977). But most importantly in relation to the microanalysis of interaction, discourses offer specific clusters of meaning, that is, interpretative repertoires, which are the foundation of the moment-to-moment negotiation of meaning in interaction.

While Foucault's important landmark studies of how the structure and power of discourse shapes our understanding of sexuality and self (1978) and influences our structuring and organization of the penitentiary system (1977) have had an immense impact on the social and human sciences, it is a form of analysis that is one step removed from the actual doings and sayings of concrete subjects. As Wetherell and Potter describe in a critique of Foucault's perspective on discourse:

> One of the dangers of this view is that the social practices of discourse use often disappear from sight altogether ... The study of discourses can thus become something very like the geology of plate tectonics – a patchwork of plates/discourses are understood to be grinding violently together, causing earthquakes and volcanoes, or sometimes sliding silently one underneath the other. Discourses become seen as potent causal agents in their own right, with the processes of interest being the work of one (abstract) discourse on another (abstract) discourse, or the propositions or 'statements' of that discourse working smoothly and automatically to produce objects and subjects. (1992: 90)

This does not mean, however, that the notion of discourse as a structuring element of thought and action cannot be applied in more grounded forms of analysis that focus on the micro-level of processes of meaning. The interactional perspective advocated by Potter and Wetherell (Wetherell, 1998, 2005; Wetherell & Potter, 1988, 1992) and proposed in this book is precisely about applying a poststructuralist perspective on language and the notion of discourse to describe how structures of meaning and culturally established 'truths' are used actively as resources in the production and negotiation of meaning between interlocutors in interaction. Although the notion of discourse is compatible with an interactional approach to the negotiation of meaning, I will refrain from using it in this study and rather use the notion of interpretative repertoire, which in a similar way defines the structures of meaning that are used as resources in interaction. The point of this is to steer free of the conceptual baggage and methodological confusion that surrounds the term discourse and in a way has created its own inescapable structure of meaning, which hinders the potential of its application.

The notion of interpretive repertoire brings attention to the language use as a co-produced resource, while the notion of Discourse in the

Foucauldian sense highlights the structuring properties of discursive formations to a greater extent. Thus, the notion of interpretive repertoire is more compatible with the processual and dynamic qualities of a poststructuralist framework that I find useful for the analysis of language-in-interaction. Furthermore, the term *repertoire* showcases how structures of meaning that any given individual has access to and uses in interaction are a generated outcome of a history of participation and practice in a range of different contexts and communities. This resonates with the sociolinguistic notion of language as contextual, which is made slightly more concrete, but also potentially problematic, by the notion of speech community. The difference between interpretative repertoires and discourses is, in other words, that repertoires are flexible and used for local, interactional purposes whereas discourses in Foucault's sense have more of a monolithic quality to them. Different repertoires are used as resources for specific interactional purposes (Potter, 1996: 131; Wooffitt, 2005: 154) and they can in this way be used as a tool for a bottom-up rather than a top-down form of analysis.

Another quality of the notion of repertoires is the way it highlights the historic dimension of meaning-making, the fact that face-to-face interactions are not situated in a void in time and space but are made possible by previous interpretations, interactions and negotiations of meaning. It describes the more or less established linguistic, discursive and ideological structures that the individual uses as cultural resources in interaction. In a similar vein, Gumperz uses the term *verbal repertoire* in 1964 to describe 'the totality of linguistic forms regularly employed in the course of socially significant interaction' (Gumperz, 1964: 137) and emphasizes that the verbal repertoires supplied the resources for accepted and recognizable ways of speaking and communicating from which a speaker can choose in accordance with the meaning they want to convey (Gumperz, 1964: 137–138).

What is important to note about Gumperz's use of the term *verbal repertoire*, and later *linguistic repertoire* (Gumperz, 1972: 20), is that he sees the linguistic repertoire as corresponding to a specific speech community, which is the unit of analysis developed within Ethnography of Speaking as a substitute for broader linguistic or cultural units or groups (Gumperz & Hymes, 1972). It can then be said that Gumperz studies linguistic or verbal repertoires by identifying a speech community, such as the Khalapur community in India and the Hemnesberget community in Norway, and by describing the structure of the repertoire available to the members of these communities as manifested in talk-in-interaction (Gumperz, 1964).

As described by Bakhtin, words and meaning always reflect both previous and future meanings, and are thereby fundamentally contextual, historical, ideological and not least ambiguous. The individual utterance can therefore be used as a point of departure for the disclosure of this contextuality:

The authentic environment of an utterance, the environment in which it lives and takes shape, is dialogized heteroglossia, anonymous and social as language, but simultaneously concrete, filled with specific content and accented as an individual utterance. (Holquist, 1981: 272)

When utterances are considered in relation to a context of meaning, history and ideology, the implication is that people via their life history and background have access to certain meanings and interpretative repertoires rather than others. Where discursive psychology thus claims to reject the idea that external factors such as culture, race, personality and cognition determine the individual, it may be argued that they insert a new determining factor instead, namely discourses, ideologies and interpretative repertoires. But the question is whether the notion of discourse, ideology, and specifically interpretative repertoires, present new analytical possibilities. As argued previously, a data-driven discursive reading opens up possibilities to describe contextual relations, based not on a priori understandings of the participants' culture and identity, but rather on the resources, interpretative and linguistic, that they can be interpreted to be bringing into play.

A final theoretical context in which the notion of repertoire has been discussed should be mentioned, namely the context of sociocultural theories of learning where the notion of repertoire is closely linked to ideas about learning as participation in communities of practice. Lave and Wenger use the term *shared repertoires* to describe resources for negotiating meaning created over time by the joint pursuit of an enterprise (Wenger, 1999: 82). Whereas the notion of repertoire employed by Potter and Wetherell is strictly discursive and semiotic, the notion used by Wenger includes routines, words, tools, ways of doing things, stories, gestures, symbols, genres, actions and concepts – or, as she says, both reificative and participative aspects (1999: 83). The repertoire, according to Wenger, has two characteristics that make it available as a resource for the negotiation of meaning: First of all it reflects a history of mutual engagement, and second it remains inherently ambiguous.

This notion of repertoire summarizes or unites the notion of linguistic repertoire and the notion of interpretative repertoire, since it combines the former's emphasis on repertoires as a product of a history of interaction and coexistence with the latter's emphasis on repertoires as clusters of meaning that are inevitably ambiguous, contestable and in flux.

I will use the notion of interpretative repertoires as proposed by Potter and Wetherell, namely as an analytic unit that can be used to situate the meaning of an utterance in a broader cultural, historical, ideological, linguistic and social context rather than the local conversational context. This situating is based on the understanding implicit in the notion of linguistic, interpretative and shared repertoire. According to this perspective, all construction, interpretation and negotiation of meaning is informed by the previous participation of any given interlocutor in other interactional, linguistic and cultural contexts of practice and the meaning produced in and attributed to these contexts. These previous contexts of practice should not be established a priori by attributing the participants to specific groups and defining them in terms of social categories such as gender, culture and ethnicity, but rather by the microanalysis of talk-in-interaction that seeks to establish the links to a broader context by inquiring into the argumentative threads of an interaction, the logic behind specific utterances and the history of meaning which make meaning-making and negotiation of meaning possible (Wetherell, 1998: 402–405).

The notion of *interpretative repertoires* is central in this book because it emphasizes the idea that meanings and categories established within a given interactional context always bear traces of processes of meaning in other, related contexts in the same way as they have potential implications for future interactional contexts. The way categories are interpreted and negotiated and the boundaries of possible ways of conceptualizing them is influenced by patterns of meaning that cut across different contexts and are anchored to larger cultural and historical contexts. In this respect, *interpretative repertoires*, as a notion and an empirical focus point, resonate with the Cultural Studies perspective that forms an undercurrent in this book. This can be seen most clearly in my inquiry into how culturally specific logics of difference manifest themselves in processes of meaning and the accentuation of how the orientations and categorizations of interactants are made (im)possible by the knowledge and subject positions produced and made available through discourse. This is a very different interest and focus from that of CA and one of the key elements that distinguishes this book from other microanalytical studies found within Conversation Analysis and interactional sociolinguistics.

What is highlighted by the analysis presented in this book and by the notion of interpretative repertoires is how social categories, groups and identities are constituted in interaction by means of a range of discursive, argumentative and social resources.

Common sense and ideology

An important contribution to the conceptualization of how categories and identities are constituted is the notion of *common sense* as formulated by rhetorical psychologist Michael Billig, since it highlights how social categories such as 'Iranian', 'Danish', 'Muslim' and 'second-language speaker' are not created from scratch but constructed from the linguistic, semiotic, discursive and social resources afforded by the specific cultural, historical and social context that the participants of a given speech situation are part of and embedded in.

The resources for processes of categorization and particularization are the words, meanings and knowledge which are recognizable and meaningful within a given cultural, historical and social context. This idea is also found in the ethnomethodological conception of common sense (Garfinkel, 1967: 76–77). Here the focus is, however, not so much on specific meanings and words but more on social organization and sense-making more generally speaking, which nonetheless includes membership categories and thereby words and meanings associated with the categories. As Sacks describes it:

> A first thing we can say about this class of category sets is that its sets are 'which'-type sets. By that I mean that whatever number of categories a set contains, and without regard to the addition or subtraction of categories for that set, each set's categories classify a population. Now, I haven't made up these categories, they're Members categories … A second thing we can say about this class of category sets is that its categories are what we can call 'inference rich'. By that I mean, a great deal of the knowledge that members of a society have about the society is stored in terms of these categories. (1992: 40)

What Sacks is describing here is how processes of categorization involve the simultaneous constitution of and use of *membership knowledge* of categories as well as the social organization of such categories. Hence, the establishment and organization of categories and its association with certain actions, behaviours, traits and characteristics involves referencing to other categories, actions and meanings that are temporarily established or treated as real, factual or beyond argumentation. While meaning is established in context by the orientations and actions of the participants, no meaning is created anew. As Billig states, following Barthes:

> The speaker can be portrayed as both master and slave. As slaves, speakers are condemned to recycle concepts, which function behind their back, or rather, through their larynxes. On the other hand, the speaker is the master of language: to speak is to assert the self, and the speaker is the hero who creates patterns of discourse, which have never been uttered before. The paradoxical nature of language-use suggests that theoretical

attempts to dissolve, or resolve, the paradox will be less convincing than accounts which express the paradox itself. (1991: 8–9)

What Billig identifies here is the fundamental condition of processes of meaning, and thereby categorization, that the establishment of meanings and categories involves and imports a history of other meanings and categorizations. For this reason, the analysis of categories related to nationality, language and religion should not only focus on that which is being established and negotiated explicitly and implicitly, but should attend to the meanings, categories and knowledge that are assumed and used as a basis for such establishment and negotiation.

Some assumptions of meaning, knowledge and categories are formulated and repeated in ways that create patterns in form and function. Such patterns can be described as interpretative resources that are used in specific contexts of interaction and in specific contexts within an interaction for particular purposes. The notion of interpretative repertoires has already been described but should be mentioned again here as examples of how ideology and common sense manifests itself and how it is tied to the specific interactional actions, meanings and functions.

Assumptions, meanings and categories are not constant and stable points of reference for various constructions of meaning between the participants. The assumptions, meanings and knowledge expressed in relation to a specific construction of meaning constitute temporary fixations of a generally dynamic process of meaning. What is assumed and what is created changes from moment to moment in interaction, depending on the actions of the participants and the sequential context. With respect to the negotiation of categories, Billig formulates this dynamic relationship between an object of negotiation and the premises of this negotiation in the following way:

Just as the arguments about particulars can lead to arguments about categories, so, it will be suggested, the arguments about the essence of categories can lead to arguments about particulars. (1996: 176)

Processes of categorization are, given their embeddedness in a culturally specific history of meaning and a history of categorization, linked to a context of common sense and ideology. Gramsci's perspective on ideology, which has received a lot of attention and support within the field of Cultural Studies, highlights the influence of intellectual philosophies on the thinking of the ordinary individual, which describes how the common sense within a given context is shaped by broader ideologies about the social world. In Gramsci's own words:

If it is true that every language contains the elements of a conception of the world and of a culture, it could also be true that from anyone's language one can assess the greater or lesser complexity of his conception of the world. (1971: 326)

What Gramsci pinpoints here is how the philosophies and conceptualizations of a given culture are carried by, and reflected in, language, but as is apparent from this quote Gramsci's notion of this relation between language and thought was rather deterministic.[2] When Gramsci argued that every man was a philosopher, he was not praising the thinking of the masses but rather highlighting how this thinking was determined and enslaved by the thinking of the ruling class (Billig, 1991: 7).

With this in mind, the notion of ideology advocated in this book is inspired by Michael Billig's interpretation of Gramsci, which is not as deterministic and much more compatible with a focus on meanings and categories as constructed rather than merely reproduced in interaction. Billig leans up against a specific passage in the *Prison Notebooks* where Gramsci formulates common sense as an expression of differing conceptions of the world (Gramsci, 1971: 324) and argues that Gramsci's depiction of the individual as a slave of ideology does not acknowledge the controversial nature of common sense. As Billig states: 'Language should not be seen to contain a single conception of the world' (1991: 21). Rather, language reflects a common sense which is dilemmatic and this dilemmatic property allows the formulation of critical opinions and attitudes as well as oppositional and polemic constructions of categories and meaning. As with the notion of interpretative repertoires, the relevance for a Cultural Studies perspective is clear in the sense that an investigation of common sense through an investigation of patterns of categorization can be seen to constitute a form of cultural analysis or indeed cultural critique. Common sense contains both the resources for ideological reproduction and stabilization and the potential for negotiation, challenge, re-establishment and change. Billig describes common sense and ideology as dilemmatic (1991) in the sense that they consist of a range of opposing positions and understandings that can be effectuated and used as resources in argumentation depending on the context of the interaction and argumentation:

It is easy to think of common-sense as consisting of the communal wisdom which stamps the thinking of all members of a particular community. However, common-sense may not be a unitary store of folk wisdom, but instead it may provide us with our dilemmas for deliberation and our controversies for argument. The dilemmatic aspect of common-sense, in short, might fill our minds with the controversial things which make much thought and argument possible. (1996: 222)

What Billig highlights here is how the sharedness of meanings and understandings within a given community is not homogenous and unitary, but is rather controversial and dilemmatic. This conceptualization of sharedness formulates an alternative to essentialist and deterministic notions of culture which is instead dynamic and highlights the ability of the individual to contribute to ideological critique and social change. As Billig states:

> The elements of common-sense can be used to criticize common-sense. In this sense, ideology does not necessarily prevent argumentation, but it can provide the resources for criticism. (1991: 22)

The notion of common sense is also used within Ethnomethodology (Garfinkel, 1967) to refer to the socially sanctioned knowledge of 'members' of society that is established through the structuring actions of such members and makes such actions recognizable. As formulated by Garfinkel:

> Socially-sanctioned-facts-of-life-in-society-that-any-bona-fide-member-of-the-society-knows depict such matters as the conduct of family life, market organization, distributions of honor, competence, responsibility, goodwill, income, motives among members, frequency, causes of, and remedies for trouble, and the presence of good and evil purposes behind the apparent workings of things. Such socially sanctioned, facts of social life consist of descriptions from the point of view of the collectivity member's interests in the management of his practical affairs. Basing our usage upon the work of Alfred Schutz, we shall call such knowledge of socially organized environments of concerted actions 'common sense knowledge of social structures'. (1967: 76)

Ethnomethodology is a strand within sociology, which was established and developed by Harold Garfinkel and Harvey Sacks during the 1950s and 1960s. The subject of ethnomethodological inquiry was, and still is, the social order and the means by which participants establish and orient to it in interaction (Hester & Eglin, 1997c). The participant perspective is thus central to ethnomethodological enquiry and the ambition is to describe the knowledge and procedures that ordinary people use to make sense of, and organize, the actions and activities that they engage in. As formulated by John Heritage:

The term 'ethnomethodology' thus refers to the study of a particular subject matter: the body of common-sense knowledge and the range of procedures and considerations by means of which the ordinary members of society make sense of, find their way about in, and act on the circumstances in which they find themselves. (1984b: 4)

Ethnomethodology and CA, which developed from it as a subdiscipline based on Harvey Sacks's lectures on conversation as well as the work of sociologists Emmanuel Schegloff and Gail Jefferson, are concerned with the competences and knowledge of individuals and the way in which they inform and enable social action (Heritage, 1984b: 241). From an ethnomethodological perspective, common-sense knowledge in this way refers to the shared knowledge within a given, and undefined, collectivity that structures our actions and social conduct. While the notion of common sense presented by Billig emphasizes the shared structures of meaning and understanding, the ethnomethodological perspective on common sense instead emphasizes shared knowledge of social structures and social organization. However, there is a significant overlap in the way that Billig and ethnomethodologists consider processes of categorization to be influenced and informed by common sense. As expressed by ethnomethodologists Hester and Eglin in relation to Membership Categorization Analysis:

MCA directs attention to the locally used, invoked and organized 'presumed common-sense knowledge of social structures' which members are oriented to in the conduct of their everyday affairs. (1997a: 3)

What is highlighted by ethnomethodology, as well as Billig's rhetorical form of Discursive Psychology, is that processes of categorization involve the negotiation, reproduction and challenge of commonly shared knowledge of categories, people and social conduct. Within ethnomethodology and rhetoric alike, common sense incorporates cultural aspects pertaining to form as well as content and links it intimately with the negotiations in and of social life.

The construction of meaning, membership categories and social relations

In order to understand the dilemmatic common sense that informs our way of categorizing ourselves and others we need to first investigate how meaning and 'reality' is established and negotiated within specific contexts by actual individuals. We need, in other words, to look closely at the construction process in which people orient to each other in particular ways and construct the category memberships of themselves and others as part of their daily activities. The fields of Ethnomethodology (EM) and Conversation Analysis (CA) have offered valuable insight with respect to how categories and knowledge are interactionally produced and organized based on resources of a shared cultural common sense that are essential to the analytical perspective that I take in this book. These are ideas that have been adapted by Discursive Psychology as well, where they are mainly applied to revisit and reframe 'traditional' psychological notions and phenomena, such as emotions, cognition and attitudes. However, I employ the toolbox of EM/CA for slightly different purposes: namely to investigate how the meaning of social categories is established and organized interactionally within a given context and how patterns in this establishment can be found across different contexts that illuminate the working of ideology and existing relations of power.

One of the central tenets of CA is the commitment to describing social action without recourse to the idealizing use of social scientific concepts that blur the characteristics of the events they seek to describe. Hence, Sacks, Schegloff, Jefferson and their followers sought to develop a method of analysis that would enable a close description of conversational events that would allow the accumulation of cases and avoid gross generalizations (Heritage, 1984b: 234).

An important principle behind this method is that of *indexicality*, which describes the fundamentally local nature of meaning-making both in relation to content and action. In the study of sense-making practices, the meaning of certain actions, words and categories is never decontextualized but situated and contextually embedded (Hester & Eglin, 1997c: 11). This notion of meaning opposes traditional sociological notions of individual actions as determined by overall sociological structures and categories. CA sees local actions as determining what those structures are rather than being products or results of their existence.

The principle of indexicality is however not only a theoretical premise but an analytical starting point, in the sense that what is being studied within EM and CA is exactly the local establishment of meaning and social order. Sacks's point was that the meaning of categories such as young, migrant etc. change in relation to the context in which they are used, in the same way as indexicals such as I, you, here, there etc. do. The meaning and use of categories must therefore be seen in relation to the local context of an interaction.

Another central aspect in the microanalysis of categorization and processes of meaning is the emphasis on the sequential organization of interaction, meaning the turn-by-turn negotiation of meaning between the interactants. The CA principle of *sequentiality* in this way describes an analytical focus on the double contextuality of actions and utterances in the sense that they are at once shaped by what precedes them and giving shape to what follows. As Heritage states, a speaker's action is at once context-shaped and context-renewing (1984b: 242). This principle is fundamental to the orderliness established by participants in interaction and which is the object of study for conversation analysts. Furthermore, it is closely related to another emphasis in CA, namely that of *paired action-sequences*, which involves the study of how the significance of any given action is demonstrated in the responses to such action by a subsequent action. As Heritage puts it:

> Conversation analysis is therefore primarily concerned with the ways in which utterances accomplish particular actions by virtue of their placement and participation within sequences of actions. It is sequences and turns-within-sequences which are thus the primary units of analysis. (1984: 245)

The principle of *sequentiality* is not only manifested in the expectations established by certain actions and in the projection of particular actions by other actions, but also in the very systematic of *turn-taking* that structures and organizes the interchanging distribution of turns of talk between the participants in a given interaction (Sacks et al., 1974). This system of turn-allocation describes the various ways in which a speaker can appoint or be appointed next speaker, i.e. ways in which a speaker can take or be given 'the floor'. There are, in brief, the following options: a speaker can appoint the next speaker, which dictates that this person takes the turn right away; a speaker can self-select himself/herself as next speaker, if there are no other speakers appointed; and finally, a speaker can continue speaking if no other participant has made use of the other rules. This system is circular and can continue endlessly.

The turn-taking model described by Sacks, Schegloff and Jefferson thus explains the principle of people talking one after the other and it is based on the assumption that all participants have an equal distribution of rights to talk. It should be noted that this model is based on ordinary interactions that are considered to be equal and symmetric and not institutional interactions such as the internship interview, where the turn-taking system and the distribution of rights between the participants may have a different realization. While the notion of ordinary conversations as symmetric and equal is problematic and may certainly be disputed, the systematics of turn-taking as an underlying principle of interaction and a fundamental premise for the principles of *sequentiality* and *indexicality* represents a valuable contribution to the study of social categories, since it illuminates the microdynamics of the processes of meaning and social organization in which such categories are constituted.

Nevertheless, the most central and valuable development within EM and CA for the approach presented in this book is the previously mentioned Membership Categorization Analysis, which was a strand of research that was opened up by Harvey Sacks in his very early lectures on conversation. What Sacks described (1972: 1972) is how individuals in interaction constantly order and re-order objects and categories into various collections or the so-called Membership Categorization Devices (MCD). Membership Categorization Devices are, however, not merely collections of categories, but refer to the entire 'apparatus' of categorization, i.e. the collections of categories plus the rules of their application. As Schegloff states:

> ... we are looking for an account for the sorts of hearings and understandings such usages get, and for the practices that get them produced in a fashion that achieves these understandings. (2007: 467)

Associating a range of objects, persons or phenomena into a certain category in this sense means simultaneously ascribing a range of characteristics, traits or descriptors to the objects within the category. This means that people/objects ascribed to a specific category are simultaneously ascribed with certain features. It also means that people/objects that have specific features, which include specific actions or behaviour, can be ascribed to a certain category. A person can thus be ascribed to, or self-apply, different categories and do so in various ways for various purposes, but the instant a different category is evoked different features, actions and characteristics of this person are also highlighted and made relevant. In this respect, processes of membership categorization are influenced by the principle of indexicality previously described. The category 'wife' for example has different category-bound features compared to the category 'waitress' and even though each category can be used to describe a female individual, they contextualize an interaction in different ways and can be used to project two different topical developments of an interaction. By using the term Membership Categorization *Devices*, Sacks emphasizes that people use categories to various conversational and social ends.

What this points to is that people have various ways available to them to ascribe other people to categories. However, while there are endless options of categorization, one category is in principle enough, which Sacks referred to as the 'economy rule'. This is important since it, as Schegloff describes, presents a starting point for making interpretations about categorizations in the sense that 'if one reference can be enough, why wasn't it?' (2007: 471). Additionally, as argued by Sacks (1972a, 1972b; Schegloff, 2007: 467) any person can be ascribed according to at least two general characteristics, age and gender, which makes any choice of categorization subject to investigation, since there will always be at least one other possible choice of category. If people could only be categorized in one way, categorization would not be a practice that could tell us much other than it being a basic premise of communication. Since categorization always involves a choice between various categories, it is a practice that is not simply automatic, but is instead related to the situated action and context of a particular interaction and to the orientations of the participants involved.

Another rule introduced by Sacks, which influences the establishment and negotiation of categories, is the *consistency rule*. From this rule it follows that once a person is ascribed to a category which belongs to a specific MCD, other persons can be ascribed to other categories within the same collection or device. In the internship interviews, for example, once the category of 'Iranian' was introduced, other categories within the Membership Categorization Device 'Nationalities' were made relevant and possible as resources of meaning. As Schegloff states: 'it does serve to inject into the scene or the activity the relevance of those other categories' (2007: 471).

A final notion related to MCA is *category-bound activities*. Certain actions are linked to specific categories through common-sense knowledge, like crying could be linked to the category of 'baby'. This means that through the mentioning of a specific kind of action, certain categories can be invoked. In the same way, performing a certain action potentially makes a certain category relevant. Schegloff (2007) notes, however, that just as categories and Membership Categorization Devices are never simply relevant in or for an interaction, the meaning of actions is also always situated and negotiable. Crying, for example, is not merely a given phenomenon that automatically activates the category of 'baby', but it is a situated practice which is given meaning as crying rather than, for example, a reaction as a result of intense laughter etc. Schegloff argues that Sacks 'treats the description of the activity as non-problematic so as to focus on the categorization of the actors as problematic' and suggests instead that 'the characterization of actions or activities is also a locus of order, and an apt candidate for analysis' (Schegloff, 2007: 472).

Although Sacks, Schegloff and other conversation analysts such as Hester and Eglin emphasize that the meanings of categories are to be considered locally situated and constructed, this is not always the case when studies are carried out in practice. Consider the following quote from Hester and Eglin's study on interactions between educational psychologists and teachers, where the very categories whose establishment and organization they set out to investigate interactionally are reified and treated as de-contextualized common-sense knowledge:

> The membership categories of the participants in the referral meetings are teacher and educational psychologist respectively. Together, they comprise the collection 'parties to a referral meeting' which is an example of a standardized relational pair of categories. These 'parties to a referral meeting' constitute the event or setting for what it recognizably is through their activity. The category predicates or category-bound activities of 'teacher' and 'educational psychologist' in this setting center around 'problem talk'. (1997c: 28)

In this quote, the categories 'teacher' and 'educational psychologist' are inferred from the predefined setting of the interaction rather than the researchers' unravelling and demonstrating the way the participants orient to and co-construct these categories. This seems to go against the principle of relevance and in fact their own description of the researcher's task at hand. Consider, as a final example of this, the following quote, which is taken from a part of the actual analysis. Here they describe the establishment of meaning around the category 'thief', but they do so by referring to the previously mentioned, seemingly pre-established other categories, which are referred to as 'contextual resources'.

> The contextual resources used in making sense of this categorization include the category membership of the subject (referred pupil), the setting (referral meeting), the category membership of the participants (teacher and psychologist) and the immediate context of the co-selected descriptions ... Furthermore, the occasioned device ('parties to a referral meeting'), its constituent categories (teacher and psychologist) and their category bound activities (talking about referral problems) all provide for the reasonable inference that the 'thieving' is not only petty but is a description of a problem for which the child has been referred to the psychologist and not to the police. (1997c: 29–30)

Here it is clear how some membership categories and category 'predicates', which is Hester and Eglin's term for *category-bound actions*, are used as a reference point or the inferential gravity for the meaning of other categories, here the category 'thief', rather than being studied as achieved and accomplished categories and actions in their own right. The problem of Membership Categorization Analysis, which is ultimately a fundamental condition of language use, is that we employ and thereby temporarily fix some categories in the analysis of the contextual establishment of other categories. As Derrida (1981, 1972) reminds us, the meaning of words, and thereby also categories, is established through an endless chain of referral from one word to the next and as we seek to explain or deconstruct the meaning of one word or category we reify and reproduce the meaning of another. It is, in other words, impossible to describe the meaning of a category without importing and making use of another category just as it is impossible to explain the meaning of a word to a child without using another word that may be equally unknown. In this way the study of categorization processes always involves the momentary foregrounding and analysis of some categories and the momentary fixing of other categories. This does not make it futile to study categorization practices, nor does it challenge the principle of relevance, but it is a premise of any kind of analysis that focuses on processes of meaning.

The study of patterns of ideology and social relations of power

There are many similarities between the analytical approach of this book and the Conversation Analytical approach with respect to the way social categories and processes of meaning are perceived. Both consider social categories as something that individuals produce, ascribe to, negotiate and challenge locally in social interaction and there is a shared interest in how language is used to categorize and construct reality in various ways for various purposes, thereby making some categories and memberships more or less relevant. Having said that, I use EM/CA merely as a toolbox, which is a means to an end rather than an end in itself. The analysis presented here thus follows the critical line of investigation and the general epistemological positioning of Discursive Psychology (DP). This distinction calls for a more elaborate outline of the difference in positioning and analytical focus of DP and CA.

The analytical tools applied within DP are to a large extent the same as those used within EM and CA but the analytical attention is more focused on 'how psychology and reality are produced, dealt with and made relevant by participants in and through interaction' (Hepburn & Wiggins, 2005). While this slight difference in analytical focus of DP in relation to CA is first and foremost related to DP's aim of formulating an alternative to cognitive social psychology, it is also related to a more pronounced inspiration from poststructuralist and social constructionist ideas about the individual and the social reality as constituted through language processes. This influence is however more pronounced in the beginning of DP's establishment and seems to be less central in some of the more recent studies (Hepburn & Wiggins, 2005; Stokoe & Edwards, 2007; Stokoe & Hepburn, 2005; Antaki, 1994; Antaki *et al.*, 2005; Antaki & Wetherell, 1999).

Whereas the goal of conversation analysts is to describe the local negotiations of meaning and social organization in relation to a general systematics of talk, the end goal of discursive psychologists is to illuminate broader structures of discourse and power relations as they are established at an interpersonal and interactional level. An example of the former is conversation analyst Lorenza Mondada's study of ways of 'doing being plurilingual' in international work meetings (2004). An example of the latter is discursive psychologist Susan Speer's study of how gender is constructed in various ways during psychiatric interviewing of transgender candidates for a sex change operation (Speer & Parsons, 2006, 2007).

Although the fundamental premise within DP is that different social categories are made relevant in relation to various locally situated actions and activities, a focus on specific social categories, in Speer's case gender, is chosen, since the construction of this particular category has consequences for the future lives of transgendered people. Finding out more about what constructions of gender either qualify or disqualify a person for specific future practices and privileges tells us something about the organization of common sense and the culturally salient distinctions of normality from abnormality. Such findings inform our understanding of what it means to be transgendered as well as normatively gendered.

Research such as Speer's study illuminates how meanings contribute to the production or reproduction of unequal relations of power, processes of exclusion and inclusion and hierarchies of knowledge and power. Such power-related by-products of meaning are not necessarily oriented to as such by the interlocutors in an interactional exchange of utterances, since they are not always visible to them but may be concealed in a seemingly neutral exchange over various topics. This becomes particularly evident in native/non-native interactions, where the analyst shares a cultural and linguistic membership with the native speaker. In such cases the analysts may, due to their membership knowledge, pick up on some ideologically related categorizations that are not necessarily picked up by the non-native speaker, but are none the less influential to the overall interpretation of the interaction.

This form of analysis would by some representatives of 'core' CA be considered problematic, since it uses pre-established knowledge about the participants to inform the analysis and furthermore associates the various categorizations with various power relations. From a discursive perspective, however, the membership knowledge of not only the participants but the researcher as an informed bystander needs to be included in order to grasp the fuller picture of what is going on. This position is related to a difference in analytic goals and perspectives of this book and CA. While I apply CA and Membership Categorization Analysis as part of an ideological and cultural critique, CA studies generally refrain from taking this step and stick to the illumination of the apparatus of talk-in-interaction and how it is realized in different contexts. The central reason why most CA studies maintain an analytical emphasis of the interactional level is their adherence to the CA principle of *relevance*, which has been an object of dispute between CA and DP. In his 1997 paper 'Whose text, whose context?', Schegloff describes the principle of *relevance* in the following way in relation to a critique of critical forms of discourse analysis that use contextual knowledge of the participants as a descriptive point of departure:

> The reservation I wish to feature here is that such analyses make no room for the overtly displayed concerns of the participants themselves, the terms in which they relate to one another, the relevancies to which they show themselves to be oriented. Such analyses insist instead on characterizations of the parties, the relevancies, and the context, to which the *analyst* is oriented. (1997: 174)

Schegloff (1997, 170) has two main points: (1) before relating cultural or interactional artefacts to a political, economic and cultural context, we must understand their constitution as objects in their own right; (2) For each inquiry researchers make, we have to establish and re-establish what constitutes the relevant social context. What he is advocating here is that research should be unmotivated by specific research interests and should be guided by concepts relevant to the participants rather than analytical concepts relevant to the researcher.

Michael Billig (1999) contests Schegloff's portrayal of the method of CA as unmotivated and uninfluenced by assumptions about the participants and the interactions studied. He argues that CA is not, as claimed, neutral in its investigations of talk-in-interaction and that they too impose certain pre-established categories and conceptualizations of the social world upon their analytic object. In Billig's words, 'CA contains its own ideological and sociological assumptions' (1999: 544) that are manifested in a 'foundationalist' and 'specialist rhetoric' found in the portrayal of CA formulated by Schegloff and others (1999: 543). By this he means that

CA research is first of all guided by assumptions about the social world as characterized by equality between the participants regarding rights to speak and act. This is what he refers to using the term *foundationalist rhetoric*. Such assumptions become problematic, Billig argues, when looking at interactions that are overtly influenced by power relations, which is, as shown in Chapter 2 and in the previous example, the case in the internship interview. Secondly, CA is guided very explicitly by what Billig refers to as *specialist rhetoric*, namely an extensive terminological framework that seeks to objectify the actions and behaviour of interlocutors, but simultaneously represents and constructs such actions in a very specialized and theoretically informed way.

The analytical perspective presented in this book aligns with the argument presented by Billig that all forms of research of talk-in-interaction are ideologically and theoretically informed (1999) as well as with the argument presented by Billig (1999: 544) and Schegloff (1997: 174, 180, 184) that critical forms of discourse analysis should be based on fine-grained analysis of actual discourse. In order to ensure that the researcher's perspective enriches rather than overshadows the participant perspective, it is important that the analysis of interactions in their own right precedes the macro-perspective on broader issues of power and ideology (Schegloff, 1997: 174, 180, 184).

The difference between CA and critical discourse analysis can be summarized as a difference between empirically derived analytical categories and theoretically derived analytical categories and furthermore as a difference between aspiring towards unmotivated looking or guided (critical) looking. And yet such a distinction is of course blurred and problematic when considering actual studies within the two fields.

What is problematic in any form of analysis, whether oriented towards micro- or macro-dimensions of processes of meaning, is if a specific conceptual and terminological framework is applied without consideration of how its mere application shapes and delimits the given object of research. In this way, CA studies which isolate and claim the workings of the 'machinery of talk-in-interaction' and ignore the potential influence of broader structures of power and ideology are as problematic as critical studies of discourse that isolate and claim 'structures of power and ideology' and ignore the actions and behaviour of people.

In this book, categories such as 'internship candidate', 'employer', 'Muslim' and 'Danish' are considered and documented as relevant for the participants on an interactional level. Furthermore, analytic categories such as Membership Categorization Devices, Ideology and Culture are considered relevant on an analytic level since they can be shown to point to different, yet interrelated, aspects of the participants' actions and orientations. In short, this book's analytical motivation was not an interest in ideology or turn-taking as such, but rather an interest in exploring processes of meaning related to the employment of migrants, and more specifically within the context of the internship interview. Naturally, this choice of empirical object was influenced by an orientation towards specific categories such as 'migrants', but the ensuing analysis of the data showed that this orientation was equally relevant for the participants themselves. If they had not been relevant within the actual interviews, these empirical categories would, and should, have lost their relevance for my research as well, or at least the relevance should have been questioned. In the same way the analytical perspective of the book is informed and enabled by knowledge of the principle of turn-taking and notions of ideology, the legitimacy and relevance of these analytic categories is determined by the fact that such principles and processes were found and can be evidenced in my data.

The question of relevance is thus closely related to broader methodological principles of 'good research', defined as a systematic illustration and support of arguments, on the basis of a clearly defined object of research and a clearly defined theoretical and analytic framework. Furthermore, the question of relevance is not only determined by the orientations of the participants, but rather somewhere in the circular process of choosing, investigating and redefining an object of research. In turn, this is a process that should be data driven and participant oriented, but is always influenced by the assumptions, understandings and knowledge of the researcher. This should not be considered a problem but an unavoidable premise of research that can be a useful and valid point of departure, as long as it is acknowledged and incorporated into the analysis.

A central part of the discussion of relevance is exactly the question of the analyst's position with regard to the membership and knowledge of the participants. As described previously, EM and CA rest on the premise of membership knowledge as the resource used by participants in interaction to understand and interpret actions and to perform meaningful actions in response. Equally, this membership knowledge is the resource used by the analyst to understand and interpret actions and behaviour in interactions. This raises the question of whether a researcher can or should study interactions involving participants who have different linguistic and cultural memberships. I will not go into this discussion here, but will merely focus on the fact that the analyst is considered to import and apply their own membership knowledge in the analysis of what is going on within an interaction. Naturally it cannot be assumed that the researcher has access to the same cultural, social and linguistic resources as the interlocutors studied and this sets the limits for what can be heard and 'caught' in the analysis.

In relation to the question of relevance one could argue that such membership knowledge enables and justifies the inclusion of categories that are not being explicitly oriented to by the participants. In other words, if the analyst sees gender, power or racism then such interpretations could be regarded as a result of his or her membership knowledge of the context of the situation and the membership categories put in play.

The position that CA is advocating is very useful in the sense that it broadens the analytical gaze and allows for more inductive and also surprising findings, since it prevents the analysis from being steered in a direction of preconceived understandings and ideas about the context and the participants. However, I agree with Billig and Schegloff that the principle of relevance does not necessarily undermine or make impossible the critical ambition of many discursive psychologists, but rather brings attention to invalid or unreliable ways of doing analysis in general. As it is argued by Potter and Wetherell (1987, 1988), meticulous and thorough attention to sequences which challenge or deviate from the systematicity discovered is a prerequisite for valid and reliable discourse analysis. Although they are referring to the analysis of interpretative repertoires, the same applies to the study of categories in interaction. Even if the analytical outset is an interest in specific categories such as gender or ethnicity, the establishment and negotiation of these should clearly be demonstrated empirically to the same extent as any other identities that are made relevant during the interaction. This opens up the possibility of finding out that a given interaction was not about negotiating, for example, gender but rather about doing actions and activities that made a whole other range of identities relevant. Moreover, it allows for the discovery of how the categories of interest are interrelated with other categories and actions as their negotiation and establishment unfolds in interaction.

In this book, I aim to show how categories and processes of categorization and particularization tie in with a cultural common sense and can be used to illuminate cultural 'truths' and the way reality is constantly negotiated but also fixated in particular ways for particular purposes. As will be shown in Chapters 4, 5 and 6 the establishment of categories related to nationality, language and religion, as processes of categorization in general, is influenced by fundamental properties of language processes that are linked to ideology and hereby to the social relations of power. This conceptualization is critical in the sense that it highlights and assumes the ideological nature of common sense and recognizes that ideology and common sense contribute to maintaining and reproducing social relations of power.

According to Gramsci, by reproducing the thinking of the ruling class, the ordinary person is also confirming and submitting to their domination. Ideologies are, in other words, not only manifested in language and processes of categorization, but in certain structures of social relations that determine the domination and power of some groups and individuals. Again the aforementioned determinism resonates in such ideas and the individual is portrayed as unable to act or speak outside ideology and that even when they think they are challenging conventional or commonsensical ways of speaking, acting and behaving, they are merely reproducing the status quo and confirming its primary and superior status as common sense. A classic example of this is feminism that seeks to challenge the unequal distribution of rights, privileges and status between men and women, but can only do so on the premises created by men and thereby reproducing and confirming their domination.

The notion of power applied in this book is, like the notion of ideology, dialectical rather than deterministic, in the sense that language and interaction are regarded as both producing and reproducing a certain distribution of rights and power. Thus, the actions and behaviour of the participants in interaction both establish a certain distribution of rights and manifest already established power structures – both of these forms of power can be analyzed by describing what is said and what is seemingly assumed.

This is particularly evident in institutional interactions where assessment plays a role and where there is an unequal distribution of rights to categorize related to the distribution of rights of the participants. In a study of report card meetings between school teachers, Mazeland and Berenst (2006) show the interrelation of an overall institutional organization of particular assessment practices and local processes of categorization. The structure of the school system thus enables the actual report-card meeting event, and the school evaluation system makes it necessary to rank students in a certain way and thereby makes the pre-given categories of MAVO and HAVO[3] students relevant. Mazeland and Berenst apply Goffmann's term *situated activity system* to describe how the contextual embeddedness of the report-card meetings influences the organization of the decision-making. This contextual embeddedness includes the institutional hierarchy and the uneven distribution of power between teachers and students.

In relation to the internship interview we see a similar interplay between the local membership categorization practices and a broader institutional, social, historical and cultural context, which influences the actions and behaviours of the participants and renders some categories, actions and meanings recognizable and commonsensical and others controversial, problematic and unthinkable. As described in Chapter 1, the internship interview is enabled as an interactional event through the job-training programme, which the internship candidate is participating in as part of an employment strategy initiated by the municipality and ultimately the government. This employment strategy can be said to be a result of the large amount of migrants and refugees on social support or welfare and the increasing gap between migrants and non-migrants on the labour market. In this way, the social and economical structures contribute to creating the possibility for the internship candidate to spend a month or two on an internship, which is funded by the government through social support or welfare, all of which create the context and opportunity for the internship interview in the first place.

Not only do certain social and economical inequalities in this way enable and contextualize the speech situation of the internship interview, they also potentially influence the participation framework to project a certain distribution of rights and roles between the participants. The job consultant, for example, is paid by the government to help the candidate in his or her job search and is therefore responsible for establishing and participating in the internship interview. Although the context of the internship interview does not in any way determine a specific behaviour of the candidates, the various participants are there as representatives of a certain position in the labour market and the welfare system – that is either unemployed, employer and job consultant – and this influences the distribution of rights and actions available to each participant.

The context of the internship interview in this way presents an example of how ideologies such as those related to the welfare system, employment, the community, citizenship and so on are intimately linked to social relations of power and how all of these realms enable, inform and potentially influence particular speech situations.

It is important to bear in mind, however, that ideologies and social relations of power are fundamentally dilemmatic. Though they influence and inform social interaction, this does not imply that they determine social action. As Billig describes:

> The rhetorical repetition is more than a repetition: the slaves can order their masters into new argumentative battles. Speakers might reproduce common sense, but their reproductions will not leave ideology unchanged. (1991: 22)

In order to analyze the manifestation of ideologies and social relations of power in the actions and behaviours of individuals, one therefore has to study such actions and behaviours. The interpretation, argumentation, establishment and enactment of ideology and power cannot be predicted on the basis of a critical perspective. Ideology and power are not only reproduced but also potentially established and challenged within a specific speech situation or a specific utterance. As Billig further states:

> Each echo is itself a distortion, for none can be a perfect repetition of what was already a series of repetitions. No two contexts are exactly identical, and, therefore, no two utterances can have precisely the same meaning. Each repetition will be a creation, bringing the past towards its future. (1991: 22)

The close attention paid to the interpretation, argumentation, establishment and enactment of ideologies and social relations of power by specific participants within a specific context can thus challenge not only the assumptions and ideologies of a given time and place, but also the very assumptions and ideologies of the analyst as well.

What I propose in this book is that the methodology of CA, and not least its ethnomethodological foundation, formulates a fundamentally interpretative endeavour that can very well be used to address specific questions and social issues and is highly compatible with more critical forms of analysis. However the methodological principle within CA of 'holding off' from giving explanations on the basis of assumed identities and categories and the commitment to the 'documentation' of the relevance of such identities and categories are important in ensuring the quality of such analysis. While CA's reasoning behind committing to such principles is primarily methodological, the reasons presented in this book are furthermore epistemological or even ontological in the sense that the social world is considered to be socially constructed and more specifically constituted through language. In this way, my analysis formulates the linking of ethnomethodological principles of research and poststructuralist and socialconstructionist perspectives on identity and social categories as constructions and positions within a discursive context (Hall, 1997a, 1997b; Hall & Du Gay, 1996; Jameelah, 2011). In doing so, I am – as can be seen in the references – inspired by the British Cultural Studies tradition, and in particular Stuart Hall's approach to ideology, representation and identity. The abovementioned link is also argued and/or illustrated in the work of British sociolinguist Ben Rampton and discursive psychologists Margaret Wetherell and Jonathan Potter (Rampton, 1999, 2003, 2005, 2006; Rampton et al., 2006; Wetherell, 1998, 2005; Wetherell & Potter, 1988, 1992). What distinguishes this book from such studies is the inspiration from interactional sociolinguistics which is reflected in the emphasis on how processes of meaning involve processes of gatekeeping. What the book addresses is the boundaries of normativity and deviance that are involved in sense-making practices and the processes of inclusion and exclusion that are involved in the maintenance and challenging of such boundaries.

Analyzing gatekeeping discourse-in-interaction

The combination of perspectives, tools and concepts from Conversation Analysis and Discursive Psychology allows for the capturing of the dialectic of discourse-in-interaction, i.e. how social individuals and social life are simultaneously structuring and structured by language and discourse. The purpose of combining a CA perspective and a discursive psychological perspective is to grasp the microdynamics of discourse-in-interaction and the way that such microdynamics tie in with and reveal broader structures of discourse that influence our (inter)actions and also the possibilities of constructing ourselves and others and positioning ourselves in social life.

The tools of CA, namely sequential analysis and Membership Categorization Analysis, allow for a description of how nationality, religion and language are made relevant and the different consequences of this for the future development of the interaction. Discursive Psychology and the notion of interpretative repertoires, on the other hand, allow for a description of how certain patterns in the construction of nationality, language and religion constitute structures of meaning that are related to power and ideology. Such structures constitute part of the resources for constructing and negotiating meaning in interaction, and they are an important dimension of membership knowledge and cultural common sense.

The tools of Conversation Analysis and Membership Categorization Analysis can be used to shed light on how the participants construct, negotiate, interpret and orient to various social categories, meanings and identities and mutually co-construct what the interaction is about and where it is going. This form of analysis shows how the sequential organization and development is closely tied to the categorical work of the participants, and that in order to describe how nationality, language and religion are made relevant and the consequences of this, both perspectives must be included in a back and forth movement as described by Watson:

> What I am claiming, then, is that interlocutors' sensible production and monitoring of an utterance and of a series of utterances is both categorical and sequential. Interlocutors' conjoint orientation to the categorical relevances informs their orientation to the 'structure' of

utterance and series which in turn inform the categorical relevances. (Watson, 1997: 54)

Hence, making certain categories relevant influences the sequential development of the interaction, which again has consequences for the categorical negotiations that follow, which in turn influences ... and so forth. We will see this very clearly in Chapter 6 as orientation towards the category 'Muslim' immediately influences the distribution of roles and turns between the employer and the candidate and led to an extensive negotiation about religion. There is, however, yet another dimension of the construction of sense or meaning which is not considered in sequential CA analysis, and is only tacitly implied in Membership Categorization Analysis, namely the relation between an interactional here and now and the discourses and ideologies in which this here and now is embedded.

Sequential Conversation Analysis and Membership Categorization Analysis deal with the local establishment of meaning between participants and determine the meaning of each individual utterance by looking at how it is received and responded to by the other participants. In the search for an answer to the question that drives CA, namely 'why that now', Conversation Analysts seek to explain social action and organization by continually moving backwards in the interaction, looking at the previous utterances and actions. Within Conversation Analysis the meaning and organization of social action and language are, in other words, pursued through a back and forth movement between what occurs previous to and after an utterance.

In the ensuing analysis, various utterances or extracts will be chosen as starting points to determine how nationality, language and religion are made relevant in the interaction and with what consequences. While such starting points certainly allow a description of how the participants respond to and negotiate the utterances by other participants, it does not enable any explanation of why specific utterances occur and are made relevant in the first place. In order to understand 'why that now?' one has to move further back in the interaction, since the previous turns constitute the conversational context of this exact utterance in the same way that the utterance itself establishes the conversational context for what is to follow. Although one can always choose to include a larger extract or go further back in the interaction to look for a sequentially based explanation for a specific utterance or activity, this will only give half an answer at best, and at worst provide no answer at all. It may reveal that a specific topic or category such as nationality is made relevant in relation to a discussion of experience or problems at the workplace, which allows us to establish that the participants orient to and construct a relation between nationality and experience. However, it does not tell us anything in itself about why that relation is recognized and treated as meaningful. Not only can this question not be answered within the framework of the isolated interactional context, it is also a question that will not be pursued within CA, since it extends beyond the local organization of meaning and social action into the broader cultural, discursive and ideological organization of meaning and social action.

In the following analysis, it will be shown how the participants' constructions of nationality, religion and language background form patterns that reveal structures of meaning around the notion of culture that resonate with traditional notions of culture as institutionalized systems of thought and ways of being which determine individual thought and action. Such notions of culture are closely linked to a cultural relativist form of thinking, which has been influential since Boas (Liep & Olwig, 1994: 7). Moreover, these notions share a range of common features with the idea of the Nation State, which, as Anderson describes, evolved during the period of Enlightenment (1991: 5–7). It will be argued that patterns in the membership categorizations established within the internship interview can be said to reveal the influence of 'common-sense' understandings of culture that tie in with the negotiations of not only categories related to nationality, language and religion, but with the orientations of the participants towards each other and towards the speech situation in general.

The notion of interpretative repertoire will be used to shed light on patterns in the logic and reasoning of the participants and to reveal structures in the knowledge and understandings which are taken for granted. I will not apply theories about culture, nationality, religion or ethnicity analytically to explain the actions and behaviour of the participants, but rather to illuminate systematically appearing categorizations, assumptions and meanings related to nationality, language and religion as they are established and negotiated in interaction. The discursive psychological concept interpretative repertoire can be used to disclose such systematics and to identify and define the understandings that are brought in play from the participants' actions and utterances, rather than from theoretical considerations and definitions.

As Wetherell and Potter (1988: 177–78) describe, the identification and definition of interpretative repertoires requires a description of their systematic appearance and use throughout a larger corpus of data. Since various repertoires are characterized by their incommensurability, difference and variability in relation to a local function (Wetherell & Potter, 1988), this is done by demonstrating how their appearance in a given text or interaction is separate and different from the appearance of other opposite repertoires and by showing the participants' orientation towards this difference and incommensurability. It is not possible, based on merely one extract, to define and identify the interpretative repertoires related to nationality, language and religion that the participants are possibly drawing upon, since one extract does not reveal the variability of argumentation and meaning, and thereby also the incommensurability and difference that define different repertoires. The following analysis will therefore examine and compare the various categorizations related to nationality, language and religion throughout the entire data-collection.

While the concept of Membership Categorization Device is, as mentioned, a useful tool to describe how the establishment of certain categories and category-bound activities establish and organize the social world in a specific way, the following analysis illustrates and argues that it falls short of capturing the systems of reasoning that can be said to inform processes of categorization and link them to ideologies and common sense. The notion of interpretative repertoire, on the other hand, illuminates this dimension of processes of meaning and social organization. What is highlighted by the concept of interpretative repertoire and the discursive psychological perspective is that by using a certain range of words, formulations and images one can index and make relevant a specific interpretative framework that links the local categorizations, actions and behaviour of interactants to a discursive, cultural and ideological context. One could say that MCDs and categories are enmeshed with a range of interpretative repertoires and can be identified in relation to these, but that an interpretative repertoire is never confined to a single category or a collection of categories and can only be identified in relation to patterns of categorization. For example, the notion of MCD can be used to describe how Islam and other religions are made relevant through the orientation towards the scarf and the use of the category 'Muslim'. It cannot explain however, the particular ways in which the category 'Muslim' is interpreted, negotiated and defined within this particular context and the patterns of meaning related to this category that are informed by the particular historic, ideological and cultural context which the internship interviews are situated in. The MCD religion and the category 'Islam' as part of this could in other words be activated and applied in very different ways in other interactional contexts where it would constitute an element of a completely different interpretative framework. The words and meanings used and produced could in such cases form very different patterns of meaning. This will be illustrated and discussed further in Chapter 6 where I show an example from an internship interview at a Muslim kindergarten. While the MCDs and categories activated here are the same, the interpretative frameworks applied and manifested in the discussion of Muslims is very different. By looking at both membership categorization and interpretative repertoires, one can illuminate the interrelation of locally produced meanings and social organization and broader structures of meaning and ideology.

The combination of Membership Categorization Analysis and the analysis of interpretative repertoires provides the means to investigate *gatekeeping* in internship interviews, or more specifically, how membership categories related to nationality, language and religion are established, negotiated and evaluated in internship interviews and how this systematically establishes a particular distribution of rights, knowledge and status between the participants.

During all of the internship interviews, at one point or another, one or some of the participants oriented to either the national, religious or language membership of the candidates, which was related to an either implicit or explicit orientation to the category of 'Danes' and an implicit or explicit exclusion of the internship candidates from this category. What will be argued and illustrated in the following analysis is how categorizations related to nationality, language and religion are highly influenced by common-sense notions of culture as a particular 'way of doing things' and a 'system of values and practices'. While culture was in some cases explicitly topicalized, in most cases it was implicitly made relevant through the topicalization of nationality, language or religion, but the general outcome was an increased focus on the difference or otherness of the candidates in relation to the nationality, language, 'culture' or religion of 'Danes'. A major part of the analysis will consist of describing and comparing the various ways in which the participants orient to and construct actions, things or people as culturally related. The analysis will show how making cultural membership or cultural otherness relevant influences the future development of an interaction and how members' categorizations related to nationality, language and religion reveal processes of gatekeeping that are fuelled by and reproduce ideologies and common-sense assumptions related to immigration, language learning, culture and religion.

The analysis is structured in a way that first separates the three different ways that I found the participants orienting to the cultural otherness of the candidates, and second seeks to compare them in relation to more general patterns in form, function and content. Chapter 4 looks at how Danish 'culture' is made relevant in relation to categorizations of nationality and argues that nationality or national group membership is not only associated with a specific place of birth, but also with a specific organization and understanding of reality. Chapter 5 examines how Danish 'culture' is made relevant in relation to categorizations related to language and linguistic resources. More specifically, the construction of specific speech communities is linked to specific systems of knowledge and used as criteria of distinction and exclusion from another system of knowledge, namely Danish 'culture'. Chapter 6 investigates how religion is made relevant and similarly used as an explanation for actions and understandings that are constructed as different from and incompatible with common practices and common sense in Denmark. In Chapter 7 these findings are considered in relation to the notion of gatekeeping and discussed as more general strategies of inclusion and exclusion.

Notes

(1) For further introduction to Discursive Psychology see Edwards and Potter, 1992; Potter, 2005; Potter and Wetherell, 1987; Wetherell and Potter, 1988; Wetherell and Potter, 1992; Wooffitt, 2005.

(2) Gramsci uses the idea that one can assess the greater or lesser complexity of a person's conception of the world through that person's language to criticize incomplete language learning and the speaking of dialects. He argues that a person speaking with a dialect can only have a 'limited and provincial' intuition about the world and that it is therefore necessary to at least learn the national language properly (Gramsci, 1971: 325). This aspect of Gramsci's ideas about common sense, ideology and language is of course highly problematic and out of line with the perspective on language, culture and ideology presented in this book.

(3) MAVO refers to a mid-level type of secondary school and HAVO refers to a higher-level type of secondary school (Mazeland & Berenst, 2006).

4 When Background is Foregrounded – Nationality and 'Ways of Life'

> *What we have to do is to try to construct what a procedure might be for determining what it is that's being referred to when somebody says 'you', 'we', etc.* (Harvey Sacks, Spring 1966 (1995: 333)

This chapter investigates how nationality is made relevant in relation to the assessment and evaluation of the candidates in the internship interview. Throughout nearly all of the interviews, categories related to nationality were introduced by the participants.[1] Sometimes they were used to account for the actions, experiences and competences of the candidate and other times they were used as resources to characterize the work involved in the internship. It will be shown that in all cases this orientation towards nationality involved an opposition to the category 'Danish' and a simultaneous disaffiliation of the candidate with this category.

Other studies have been made on topicalizations of an ethnic group membership in interactions between native speakers and non-native speakers, but they are not limited to dealing with only how ethnic group memberships are established and the consequences of this. In a study of multicultural workplaces, Dennis Day (1998, 1994, 2006) describes how the ethnicity of employees with a non-British background is continually made relevant in informal conversations between co-workers. He describes how, as a consequence, the employees' competences and qualifications in relation to specific activities at the workplace were put in doubt. Day coins this phenomenon as ethnification, and it bears close resemblance to some of the findings that will be presented in this chapter. In fact, I will argue that what Day describes is another example of gatekeeping, following the (re) definition presented in this book.

A different study by Roberts and Campbell shows how in British job interviews differences in communicative style and linguistic capital with born-abroad applicants are considered an expression of insufficient work competence (2006: 102–104). Furthermore this study shows how foreign work experience is often discredited in these job interviews on the grounds of the employers' prejudices (2006: 118). A final central observation from this study has to do with the effects of orientations towards nationality. Roberts and Campbell describe how the interviewer perceives it as negative and unpleasant when born-abroad applicants make their ethnic background relevant in a job interview because it dissociates them from the interviewer in terms of both work and ethnicity (2005: 207). Topicalizations of ethnic membership are in other words found to create social distance between the participants. This is an issue which will be dealt with in the following as well.

Both of the studies mentioned deal with ethnicity rather than nationality and the contexts examined are obviously different. However, as will be clear from the following analysis, their descriptions of the workings and effects of interactional orientations towards ethnicity are still relevant to the present study. As it turns out, in real-life interactions such as workplace interactions, job interviews and internship interviews, it often becomes difficult to distinguish between categorizations of nationality, ethnicity and not least culture. While nationality, ethnicity and culture can be described theoretically as distinct categories, members often oscillate between and even conflate these notions. That is to say that nationality is sometimes established as synonymous with or implicative of ethnicity or culture. Similarly, the 'culture' of a given individual is spoken about in ways which implies its linkage to a certain nationality. The analysis will not focus on teasing culture and nationality apart but will rather emphasize how the participants construct and use these categories, at times as separate and at times as interchangeable phenomena. What is involved in an orientation towards nationality or culture, I will argue, is an orientation towards the other as 'an other' or 'a stranger' (Ahmed, 2012) and the attempt to interpret this otherness in terms of nationality or culture.

This chapter is structured around a detailed analysis of a particularly lucid example of how nationality is in many cases made relevant in relation to a discussion of what the candidate can learn from the internship, i.e. in relation to the issue of previous versus future experiences. The example will show how nationality is often used as an interpretative resource in the assessment of the candidate and in relation to the topicalization of assumed problems or benefits that a future internship may bring.

Other examples will be included along the way to further illustrate this main argument and to shed light on some of the deviant cases in which nationality is being topicalized in different ways, for different purposes and with different effects. For example, cases where the topicalization of nationality is made by the candidates, contrary to those made by the employers, tend to diminish rather than increase social distance between the participants. These deviant cases, however, further support my central argument that all topicalizations of nationality or culture have gatekeeping effects on account of their establishment of difference and asymmetry between the participants.

Nationality as a Barrier

When nationality was topicalized by the employers it was mostly done in relation to an assessment of the candidates' previous experiences and not least in relation to questioning the relevance of this experience. The first example is taken from an interview with a Colombian candidate for an internship as a teacher at a school.

The extract follows a short discussion of the importance of the intern's previous experience with teaching pre-school children in Colombia, where she had trained and worked. Previous to the extract, the participants have been discussing the length of the internship, and the employer has suggested that the three months period is a bit short in order for the candidate to experience the full development span of the children during the year. The candidate has responded to this by pointing to her previous experience from Colombia, and the extract begins with the employer's response to this.

It is not the initial mentioning of the category Colombia which is of interest here but rather the following renewal of the relevance of this category made by the employer. This leads to an extended negotiation of the meaning and significance of the category membership of the candidate, which potentially throws into doubt the relevance of the candidate's experiences and hereby poses a problem and a barrier for the candidate.

Extract 10 Colombia[2]

```
 8    HO:    Men jeg vil tro  (.) sådn (.) uden at vide  noget som helst om
 9           But I would think (.) like  (.) without knowing  anything  about
10
11    HO:    Colombia så vil jeg tro at man i en børnehaveklasseforløb her går
12           Colombia I would think that you in a pre-school class  here go
13
14    HO:    (.) fra  (.) en meget mere (.) >hvad skal man sige< (.) regelstyret
15           (.) from (.) a  much  more (.) >what can  you say< (.) rulegoverned
16
17    HO:    indgang i skolen til en meget mere hvas øøh (.) a man ka- ik- sige
18           approach to school to a much more  wha- eeh (.)  ya- you can't say
19
20    HO:    normstyret men [alligevel s
21           valuegoverned [but still s
22
23    EM:                   [MEGET MEGET LÆRIN[G >leg og læring< er blandet
24                          [A LOT A LOT OF LEARNING >play and learning< is mixed
25    EM:    [sammen ik-=
26           [together right-
27
28    HO:    [ja]
29           [yes]
30
31    HO:    =ja=
32           =yes=
33
34    IN:    =ja  (0.2) [ja meget meget (der)
```

(Continued)

```
35              =yes (0.2) [yes very very (there)
36
37      HO:             [>'hvor hvor'< hvo:r hvor børnenes egen
38                      [>'where where< whe:re where the childrens own
39
40      HO:     forvaltning    (0.4) er ret   stor fordi=
41              administration (0.4) is pretty big because=
42
43      IN:     =ja:.  (.) der  er ligesom en introduktion til i skole faktis-=
44              =Ye:a. (.)there is sort of an introduction to in school actual-=
45
46      HO:     =ja (.) nå=
47              =yes (.) oh=
48
49      IN:     =i- der i Colombia   [(.)så de ko:mmer å:  (.) la:ngsommere de=
50              =in- there in Colombia[(.)so they co:me an- (.) slo:wly      they=
51
52      HO:                          [ja]
```

In the beginning of the extract we see how the employer (HO) makes an assessment (line 10) of the kindergarten system in Colombia by comparing a rule-governed and a norm-governed kindergarten system. Anita Pomerantz (1984: 45) argues that in making an assessment, a person simultaneously claims knowledge of that which she or he is assessing. In this case, however, HO is explicitly moderating her claims to such knowledge, which can be seen as an orientation towards the internship candidate's privileged claim to knowledge vis-à-vis her being Colombian. HO's utterance 'But I would think without knowing anything about Colombia' renews the relevance of the category Colombia and simultaneously expresses the implication that the other participants in the interaction know (or know more) about Colombia. IN's membership is indirectly re-emphasized by HO's utterance, since the candidate, as mentioned, has already introduced the category Colombia and has associated herself with it and it cannot be applied to any of the other participants.

While the mentioning of Colombia makes the national category membership of the candidate relevant, it simultaneously makes the national category membership of the other participants relevant. Using the terminology of Membership Categorization Analysis, one can say that as the category Colombia is used, the Membership Categorization Device (MCD) country is activated, which automatically makes other categories within that MCD relevant. Furthermore, following the consistency rule as coined by Harvey Sacks, the use of one category within a Membership Categorization Device to categorize a person makes it possible to use other categories within the same MCD to categorize other persons. He describes this principle in the following way:

A second rule I call 'the consistency rule'. It holds: If some population of persons is being categorized, and if a category from some device's collection has been used to categorize a first member of the population, then that category or other categories of the same collection may be used to categorize further members of the population. (1972b: 333)

This is an important point with respect to not only this example but also membership categorization practices as such – namely, that any type of membership categorization establishes a range of potential differences and similarities between the participants. It is the negotiation and realization of such differences that determine their effects and consequences for the distribution of power within the interaction.

In this particular example the difference between categories and thereby category members is defined by HO as a difference in kindergarten systems. HO describes a movement from ('*går fra*') Colombia as a system characterized by rules to ('*til*') Denmark as a system characterized by norms or values. She is backed up in this by her colleague in line 22 who adds to the characterization by stressing the importance of learning through play. In other words, the implication seems to be that learning through play is closely related to a norm- and value-governed system, and that this represents a contrast to a more formal learning environment dominated by rules.

There is some ambiguity about the meaning of the word '*her*' ('here') in line 12, since this could be referring to either Denmark, considering that the interview is taking place in Denmark, or to Colombia, since Colombia has just been mentioned. In any case HO is describing a move from one setting to another by using the construction '*går ... fra ... til*' ('go ... from ... to'). Another ambiguity springs from the fact that the described movement can be of a geographical nature (from Colombia to Denmark) or a historical nature, referring in that case to a pedagogical development 'here' ('*her*') in Denmark. This ambiguity is not resolved till the end of the extract which provides an opportunity for IN to challenge the proposition of HO, which I return to shortly. The central point which I wish to make here is that HO and EM make Colombia relevant in the negotiation and co-construction of the meaning of '*børnehaveklasseforløb*' ('pre-school class'), and they do so by using the categories '*regel-styret*' ('rule-governed') and '*norm-styret*' ('norm-governed') as a basis of comparison between two (geographical or historical) contexts.

Having argued then that the use of the category Colombia indirectly affiliates IN with Colombia and the other participants with Denmark, the following characterization of rule-governed versus norm-governed can be heard as distinguishing between the formerly mentioned country, Colombia, and the country where the other participants are from, namely Denmark. This supports the interpretation that the development being described with the '*fra-til*' ('from-to') is in fact a geographical rather than a historical one. What is central, in any case, is that by this 'from-to' construction the norm-governed system is constructed as the present 'now' and the rule-governed as the past 'then'. Furthermore, it is central that by linking the category Colombia with a specific kindergarten system, HO and EM show that they orient to and construct Colombia not only as a nationality but also as a 'culture' characterized by a specific value- and norm-system, which is manifested in a specific organization and structure of kindergarten.

Before describing the further development in this negotiation of kindergarten and the way it ties in with a negotiation of Colombia and ultimately the identity of IN, a couple of things should be noted about the format of HO's utterance. What is interesting to note in particular is how it contributes to the sequential development of the exchange and ties in with the negotiation of meaning taking place. From a Conversation Analytical perspective all utterances, their format, their sequential placement and their timing have a specific function, which is constantly negotiated between the participants. The specific construction of a specific utterance thus signals a potential meaning and simultaneously projects a future development of the interaction. From this extract it is clear how institutionally defined roles and rights of HO and EM are manifested in the formatting and distribution of utterances involved in the categorization of IN.

The hedging and hesitation in HO's initial utterance such as '*så vil jeg tro*' ('then I would think'), and '*sådn*' ('like') in line 10 and 13 in this case indicates a reluctance on HO's behalf to make claims about Colombia and suggests potential future delicacy. This format can be said to have a social function and an interactional function. The social function consists of preventing or decreasing the chances of a negative response to her claim and the interactional function is the elicitation of a response from the other participants. Word-search and signs of hesitation may invite others to finish an ongoing utterance (Nielsen *et al.*, 2005). This elicitation proves successful, as EM responds by taking the floor in line 21 where she elaborates on HO's characterization.

The Sequential and Structural Manifestation of Institutional Roles and Rights

The sequential description of HO's and ME's exchange from 10 through 19 reveals how an opportunity is established for IN to challenge the suppositions of HO in a way that avoids conflict. In a high-stakes institutional encounter like the internship interview, the candidates may wish to challenge a given categorization made of them, but it needs to be done in a way that does not challenge the situational identities (Zimmerman, 1998) expected within the participation framework (Goffman, 1981). While the candidates need to 'pass' as suitable and competent employees, they also need to 'pass' as interviewees, and failing to do the latter will mean that they fail in doing the former as well. Identifying ways and moments in which to challenge unfavourable categorizations that do not infringe on institutionally defined rights (or lack of) is in this way central. A sequential analysis of the exchange between HO and EM reveals how such a moment presents itself in this example.

First (line 10), HO elicits a response to her characterization, which she receives from EM, who then elicits a confirmation of her addition. Then, HO and EM produce agreement on a characterization of a specific pre-school system as being norm-governed (lines 10–2), with play and learning being integrated. Finally, with EM's utterance in line 23, the contrasting element of this characterization is backgrounded and a more specific characterization of one specific system is foregrounded. This shift from a more contrastive and comparative description of pre-school to a more defining characterization of its content postpones the solving of the ambiguity in HO's initial utterance, since it enables IN to meaningfully confirm and support EM's elaborative utterance without having to deal with the contrast set up by HO.

The opportunity for IN to take the floor presents itself in line 35, where HO has confirmed EM's utterance. IN uses this opportunity to confirm what has just been said by EM and confirmed by HO. She does this by using what Pomerantz (1986) refers to as an extreme case formulation, namely 'meget meget der' ('very very there'), which is described as a device used to legitimize a claim. In this example, it has the function of showing and emphasizing alignment with the descriptions offered by HO and EM, but it comes off as ambiguous, since it lacks a verb and it is unclear what 'der' ('there') refers to. What nevertheless links it to EM's utterance is the fact that IN is repeating her wording, thereby showing alignment to the description EM has just given. By not picking up the contrasting element offered in HO's initial utterance and giving a non-specific confirmation of the following, IN contributes to the move away from a discussion of national difference manifested in two different pre-school systems to a discussion of pre-school as such.

What is interesting here then, and which does not become clear for HO until later in the interaction, is that even though IN seems to confirm the characterization of Colombia and Denmark co-constructed by HO and EM, she is more likely merely expressing recognition of the Danish school system. Her following description of pre-school as 'sort of introduction to schooling' in line 44 does not support HO's characterization of the system in Colombia. Rather, it describes the function of a pre-school system, which seems quite similar to the function of pre-school in Denmark. While it is unclear whether this description refers to schools in Colombia or Denmark, the following response from HO in line 47, *'ja nå'*, ('yes oh') suggests that she interprets IN's description as a reference to Colombia.

At this point, IN has not yet had a chance to continue her description of pre-schools in Colombia, since she is overlapped by HO in line 38, who continues her previous characterization of differences between Colombia and Denmark. She does this by using the words *'hvor hvor'* ('where where'), which is syntactically constructed as a continuation of a previous sentence and can be interpreted as a way of signalling that she had not finished talking and of linking her present utterance to her previous one. Furthermore, in using the word *'hvor'* ('where') she re-emphasizes that what she is describing is a specific context rather than a general understanding of pre-schools. This other setting, namely Denmark, is then further defined as a place where children learn to be responsible and monitor their own behaviour.

IN displays understanding of what HO is describing (line 44), first by giving the affirmative response *'ja'* ('yea') to HO's utterance. After a short micro-pause she then continues with what seems to be an elaboration of the description of pre-school that HO is making. The fact that she uses the indexical *'der'* ('there'), makes it ambiguous whether she is talking about Colombia or Denmark, which is an ambiguity that is carried on from HO's previous use of the indexical *'hvor'* ('where'). IN's utterance in line 44 can, in other words, be understood as describing the pre-school system in Colombia *and* in Denmark.

In line 47 the employer responds immediately with a confirming 'yes', which suggests that she interprets IN's utterance as a confirmation and an elaboration of the system in Denmark. However, after a micro-pause HO changes this into *'nå'* ('oh'), which within the CA literature is described as a change of state token that indicates some kind of realization or change in understanding (Heritage, 1984a). As Heritage describes:

> It is now well established that the particle *oh* is frequently used to acknowledge new information, e.g. answers to questions … and that it commonly functions as a minimal 'third turn' expansion, i.e. one with sequence-closing import, to question/answer adjacency pairs. In such contexts, where *oh* is produced as a response to information of some kind, it functions as a 'change of state' token; it registers, or at least enacts the registration of, a change in its producer's state of knowledge or information. (2006: 311)

The use of the particle *oh* has thus been described as a response to information that displays a registration of a change in the producer's state of knowledge or information which has the function of closing a topic. In Denmark, the use of the change of state token '*nå*' ('oh') has been described by Mie Femø Nielsen (2002: 92–94), who argues that it is a way of signalling a change in the speaker's level of informedness and a change in their attitude, which seems likely in this case. Hence, HO shows that she realizes that IN is actually describing something about Colombia, which is new to HO and at least challenges the contrastive description HO has given of Colombia and Denmark.

Interactional Opposition to Differentiation and Hierarchization

This point represents a turning point in the distribution of talk between the participants on the subject of Colombia, which can be argued to be related to a more general change in footing, as defined by Goffman, between HO and IN. Goffman describes how 'a change in footing implies a change in alignment we take up to ourselves and others present as expressed in the way we manage the production or reception of an utterance' (1981: 128), and such a change arguably takes place upon the aforementioned change of state token. As it will appear from the following part of the example, IN now launches into a fuller and more detailed description of the Colombian pre-school and is given space to do so by HO and EM. While the initial part of the interaction was influenced by the authoritative stance of HO, who seemed to push her description of the Colombian system as contrastive to the Danish system, the footing now changes as HO becomes the recipient and IN becomes the primary speaker and furthermore displays authority regarding knowledge about the Colombian system. IN is in other words using her interactional resources to counter the othering of her which is accomplished through a hierarchization of the categories Colombia and Denmark, rule-governed and norm-governed.

Extract 10 Colombia *(continued)*

```
|53                      [yes]
|54
|55    IN:    =tilpasser sil tiden tidel (.) til øøhm (.) øh farske
|56           =adjust   (sil) time (tidel)(.) to  eehm (.) eh difficoul
|57
|58           >forskellig-< farver   de   skal lære  i
|59           >different-< colours they must learn in
|60
|61    HO:    ja
|62           yes
|63
|64           (0.4)
|65
|66    IN:    øøh (0.3) i klassen (0.4) det er meget meget langsomt men også
```

(Continued)

```
67              eeh (0.3) in class  (0.4) it  is very  very   slowly  but also
68
69    IN:       (0.4) de   er me:get klar over for (0.2) de forventer at
70              (0.4) they are very  clear about (0.2) they expect   that
71
72    IN:       børnene      nå    nå:  nå de   er færdige med børnehaveklasse,
73              the children when- whe:n when they are done  with pre-school,
74
75    IN:       (0.4) så de   er  klar til at ta- i   skolen   og  de   er  klar
76              (0.4) so they are ready to   go to the school and they are ready
77
78    IN:       til tiden og de   er  klar til øh .hh til a argumentere hvad de
79              in time and they are ready to eh .hh to  a  argue      what they
80
81    IN:       tænker    om    å  (0.2)
82              are thinking about an- (0.2)
83
84    HO:       ja  (0.2) ja
85              yes (0.2) yes
86
87              (0.6)
88
89    HO:       Arhm det lyder  jo       ikke så   forskelligt=
90              well that does (hedge)  not  (hedge) sound so different=
91
92    *EM:      [=ne:j
93              [=no:
```

After the change of state token by HO, IN immediately continues her turn in line 49 by specifying that she is talking about Colombia, which indicates that she catches on to HO's utterance as a display of confusion. In other words, she accounts for or explains her previous utterance as a response to HO's change of state token The description IN gives paints a very positive image of the system in Colombia from line 49 to 81, which stresses that learning how to go to school is a slow process (lines 49, 66), where the students adapt to time (lines 55, 78) and learn about different colours (line 58) and about how to express their thoughts (lines 78–82). She is in other words negotiating and redefining the membership category 'Colombia' by highlighting different features or attributes of the Colombian pre-school.

It is important to note how the behaviour and response of HO facilitates IN's extended explanation stretching over several units and turns, or what in the CA literature is referred to as a multi-unit-turn. Multi-unit-turns are to a greater extent single-unit turns, something that needs to be jointly accomplished by the participants (Nielsen & Nielsen, 2005), since it demands that the speaker uses several different strategies to keep the turn or that the other participants refrain from taking the turn in the various places where they can. Hence, IN makes various short pauses, where another speaker might have taken the floor, but as they don't, IN interprets this as an encouragement to go on. The other participants can support this by signalling to the speaker that he or she should continue talking by using nods, smiles or words like 'yes' or 'mhm'.

This form of listener behaviour, which is prevalent during extended turns of talk, has been described by Schegloff as *continuers* in a specific study of the use of 'uh huh', which is the English equivalent to the Danish 'mm' or 'mhm'. He describes how the most common function of *continuers* is to 'exhibit on the part of its producer an understanding that an extended unit of talk is underway by another, and that it is not yet, or may not yet be (even ought not yet be), complete' (Schegloff, 1982: 81) However, Schegloff also argues that continuers can have other functions as well, such as expressing enthusiasm and encouragement on behalf of the listener, or they can mark agreement and their particular meaning should for this reason be analyzed in relation to the sequential context in which they occur (Kjærbeck, 1998: 69).

In the present example, the continuer in line 52 seems to encourage IN to continue speaking, which is supported by the minimal response in line 61 and the encouraging 'yes' in line 84. However, since IN does not continue speaking here, HO supplies another 'yes' after a short pause, which simultaneously presents a final opportunity for IN to take the turn as well as recognition of what she has previously stated. Since IN does not offer any further elaboration, HO finally takes the floor in line 89 and responds to IN's multi-unit description of the system in Colombia with a summarizing statement, which can be said to be formatted as what is referred to as a *formulation* within CA.

The action of formulating was first described by Garfinkel and Sacks in 1970 as a description or summary by a person of his/her own actions or the actions of others as a means of establishing a joint understanding of an ongoing activity (Antaki *et al.*, 2005: 627). In Garfinkel and Sacks's words formulations are a conversational means to

> treat some part of the conversation as an occasion to describe that conversation, to explain it, or characterize it, or explicate, or translate, or summarize, or furnish the gist of it, or take note of its accordance with rules, or remark on its departure from rules. That is to say, a member may use some part of the conversation as an occasion to formulate the conversation. (1970: 350)

Formulations are a way to display an understanding of what is being talked about (Drew, 2003: 297). This can be done by either summarizing the *gist* of what has previously been stated, or by suggesting the implications or the *upshot* of it, the former involving the deletion, selection and rephrasing of what has been said and the latter involving the extraction of an implication of it. The present example may be said to be a mixture of an upshot and a gist formulation in the sense that it is at once rephrasing what the internship candidate has said and extracting an implication from it ('well that does not sound so different'). Heritage and Watson (1979: 159) later described how formulations were formatted as adjacency pairs and involved a preference for agreement in the sense that a formulation invited and projected a confirmation by the next speaker (Antaki *et al.*, 2005: 627). This observation is supported by the present example where EM confirms HO's formulation in line 92. EM and HO in this way co-operate in summarizing the gist and upshot of what IN has described.

Antaki *et al.* describe how formulations in a psychotherapeutic institutional context are used by the professional as a means to sharpen, refine and clarify the client's accounts and thereby give it a form that enables a following diagnosis (2005: 627). Thus, a formulation can have the function of pressing the solution or conclusion of a topic of discussion. Apart from this function of contributing to closing a topic down (Heritage & Watson, 1979: 152), which is seen in the present example, formulations can furthermore have a supportive effect in that they display understanding. This is found in interview situations such as the internship interview or language testing interviews as demonstrated by Brown (2003: 10–11).

With her repeated '*ja*' ('yes') in line 84 and her formulation in line 89, HO can in this way be said to signal that she has understood IN's description, confirms it and hereby simultaneously recognizes that her own previous description of Colombia must be re-evaluated. HO hereby manages to close the topic and finally solve the ambiguity, while having allowed IN plenty of time to offer additional information.

The Linking of Nationality and Culture

This example shows how the nationality of the candidate is made relevant by HO outlining a contrast between the membership categories 'Colombia' and 'Denmark' through describing differences in the features of their respective pre-school systems. This creates a potential problem for the candidate, since the contrast suggests the incommensurability between a rule-governed (Colombia) and a norm-governed (Denmark) system. The mentioning of the country Colombia sets up a case of special relevance for the candidate who is hereby indirectly associated with not only 'Colombia' but also the rule-governed pre-school system, which HO attributes to the category 'Colombia'. Simultaneously, IN is dissociated with the category Denmark and the norm-governed system through the consistency rule and the contrasting description of the two 'systems'. This potentially questions the value of the candidate's experience, which as mentioned was the topic of discussion previous to the extract, and thereby her competence as a pre-school teacher. The fact that nationality is made relevant has, in other words, the same negative effect in this example as is described in the study by Roberts and Campbell.

What is central about the example is that it illustrates how the meaning of nationality is closely linked to a notion of 'value systems' that are taken to define and dictate the actions and behaviour of its members. I would argue that what is being formulated in this interaction is a conceptual link between notions of 'nationality' and notions of 'culture'. Furthermore I would argue that this conceptual link provides the premises for constructing nationality as a barrier, since culture or a specific 'way of life' is seen to define the actions and behaviours of the candidate.

Another example of this is the following extract from a different interview at a residential home where the intern's Iranian nationality is introduced in relation to a discussion of her previous experience with caretaking. Here it is even clearer than in the previous example how the negotiation of national category memberships is involved in the negotiation of individual work experiences and how this entails a negotiation of 'cultural differences'. The membership knowledge of the participants, in other words, seems to imply a conceptual link between the notion of nationality and the notion of culture, which means that differences in terms of national category memberships imply 'cultural differences'.

Extract 11 **Tradition**

```
329
330  IN:    Fordi de meget eeh svært eh men eeh .hhh eh jeg tror det tradition
331         øh min tradition de:t tæt på eehm .mthh de:t for eksempel hvis jeg
332         eh arbejder med eh gammel mennesker .hhh eeh
333         (1.5)
334
335         Because it very eeh difficult eh but eeh .hh eh I think it tradition
336         eh my tradition i:t is similar eehm .mthh i:t for example if I
337         eh work with eh old people .hh eeh
338         (1.5)
339
340  IN:    Iehm hfm. jeg ved lidt fordi eh i: .hh mit hjemland .h eh vi
341         passer øh i gammel mennesker
342
343
344         Iehm hfm. I know a little because eh in: .hh my homecountry .h eh we
345         look after eh in old people
346  (0.5)
347  (HO:)  mm
348         (0.5)
349  IN:    Men jeg tror jeg kan eh jeg kan lære bedre .hh e:h om eh .mthh •
350         hvordan skal jeg opføre med eh gammel mennesker
351
352         But I think I can eh I can learn better .hh e:h about eh .mthh
353         how I shall behave with eh old people
354  (0.8)
355  HO:    Hvordan du skal op[føre dig]
356         How you shall be[have yourself]
357  IN:                     [ja:]
358                          [ye:s]
359  HO:    ja=
360         yes=
361
362  HO:    =ja
363         =yes
364  (0.2)
365  HO:    ja
```

In this first part of the example we see how, as in the previous example, the topicalization of nationality is initially made by the internship candidate as part of an argumentation for previous experiences with the field of work that she will engage in during her internship. The participants have been talking about the candidate's expectations of the field of work and she has been describing how she expects working with elderly people to be difficult since they are very sensitive. This is then followed by the claim in line 340 that she has some previous experience with this from her home country. The mention of previous experience is not followed up by the employer, which results in almost a minute-long pause, only broken by an 'mm', supposedly uttered by the employer. The candidate then mitigates her claim of having experience by stating in line 349 that she can 'learn better' how to behave with the elderly and this is followed up by the employer who makes a formulation of the final part of IN's utterance, thereby putting emphasis on how the candidate is to behave. While the national category membership of the candidate is in this way initially associated with particular experiences that would be useful for the internship, this attribute is de-emphasized at the expense of an emphasis on learning how to behave among the elderly. As we can see in the following part of the example, the job consultant plays an important role in this as well as in the other interviews by being the one who summarizes and assists the contributions of the candidates which influences the topical and interactional development. Here, CO makes a formulation of what IN has been saying that specifies particular elements of it and summarizes the somewhat fragmented argument which IN has presented as a more congruent whole.

Extract 11 Tradition *(continued)*

```
---   ...      ,-
366            yes
367   (0.3)
368   CO:      Ja hun [me]ner hvordan hun skal så arɔejde og pleje og be[han][dle]
369            yes she [me]ans how she shall then wo-k and care for and tre[at]
370
371   IN:      [.mtsk]
372            [.mtsk]
373   HO:                                                             [ja]
374                                                                   [yes]
375   EM:                                                             [ja]
376                                                                   [yes]
377   HO:      ja=
378            yes=
379
380   IN:      =ja=
381            =yes=
382
383   HO:      =ja
384            =yes
385
386   CO:      og det det [(   )]godt at det har vi så talt også- tidligere om •
387            And that's it [(   )] good that we have talked also- earlier about
388   %                     [(noise in the background)]
389   *CO:     det fordi hun har også været på besøg hos andre plejehjem og
390            der har hun så talt om .hh at øøhm at fordi at hun kommer
391            fra Iran og man har en tradition [for] og [passe og pleje og
```

```
392              respektere ældre mennesker
393
394              it's because she has also been visiting other residential homes and
395              there was she then talked about .hh that eehm that because she comes
396              from Iran and one has a tradition [fo~] and [ta]king care of and
397              respect'ng elderly people
398    HO:                                          [ja]
399                                                 [yes]
400    (HO/EM:)                                                         [ja]
401                                                                     [yes]
402    IN:      [ja]
403             [yes]
404
405    HO:      [ja] ja
406             [yes] yes
407
408    CO:      så tror hun at hun kan bruge det (.) i sit arbejde
409             Then she thinks that she can use it (.) in her work
410
411    HO:      ja:|
412             ye:s|
413
414    CO:      på et plejehjem •
415             in a residential home
416
417    HO:      ja
418             yes
419
420    CO:      med den
421             with the
422
423    HO:      ja
424             yes
425
426    CO:      [den] [den kul]turelle [led][ik]
427             [the] [the cul]tural   [way][right]
428
429    HO:      [ja] [|j:a|]           [ja] [.hh]ja
430             [yes] [|ye:s|]         [yes][.hh]yes
431
432    HO:      .h jo men det er [rigtigt]
433             .h yes but that is[true]
434
435    IN:                       [(tak] ska du [have
436                              [(thank]you)
437    HO:                                    [altså der er øh vi skal have meget
438                                           [that is there eh we have to have a lot
439             stor respekt her
440             of respect here
441
442    IN:      mja
443             myes
444
445    HO:      for for ældre [men]nesker vi har jo en anden kultur end den du
446             for for elderly[peo]ple    we have a differert culture than the one you
447
448    IN:                    [ja:]
449                          [ye:s]
450    HO:      [kom]mer fra ik men .hh men
451             [come]  from right but .hh but
452
453    IN:      [ja:]
454             [ye:s]
455
456             (0.3)
457    HO:      li:ge ligegyldigt så skal man også have respekt for e:h for [eh de |
458             nevertheless one should also have a lot of respect for e:h for[eh the
459    IN:                                                                   [ja det
460                                                                          [yes that
461
462    HO:      ældre menne]sker her ik
463             elderly people here right
464
465    IN:      er rigtigt]
466             is true]
```

In line c368 we see how CO's formulation first unpacks and specifies IN's previous use of the word *'opføre'* or 'behave' with three category-bound activities – namely how to 'work', 'care for' and 'treat' the elderly. She hereby makes these three categories central descriptors of the field of work they are discussing, namely 'health care help', and simultaneously makes them descriptors of the members of this category, namely 'health care helpers'.

She then continues her formulation in lines 386 to 392 by specifying IN's mentioning of the category 'home country' as being 'Iran' and through the notion of 'tradition' she relates the mentioned activities to the activities of 'taking care of' and 'respecting' the elderly, which are then bound to the category 'Iran' and hereby to the members of this category, namely IN. CO's formulation in this way works in support of IN's previous claim to experience but at the same time the way it is formatted as a report of what IN 'has talked about' (line 390) and 'thinks' (line 408) throws the applicability of her 'Iranian' membership into question, which invites a confirmation or rejection from the other participants. If CO had instead claimed co-ownership of the assumed link between the category 'health care helper' and the category 'Iranian', for instance by continuing the 'we' format used in line 386 rather than shifting to the 'she'-format in lines 389, 390 and 408 the supportive effect would have been stronger or less ambiguous. As it is here, the formulation of how IN's previous experiences vis-à-vis her membership of the category 'Iranian' is turned into a question of whether IN can 'use *it* in her work as a health care helper' (my emphasis) and the 'it' is finally conflated rather vaguely as 'in the cultural way' (line 426).

HO responds in line 432 by accepting the assumed relation between on the one hand the activities of 'work', 'care for' and 'treat', bound to the category 'health care helper', and on the other the activities 'taking care of' and 'respect', bound to the category 'Iranian' and thereby she seemingly accepts the applicability of IN's experiences and her ability to undertake the future internship. However, she picks up the 'cultural element' that CO initially introduced to suggest a similarity in behaviour and experiences and recycles it in a way that highlights cultural difference. After her confirmation in line 429 she continues immediately by emphasizing that there is a great need for respect 'here' which, following the consistency rule formulated by Sacks, is a location category that indexes another national context than 'Iran' – namely 'Denmark'.

What is clear here, as was also the case in the previous example, is such location categories have deeply rhetorical and conversational functions such as making distinctions between not only locations but also members. As Lepper describes, based on the work of Sacks and not least Shegloff, who has elaborated his work on location categories, they are contextual devices that are not merely used to designate places but to 'generate distinctions and provide inferences about speakers and hearers' (Lepper, 2000: 26). Here, as in the previous example, we see a very good demonstration of this function, since HO's use of the location category 'here' establishes a distinction between two national categories and contexts, namely 'Iran' and 'Denmark', and this distinction is then used to infer 'cultural differences' . The notion of respect, which was initially used to accentuate the experiences and knowledge of IN, is now used in an ambiguous way through the vague wording *'ligegyldigt'* or 'nevertheless': on the one hand it can be heard to highlight a common feature of both national contexts, that is as *something that cuts across* the cultural differences, and on the other hand it can be heard as something particularly necessary *because* of the cultural differences. IN responds by confirming HO's utterance in line 459, and since she does not elaborate on her response and thereby also her understanding of HO's utterance, both the emphasis on cultural difference and the need for respect in the Danish health care context is left unchallenged. IN's and CO's co-constructed argument for the applicability of IN's experiences based on a link between the members and category-bound activities of the categories 'health care helpers' and 'Iranian' is in this way challenged and turned into an argument for cultural difference and the need for 'respect'.

What we see from both examples is how the category of nationality or culture is established through opposition and difference by the employers and how this difference is potentially challenged through the emphasis on concrete activities and experiences by the candidates and the job consultants. Location categories are in this way an important resource for making inferences about the experience and knowledge of the candidates. However these location categories are only useful as a resource for processes of categorization because of their capacity to carry with them a range of ideas about the meaning of these places, which is revealed in the links made between places and norm-systems.

In the first example the location category 'Colombia' is implicitly defined through opposition from the norms and practices of the location category 'Denmark', or in other words it is defined by that which it is not, and the candidate is thereby also constituted through her 'otherness' and non-Danishness. As the candidate negotiates this through her elaborate descriptions of the Colombian pre-school, she manages to implicitly challenge the association of Colombia and non-Danishness and offer an alternative range of concrete practices that are acknowledged by the other participants as compatible with and similar to the Danish system. A construction of cultural opposition and difference is negotiated and changed into a joint construction of cultural similarity. This change can be said to be crucial for a recognition of the candidate's experience, and ultimately for a positive assessment of her future possible contribution to the school.

In the second example, the same occurs, although in the opposite order: the candidate presents experiences and activities that are conceived to be bound to the category health care helper by linking such experience and activity to the location category 'Iran'. But this orientation towards nationality is then picked up by the employer and used as a basis for the emphasis on cultural difference, rather than cultural similarity. Both examples in this way showcase where the employers conceptualize nationality as barriers and this is in the first case negotiated and in the second case challenged by the candidate and the consultant.

It is, in other words, not merely the relation established between the candidate and particular location categories that is central to the differentiation and hierarchization produced between the participants. Rather, it is the ideological traces of meaning linked to not only location categories, but also other categories, that are central to the otherness of the candidate and in this way to the gatekeeping processes that take place.

The Workings of Ideologies in the Work of Categories

Thus far, the analysis has illuminated processes of categorization and membership ascription within specifically limited sequential contexts. Within the boundaries of the various segments, the actions and utterances of the participants have been described in relation to the previous actions they respond to and the future actions they project. The CA/MCA framework has thus far enabled the description of how meaning and social organization related to categories Colombia, Danish, rule-governed and value-governed is achieved and produced between the participants. It has, however, not provided insights about why such categories were made relevant and meaningful at particular moments nor has it pointed to the traces of meaning involved in the naturalized assumptions and ideas about the differences between Colombia and Denmark. In the remaining part of the analysis around how categories related to nationality are made relevant, a somewhat broader perspective is applied on how categorization and categories tie in with particular structures of meaning manifested in the systematic application of particular interpretative repertoires by the participants.

As mentioned previously the two main Membership Categorization Devices being established in Extract 10 (Colombia) are the MCD 'Country', made up of the categories Colombia and Denmark, and the MCD 'Kindergarten' made up of the categories value-governed and rule-governed. These two MCDs are constructed as related to each other in a way that the category Colombia in one MCD implies or determines the category 'rule-governed' from the other MCD. From a CA perspective, this inferential process may be seen to be guided by a combination of the principles 'a case of special relevance' as defined by Day (1998), and the 'consistency rule' as defined by Sacks (1972a, 1972b). It can, however, also be described from a poststructuralist linguistic perspective, which highlights how meaning is carried by words as the traces of a process of *différance*, or differentiation or deferral, from other meanings. In this light, the meaning of Colombia, as it is mentioned by HO, already carries with it other meanings of other words such as 'Denmark' or 'country'. By putting it in the context of other words such as *'børnehaveklasseforløb'* ('kindergarten programme'), *'regel-styret'* ('rule-governed') and *'norm-styret'* ('norm-governed') the many potential meanings of the word are temporarily backgrounded, while others are foregrounded. This is, however, a contextually specific process which is not controlled by a person uttering a word and putting it in a specific conversational context; rather it is a process taking place between people in interaction and between language production and language interpretation.

The link between a specific pre-school system and a national context, which is not questioned but rather elaborated on by EM, seems to suggest a shared interpretative resource in which nationality is implying culture and culture is considered to determine a certain institutional and social organization and a specific set of values regarding teaching, education and child-rearing. Implicit in HO's utterance is, in other words, the assumption that pre-schools within a specific national setting are organized and run according to a specific cultural organization and can therefore be described as a whole. Such an understanding of culture as determining social and institutional organization is closely related and similar to a functionalist understanding of culture. An understanding that is not only the foundation of much research in intercultural communication, but an understanding that has also, due to its dominance within and beyond anthropology, reached wide recognition and spread in the media and among the general public. When Colombia is made relevant and associated with rules and a different system, characterized by norms as well as a mixing of play and learning, it is an expression of a highly ideology-laden construction of valorized opposition.

What are being established here, I would argue, are not merely two different types of pre-school systems or two different countries, but rather two different value-systems and belief-systems regarding child-rearing and education, which is taken to correspond to two different national or cultural contexts. In this way, Extract 10 reveals that the participants draw on and construct a certain understanding of nationality as implying a specific 'culture' which determines norms and values as well as individual action and experience. This interpretative resource is used not only in this extract, but also in other parts of this specific conversation and in some of the other internship interviews.

Culture as a Barrier

Wetherell and Potter, in their study of racism in New Zealand (1992: 129-134) identify two opposite cultural interpretative repertoires, 'culture as heritage' and 'culture as therapy', that can be said to resemble the formulation of culture in the two extracts. 'Culture as heritage' formulates an understanding of culture as traditional and unchangeable and links to ideas about culture clash and culture shock, art, rituals and traditions (1992: 129–131). This understanding of culture as a source of conflict and clashes can be said to resemble the formulation of culture as a barrier in Extract 10 (Colombia). 'Culture as therapy' on the other hand describes an understanding of culture as an individual right and necessity – something that is linked to identity, values, roots and pride (1992: 131–34). This understanding emphasizes culture as a positive thing that defines an individual's uniqueness, and in this sense it resembles the understanding of culture as a resource. An example of this is formulated in Extract 34 (Music and dancing) which will be elaborated on later.

When comparing the two previous extracts (10 and 11) and considering them in relation to the findings of Potter and Wetherell, one can say that the general understanding of culture as an absolute entity that determines individual action finds its unique expression in two different interpretative repertoires, namely 'culture as barrier' and 'culture as resource'.

These can be defined by their opposition, and the way they are applied in relation to different conversational functions and contexts. As we can see, the interpretative repertoire 'culture as resource' is used in Extract 11 (Tradition) in relation to a positive assessment of the cultural 'baggage' that IN is associated with. The conversational context for this extract is the previous positive announcement by HO about the assessment of IN as a possible intern. Alternatively the repertoire 'culture as barrier' is used in Extract 10 (Colombia) in relation to a negative assessment of IN's cultural background and her experience from Colombia, whereby the conversational context was a discussion of the internship's short duration being a problem. This difference in the function and context of the use of the two different formulations of culture indicate that different interpretative repertories can be used as resources in different lines of argumentation – in this case, respectively for and against the making of an internship agreement.

The following example, Extract 12, also constitutes a case of nationality being established as a barrier and it furthermore exemplifies the linking of nationality and culture that has been described in Extracts 10 and 11. This extract is taken from an interview with a male candidate from Somalia, who is being interviewed for an internship at a fruit farm. The candidate is a trained agronomist and has worked as one in Somalia. The interview took place while the employer was giving the candidate a tour of the orchard, explaining the kind of work he would be involved in. At this point in the interview, the employer has just stated that she probably won't be able to teach the candidate anything professionally. She then goes on to explain what she imagines that he will get out of the internship instead.

Extract 12 Danish

```
73    HO:    Men jeg kan give dig en fornemmelse af (0.6) hvad der sker
74           But I can  give you  a sense         of (0.6) what happens
75           (0.8)
76    HO:    Hvad det er vi lægger vægt på og hvordar vi gerne vil (0.2) øøh
77           ha' vores produkter
78
79           what it is we  emphasize      and how we would like to have (0.2)
80           eeh our products
81
82    IN:    mm=
83    HO:    =øøh vores butiksform
84           =eeh our way of the store
85           (0.6)
86    HO:    Du kommer i kontakt
87           You will be in contact
88           (0.2)
89    IN:    jae=
90           Yea=
91
92    HO:    =hvis du kommer ind til mig i butikken her så har du kontakt
93           med nogle [kunder] nogle der taler dansk
94
95           =if you come with me in the store here you have contact
96           with some [clients] some that speak Danish
97
98    IN:                [ja]
99                       [yes]
100          (0.4)
101   IN:    ja=
102          yes=
```

What I would like to draw attention to in this example is the description of what the intern will be able to learn or gain from the internship. The extract begins with HO giving a three-part list of the things that HO can 'offer' IN during the internship, namely a sense of *'hvad der sker'* ('what happens'), *'hvad det er vi lægger vægt på'* ('what it is we emphasize'), and *'hvordan vi gerne vil ha' vores produkter'* ('how we would like our products to be'). While the first part of the list is formulated neutrally (what happens), the second and third part are formulated personally (we emphasize, and we want) which establish the category 'we' and associate it with the activities of producing something. Since HO is the one establishing the 'we' she is automatically constructed as a member of the category, while IN is excluded from the 'we' through HO's initial construction of IN as the 'learner' and herself as the 'teacher' or 'mentor' in the utterance 'I can give you a sense of'. After a minimal response from IN, HO elaborates with what seems to be a summary of the list, namely *'vores butiksform'* ('our way of the store'), which again emphasizes her relation to the category 'producers' and elaborates on the definition of this category by associating it with not only production, but also selling the products and doing it in a specific 'way'. Up until this point, what has been established is, in other words, the category 'farmers' which is associated with a specific practice, that of producing and selling products.

What HO seems to be doing with this description is to present the terms of the internship in the sense 'this is what you are going to get' and this projects looking for a kind of acceptance from IN, which would constitute an agreement about the contents of the internship. However, this response fails to materialize, and after a 0.6 second pause HO continues her description of what IN will gain from the internship, but now taking it in what seems to be a different direction. In line 86 she states that IN will 'be in contact' but she pauses for 0.2 seconds which elicits a 'yea' from IN. HO then restarts in line 92 with a hypothetical construction, which emphasizes that *if* IN comes to work with HO in the store, *then* he will have contact with some clients, and she finishes off by specifying in line 93 that it will be someone who speaks Danish. Thus, HO moves from what can be learnt about the products and the selling of the products and the 'way of the store' to the interaction with the customers, and, more specifically, Danish customers.

I would argue that the category 'Danish' is made relevant here through a categorical link being implicitly made between the previously constructed category 'farmers' and the category 'Danes'. The interactional and interpretative resources that enable this are partially to be found in the sequential context of that given moment in the internship interview, which is furnished by the categorizations of HO. Furthermore, it is informed by the speech situation as such, and the discursive and ideological context in which it is embedded. Finally, it is partly related to IN's transportable identity as second-language speaker, which can be said to be made potentially relevant through IN's minimal responses. The latter will be dealt with separately in Chapter 5. The former two aspects tie in with the previous argument that the membership categories established in relation to language, religion and nationality are informed by assumptions about Danish culture as a 'system of thought' and that the category membership of the candidate is established in relation to processes of distinction and differentiation between this 'system of thought' and the system of thought that the candidate is associated with.

When looking at the shift from talking about the products and the selling of the products to talking about the contact with the customers, it is not formatted as presenting something new or different from the previous, but rather as an elaboration or summary of it.

In this light the move from line 83 to 86 seems meaningful and more like a topical glide,[3] since 'coming into contact' and the more elaborate 'contact with some clients' can be read as a category-bound activity to the category 'grocers', which is made relevant with the introduction of the category *'butik'* ('store'). What still needs to be explained, however, is why HO changes 'with some clients' to 'some that speak Danish'. This change or supplement, I will argue, is related to the categorical opposition between *'vi'* ('we') and *'du'* ('you'), which is introduced and continued from the beginning of the extract. This, in combination with the suggestion of a specific 'way' of the store and the farm, makes relevant not only the professional but also the cultural and linguistic otherness of the candidate and paves the way for the specific topicalization in line 93.

The Internship as a Solution to Overcome the Barrier of Culture

To continue this line of thought, the category 'we' is established right in the beginning of the extract and HO is constructed as a member of this category who, based on this membership, can introduce IN as a non-member of the category 'we' and its practices, norms and standards. While it seems that the members of the category 'we' are the people at the Orchard, this is never made explicit and is difficult to infer from the activities that are attributed to the members such as 'we value', 'we would like our products'. These activities could be interpreted as bound to the category 'farmers' or 'grocers' in general, and it is not specified whether HO is speaking as a member of such broader categories or as representative of 'farmers' at her Orchard particularly. What is clear, however, is that IN is constructed as a non-member of the 'we,' since HO is precisely describing something she is able to give IN a sense of. In this light, it seems likely that the category HO is referring to 'we' as is the smaller category of 'farmers at the Orchard'. But since this is never specified, she is simultaneously indexing another category of grocers or farmers of which IN is not a member, namely the category 'Danish farmers'.

The ambiguity or possible conflation of the category 'farmers at the Orchard' and 'Danish farmers' is made even more pronounced in line 83 where HO summarizes the previous category-bound activities as a specific 'butiksform', which I have translated as 'way of the store' but which is actually more abstract in that it does not refer to a specific store, but rather to a 'way of running the business' in general. This can be said to index a broader context of 'store practice' than merely the orchard, while indicating a specificity of 'ours' in relation to 'yours'.

While it is not possible to determine whether she is doing one or the other, or even both, the unspecified category of 'we' referring to an infinite community of farmers, followed by a specification of a specific 'way' of the store and finally a specification of the clients that frequent the store, namely 'some that speak Danish', works to establish and make relevant the category of 'Danish farmers'. Even if one should disagree with or contest the argument that the category of Danish farmers is made potentially relevant at the time of the first unspecified 'we', there is no doubt that 'Danish' is established as the relevant category membership in line 92, and that this informs or specifies the previously undefined categories of 'we' and 'our'. Following such argumentation, the utterance 'some that speak Danish' works sequentially and categorically as a summary of what is previously described and implied, namely that IN, through working in the store, will be introduced to the 'ways' of producing, farming and trading at the orchard and in Denmark more generally. IN is in other words simultaneously constructed as a non-member of the category 'people from the Orchard' and 'people from Denmark'. This argument is supported when looking at the next part of the extract where the category 'Danish' is further elaborated as something associated with more than just the language.

Extract 12 Danish *(continued)*

```
103
104   HO:    =Nogen der spørger om no:get som [ger]ne vil vide noget om
105          =Someone who asks about so:mething who [woul]d like to know about
106
107   IN:                                 [mm]
108   HO:    produkterne
109          the products
110   (0.4)
111   IN:    Jeg [f(ik      da ve    di )]
112   I    [f(ik      da ve    di )]
113
114   HO:        [Og det (.) kan man lære] lidt af også
115            [and that (.) one can learn] a little from also
116   (0.7)
117   HO:    at (0.3) jamen hvad er det folk øh går o:g og tænker o:g de smager
118          og de øh hvad sker der
119
120          that (0.3) well what is it people eh go a:nd and think and they taste
121          and they eh what happens
122   (0.8)
123   HO:    Øøhm så jeg lægger sådan set nok meget op til at du får nogle
124          oplevelser
125
126          Eehm so I am kind of eh encouraging a lot that you get some
127          experiences
128   (0.8)
129   HO:    som du så kan bearbejde o:g øh o- tage med dig hvor du nu skal læ:se
130          eller hvad du nu skal læ:se eller øh videre frem
131
132          that you can then digest a:nd eh a- take with you wherever you will
133          stu:dy or whatever you will stu:dy or eh further ahead
134   (0.3)
135   IN:    mm
136
137   HO:    øhm
138          ehm
139   (2.6)
140   HO:    For ligesom at komme lidt tæt på:
141          To kind of get a little closer to:
142   (0.8)
143   HO:    noget der er lidt mere dansk måske ik o- d- end bare lige at gå bag
144          kulisserne
145
146          something that is a little more Danish perhaps right o  d  than just
147          walking behind the scenes
```

The second part of the extract overall consists of various accounts offered by HO for why IN should come work at the store, and these accounts are centrally focused on the various ways in which it will represent a chance for the candidate to meet and experience Danish life. In line 104 HO offers an elaboration of the category 'Danish customers', which was established in the previous lines. The category is associated with the category-bound activity 'asking questions about the products', which together with the utterance 'some that speak Danish' in line 93 implies what is finally stated in line 114, namely that this is another thing which IN can learn from when working in the store. This supports what was argued earlier, namely that when HO is constructing an 'us' which IN can learn from, this us refers to both workers at the orchard and Danes more generally, since the practices to be learnt are now made to include not only producing and selling the goods but interacting with Danes speaking Danish. It is, however, not yet specified what is to be learnt from the latter; rather it is quite abstractly stated that 'that one can learn a little from also'.

What is described in lines 117–118 is not how customers 'ask about something' but rather how they 'think' (*'tænker'*) and 'taste' (*'smager'*) and 'what happens' more generally, which is a more abstract description that is similar to the previous formulation *'butiksform'* ('way of the store'). Since this, again, does not receive any response or uptake from IN but is followed by a 0.8 seconds pause, HO makes yet another statement from lines 123 to 143 which again relates back to the topic of what she can 'offer' and again initiates a closing of the topic by summarizing and repeating what she has said.

This time the utterance is more specifically formatted as a summary in that she explicitly describes what she wants to propose, namely 'eehm so I am kind of eh encouraging a lot that you get some experiences'. Again, IN only responds minimally, which elicits a hesitation marker from HO followed by a very long pause (2.6 seconds). When this still does not elicit any uptake from IN, HO takes the floor again in line 140 and states the purpose of what she is proposing, 'To kind of get a little closer to', which implies a distance between IN and what HO offers and represents. While HO can from an interactional perspective be described as affiliative in her invitations and suggestions to IN, she is inevitably, from a Cultural Studies perspective, reproducing a differentiation and othering of the candidate in relation to 'our ways'. HO does not finish this utterance, however, till after a 0.8 second pause, where she summarizes what is being offered – namely 'something that is a little more Danish than just walking behind the scenes'. Again, as described in relation to Extract 10 (Colombia), we see in this example how a valorized opposition is created between Danish culture and 'foreign' or 'other' cultures. This happens as the category Danish is made relevant and associated with specific norms, practices and values related to producing and selling fruit, which the internship candidate is encouraged to learn from. What is central in this extract as well as Extract 10 (Colombia) is that Danish culture is constructed as primary, and the distinction of and difference from 'the other' culture is assumed and unspecified.

To summarize, I have aimed to show how nationality is made relevant in Extract 12 (Danish) by two moves: first of all how HO constructs an unspecified category 'us', which indexes a context of farming at the orchard and a broader national context; and second how HO dissociates IN from it by orienting to him as a 'learner' or an 'intern'. The unspecified description of a range of general practices, standards and values which IN is to 'learn' constructs the candidate as a professional outsider. Furthermore it furnishes the conversational context for constructing him as a cultural and linguistic outsider or an 'other' as well. In other words, culture is made relevant long before it is made explicit. While this threatens to undermine the value of IN's experience and competence, the implicit way in which it is done makes it difficult for IN to engage with or negotiate the relevance of culture, which he does not do at any point in the interaction.

In Chapter 5 I will describe further how the minimal contribution and participation of IN can be said to contribute to making the category of second-language speaker, and thereby culture, relevant. The central point I wish to make here is that the establishment of the category Danish is informed by an understanding of a certain 'way' of doing things and a certain 'attitude' towards farming, producing and selling and certain 'value' regarding the quality of the produce. This 'way' of feeling, believing and acting associated with the category Danish resembles how, in the previous example, the category Danish was related to a particular norm-governed system in Danish pre-schools. Extract 12 is in this way yet another example of how nationalistic ideologies about cultural difference and cultural clashes are manifested in the application of the interpretative repertoire 'culture as barrier' and of how the application of this repertoire foregrounds difference rather than sameness.

When Candidates Categorize Themselves in Terms of Nationality

The examples shown so far illustrate how topicalizations of nationality by the employers can either be used as part of a valorization or devalorization of the candidates' experiences which in both cases creates social differentiation and distance. This is not necessarily a conscious strategy but an effect of the membership categorization processes taking place. When looking at the orientations towards nationality made by the candidates they appear to be part of a different aim altogether, namely diminishing membership category differences and the social distance between the participants. Consider Extract 13, an extract from a follow-up interview at a residential home. The participants are discussing how the internship has been going so far and the candidate describes how her negative expectations have been challenged since everybody has been really nice to her.

Extract 13 A Danish workplace

```
28      (EM:)     .hja så
29                .hyes so
30      (1.2)
31      CO:       så- så det altså Vesta sagde jo det gik fint thh. (.) hvad synes
32                du selv det går
33
34                so- so that like Vest said   that it went fine thh. (.) how do you
35                think it is going
36      (0.6)
37      IN:       jeg synes og:så (.) ah (0.3) det går fint
38                I think al:so (.) ah (0.3) it is going fine
39
40      EM/CO:    mm
41      (0.5)
42      IN:       A jeg jeg har haft noge:n anden (1.1) billede om det hele
43                and I I have had so:me other (1.1) idea about the whole thing
44
45      EM/CO:    mm
46
47      IN:       ja
48                yes
49
50      (0.4)
51      IN:       jeg tænker de:t det er dårlig
52                I think tha:t it is bad
53
54      (0.8)
55      EM/CO:    ja
56                yes
57      (0.3)
58      IN:       o:g jeg har aldrig været på en øh arbejdsplads
59                a:nd I have never been to a eh workplace
60      (0.8)
61      IN:       o:g jeg hørte også at øh danskerne de: de ville komme i kontakt
62                a:nd I heard also that eh Danes the:y they would come in contact
63      (0.4)
64      IN:       Me:d os indvandrere
65                wi:th us immigrants
66      (0.5)
67      IN:       Men jeg synes det er korrekt he he det fordi alle de ha •
68                været dejlige med mig
69
70                But I think that is correct he he it because everyone they have
71                been lovely to me
```

What should be emphasized here is how IN in line 61 makes the category 'the Danes' relevant and opposes this to the category 'immigrants' while affiliating herself with the latter and thereby opposing herself with the former. The logic of opposition that has previously been illustrated in the membership categorizations of the employers is here established by the candidate. While in the previous examples it was clear that the 'othering' of the candidates was related to a discussion of the candidates' previous work experiences, it is here related to a positive evaluation of the behaviour of the Danes as part of a positive evaluation of the internship. In lines 42 to 58 the candidate is describing a change in her perception of Danes, that she had expected it to be 'bad' to be at the workplace but that it is going fine. Social distance is in other words diminished through positive evaluation even though a social differentiation is inevitably involved. The same thing is found in Extract 14, taken from a different follow-up interview at a different residential home.

Extract 14 The first encounter

```
45
46
47    HO:    Det var os- første gang at jeg mødte:
48           It was also first time that I met
49
50           danskere faktisk s[å d]i eh=
51           danes actually s  [o th] eh=
52    HO:                      [ja ]
53                             [yes]
54    CO:    ='ah'
55            ah
56
57    HO:    j[a
58           y[es
59
60    CO:     ['ja']
61            [yes]
62    (0.3)
63    HO:    ja
64           yes
65
66    IN:    Jeg var lidt genert men [nu]det går godt synes jeg
67           I was a little shy but  [now] it is going well I think
68    HO:                            [ja]
69                                   [yes]
70    IN:    (.) går meget godt
71            going very well
72    (0.5)
73    CO:    Så det er første gang ogs du har arbejdet sammen med danskere?
74           So it is the first time als you have worked with danes?
75
76    IN:    ja=
77           yes
78
79    CO:    =ja (.) [ja]
80           =yes    [yes]
81
82    IN:            [det] er første gang
83                   [it] is first time
84
85    CO:    ja hvordan var det
86           yes how was it
87    (0.3)
88    IN:    det var: (0.5) dejligt
89           it was lovely
90    (.)
91    ( )    'ja'
92           yes
93    (0.4)
94    IN:    så sjov .heh .he
95           so fun
96
97    CO:    ja
98           yes
99
100   IN:    .heh he. .hheh ja
101                        yes
102   (1.2)
103   CO:    Altså være på dansk arbejdsplads
104          That is being in a danish workplace
105
106   IN:    ja
107          yes
108   (.)
109   CO:    Har det overrasket dig
110          Has it surprised you
111
112   (0.6)
113   IN:    e:h ja: det er meget anderledes i: .hh
114          altså i mit land og eh så Danmark det meget anderledes det er
115          meget forskellig
116
117          e:h yes: it is very different i:n .hh
118          that is in my country and eh so Denmark it is very different it is
119          very different
120
121   (0.7)
122   IN:    altså: hvordan de: mm arbejder å
123          that i:s how the:y mm work and
124   (0.5)
125   CO:    Hvorda- hvordan kan du sige lidt om det=
126          How- how can you say a little about that
127
128   IN:    =ja altså (0.3) .hh altså: jeg mener::
129          e: hvordan de eh de eh (0.5)
130          eh sk- dan jeg skal sige det heh. |
131
132          =yes that is (0.3) .hh that i:s I me:an
133          e:h how they eh they eh (0.5)
134          eh sh- how I should say this heh.
```

```
135   (0.4)
136   IN:    .h altså hvordan de snakker med fo:lk og
137          .h that is how they talk with peo:ple and
138
139   IN:    .hh altså: (.) de er meget venligere i: end
140          .hh that is: (.) they are much friendlier in: than
141
142   IN:    i mit land synes jeg
143          in my country I think
144   (0.3)
145   CO:    >meget meget< hvad
146          >much much< what
147
148   IN:    venlig
149          friendly
150   (0.4)
151   CO:    venlig.
152          friendly
153
154   IN:    ja
155          yes
156
157   CO:    ja
158          yes
159   (0.4)
160   (   )  [å:]
161
162   HO:    [så:] så der er mere .h mere hierarki der hvor du kommer fra.
163          [so:] so there is more .h more hierarchy where you come from.
164
165   HO:    .h altså .h høj taler ikke med lav og sådan [alts]å de- e-
166          .h that is .h high does not talk with low and that [that i]s the- e
167   IN:                                               [ja]
168                                                    [yes]
169   HO:    sådn- rent [sta]tusmæssigt .hh hvis man e:r er .h LEDER ikke
170          like-      [sta]tuswise .hh if one i:s is .h LEADER right
171   IN:               [ja]
172               [yes]
173   IN:    j[a ]
174          y[es]
175   HO:    [stig] eller [JEG eller] vi taler ikke med dig.
176          [stig] or   [I    or  ] we don't talk with you
177   IN:                 [DER ER SÅdan]
178                       [THERE IS LIKE]
179   (.)
180   IN:    n[ej]
181          n[o]
182   HO:    [hvor du] nej okay så[dan] ja
183          [where you] no okay li[ke] that yes
184   IN:                         [nej]
185                               [no]
186   HO:    ja.=
187          yes.=
188
189   IN:    =arj [sådan] lederen sidder bare å så de- si[ger ba]re
190          =no  [like]  the leader just sit and then the- ju[st say]
191   HO:                                                [.hja]
192                                                     [yhes]
193
194   HO:    °ja det ku jeg også tænke mig°=
195          °yes that I could also imagine°=
196
197   IN:    =ja=
198          =yes=
199
200   HO:    =°ja°
201          =°yes°
```

Here we have a similar case of the candidate making the membership category 'Danes' relevant in relation to a positive story of a first time encounter with the effect of both establishing a social differentiation and diminishing social distance between the participants. What is interesting to see in this extract however is how an initial positive evaluation of 'how people talk' in Denmark is heard and responded to in a way that steers the negotiation in the direction of a very negative evaluation of Iran due to the application of an interpretative repertoire focused on power hierarchies, status and authoritative leaders.

IN describes Danes as much friendlier than people in her home country in line 139, and HO responds to this by expanding on the herein implicit negative assessment of IN's home country by describing it as hierarchical in line 162. In lines 165–194 this is elaborated and unpacked by HO. He emphasizes that status in relation to a certain hierarchy determines who talks with whom and that the leaders do not speak to those reporting to them. In other words, HO uses IN's concrete description of Danes as friendlier (than Iranians) to make a more general and a valorized, abstract characterization of the Iranian social structure, which was not initially the focus of IN's description.

This extract is very similar to Extract 10 (Colombia), since HO also here draws on a traditional understanding of culture and uses the interpretative repertoire 'culture as barrier' as a tool for the construction of a valorized opposition between Danish values and 'foreign' values. In this case the barrier is not an authoritative rule-governed pre-school system which calls into question the value of professional training, but rather the barrier is considered to be an authoritative and unequal social structure which forms a contrast to the friendly, equal form of social interaction that the candidate has encountered during the internship. The barrier is in other words her experiences with a different form of social conduct that has to be unlearnt in order to fit in with Danish ways of interacting.

In this extract, the negative assessment and opposition is not as problematic for the candidate as in Extract 10 (Colombia), since the conversational context in this extract is the candidate's experience of the Danes rather than the employer's assessment of the candidate's professional background and experience, which was the context in the first extract. Since the candidate initially makes a positive assessment of Danes in relation to Iranians, she dissociates herself from Iranians in general and thereby from HO's supplementary characterization of the Iranian system. However, similarly to previous extracts, nationality and culture is established as a central axis of differentiation between the candidate and the employer. The three extracts in this way all indicate a systematic in the way in which 'culture as barrier' is used in the descriptions of the candidates' meeting with a Danish workplace.

Culture as a Resource

I have now shown how nationality is often oriented to as a barrier by the employers and how this orientation is based on a conceptual link between nationality and culture and influenced by a specific interpretative repertoire, namely 'culture as barrier'. I have also shown how orientations towards nationality by the candidates, contrary to those by the employers, often involve positive evaluations of Danes and thereby constitute affiliative moves that diminish the social distance between the participants while still managing to point out national contrasts. There were also cases, however, where the employers oriented to nationality in relation to a positive assessment and emphasis of the candidates' special qualifications or competences. In Extract 15, an example from later in the interview with the candidate we saw in Extract 10 (Colombia), this understanding is being expressed. Immediately prior to this extract, the employer has announced that she has had a meeting with the other pre-school heads before the interview where both pre-school classes have shown interest in having the candidate as an intern and that they will make a schedule that enables the candidate to spend time in both classes.

Extract 15 Music and Dancing

```
284   HO:    hvor begge øh team får får glæde af af (.) af den resource
285          where both eh teams will will benefit from from (.)the resource
286
287          du jo sådan set kommer med
288          you  kind of bring with you
289
290   IN:    okay
291          okay
292
293   HO:    så:
294          so:
295
296          (0.4)
297
298   HO:    Jeg kunne godt tænke mig at vide ka du sådan no:get musik
299          I  would like to know can you such things a:s music
300
301          eller: hva- (  ) danse eller [(   )]
302          or:    what- (  ) dance or    [(   )]
303
304   IN:                                  [danse] fjaf [ha
305                                         [dance] fyesf [ha
306
307   HO:                                                [Nå men .hh fordi du ka- har jo
308                                                      [Well cause .hh because you
309   HO:    ↑sikkert nogen: særlige talenter som:
310          can- probably have some special talents that
311
312   HO:    (.) kan berige os
313          (.) can enrich us
```

When the interpretative context is taken into consideration, influenced by the fact that the category Colombia has been made relevant and linked to the candidate's experience previously, then the utterances 'the resource you kind of bring with you' in lines 284–288 and 'you probably have some special talents that can enrich us' in lines 307–313 can be understood to express an expectation that IN's competences and qualifications as a pre-school teacher are specifically shaped by her culture and nationality. This is supported by the fact that HO's utterance in line 307 is constructed as an explanatory follow up to HO's utterance beginning in line 284, which makes 'knowing something about music or dancing' into something special in relation to the competences that the category 'us' supposedly does not possess (i.e. line 313). This extract can in this way be seen as a reproduction of the understanding of culture as a homogenous entity that conditions individual behaviour.

This extract differs, however, from the previous extract with the same candidate in that IN's cultural background is here formulated as a resource, whereas previously it was presented as a barrier. In previous sections of this chapter, the analysis of Extracts 12, 13 and 11 showed how the negotiation of nationality was informed by an understanding of culture as a barrier to candidates' future work and this interpretative framework was applied as the employers questioned and challenged the candidates' previous work experiences. In the present extract, however, we see a different understanding of culture being expressed as part of a positive evaluation of what the candidate is expected to bring to the table. This difference in a positive and negative realization of the same general understanding of culture, as well as the variation in the function that these two formulations of culture have in the two different conversational contexts, indicates the possibility to distinguish between them based on Potter and Wetherell's notion of interpretative repertoires and Michael Billig's notion of the contrary nature of common sense. As both Wetherell and Potter and Billig remind us, the meaning of categories and the interpretative frameworks applied in social interaction are always controversial and dilemmatic and we see clearly here how different understandings of culture are visited and applied for different purposes as part of the negotiation of the candidates' experiences.

The repertoire 'culture as resource' is however not only in play in those cases where the qualifications of the candidate are positively evaluated: it is a resource used in the negotiation of the candidate as well. This is very clear when revisiting Extract 11 (Tradition), where the competences of the candidate are actually called into question by the employer, even though the 'culture as resource' repertoire is put in play by IN and CO.

Extract 11 Tradition *(repeated)*

```
329
330  IN:    Fordi de meget eeh svært eh men eeh .hhh eh jeg tror det tradition
331         øh min tradition de:t tæt på eehm .mthh de:t for eksempel hvis jeg
332         eh arbejder med eh gammel mennesker .hhh eeh
333         (1.5)
334
335         Because it very eeh difficult eh but eeh .hh eh I think it tradition
336         eh my tradition i:t is similar eehm .mthh i:t for example if I
337         eh work with eh old people .hh eeh
338         (1.5)
339
340  IN:    Iehm hfm. jeg ved lidt fordi eh i: .hh mit hjemland .h eh vi
341         passer øh i gammel mennesker
342
343
344         Iehm hfm. I know a little because eh in: .hh my homecountry .h eh we
345         look after eh in old people
346  (0.5)
```

```
385
386   CO:    og det det [(   )]godt at det har vi så talt også- tidligere om •
387          And that's it [(   )] good that we have talked also- earlier about
388   %                    [(noise in the background)]
389   °CO:   det fordi hun har også været på besøg hos andre plejehjem og
390          der har hun så talt om .hh at øøhm at fordi at hun kommer
391          fra Iran og man har en tradition [for] og [passe og pleje og
392          respektere ældre mennesker
393
394          it's because she has also been visiting other residential homes and
395          there was she then talked about .hh that eehm that because she comes
396          from Iran and one has a tradition [for] and [ta]king care of and
397          respecting elderly people
398   HO:                                                 [ja]
399                                                       [yes]
400   (HO/EM:)                                                        [ja]
401                                                                   [yes]
402   IN:    [ja]
403          [yes]
404
405   HO:    [ja] ja
406          [yes] yes
407
408   CO:    så tror hun at hun kan bruge det (.) i sit arbejde
409          Then she thinks that she can use it (.) in her work
410
411   HO:    ja:↑
412          ye:s↑
413
414   CO:    på et plejehjem •
415          in a residential home
416
417   HO:    ja
418          yes
419
420   CO:    med den
421          with the
422
423   HO:    ja
424          yes
425
426   CO:    [den] [den kul]turelle [led][ik]
427          [the] [the cul]tural    [way][right]
428
429   HO:    [ja]  [ij:a↑]          [ja] [.hh]ja
430          [yes] [iye:s↑]         [yes][.hh]yes
431
432   HO:    .h jo men det er [rigtigt]
433          .h yes but that is[true]
434
435   IN:                      [(tak] ska du [have
436                            [(thank]you)  [
437   HO:                                    [altså der er øh vi skal have meget
438                                          [that is there eh we have to have a lot
439          stor respekt her
440          of respect here
441
442   IN:    mja
443          myes
444
445   HO:    for for ældre [men]nesker vi har jo en anden kultur end den du
446          for for elderly[peo]ple    we have a differert culture than the one you
```

We see here how IN employs the 'culture as resource' repertoire as part of the argument that she has competences within caretaking by the mere fact that there is a tradition in her home country to look after and respect the elders. CO is in this part of the extract merely responding to and supporting this argumentation by making a formulation of IN's argument. While IN initially introduces the notion of 'tradition' and links it with the category of nationality, CO is supporting this linking and defining it as 'culture'. In this way they both contribute to making culture relevant and they both use the repertoire 'culture as resource' as a means of argumentation for the competence and preparedness of the candidate. As argued previously in the chapter the argument presented by IN and CO is, however, not accepted by HO but transformed into an orientation towards cultural differences.

We see this in lines 432 to 446. It is clear from this that interpretative repertoires are resources for argumentation, in this case an argument about the work experience of IN. It is also clear that interpretative repertoires are aspects of a dilemmatic common sense and can for this reason be turned into objects of negotiation themselves by being challenged with an equally meaningful repertoire. This is what happens here in line 445, where the repertoire culture as resource is challenged by emphasizing the different cultural background of the candidate as a factor which undermines the relevance of her experience. This argument is based on the interpretative repertoire 'culture as barrier'. The extract in this way shows not only how interpretative frameworks inform local sensemaking processes within the internship interview but also that they do not determine the outcome of such processes. The interpretative frameworks being employed in negotiations of meaning are dilemmatic and are as equally open to challenge as other arguments made. The two examples shown where the repertoire 'culture as resource' was employed illustrate well, however, how the role and position of the employer is central to determining which argument wins and which interpretative premise is challenged and accepted. In the first example, the 'culture as resource' repertoire was applied by the employer as part of a positive evaluation of the candidate and was not challenged. In the second it was applied by the candidate in the same kind of argument but was challenged by the employer. While gatekeeping can in this way be said to be a phenomenon of co-construction, it is strongly influenced and reinforced by the participation framework of a particular interaction.

Summary

The examples presented in this chapter reveal various similarities in the ways in which membership categories related to nationality are made relevant and not least in the way they establish differentiation and otherness. In some cases, the nationalities of the candidates are brought forward by describing a range of practices, norms and 'ways' of doing things within a specific professional field, which is then linked to a specific national context such as Colombia, Iran and Denmark. These descriptions implicitly contrast a cultural 'other' which is considered to be the candidate and made relevant by orienting to the candidate's situated identity as a 'learner' and a 'newcomer', both with regard to the place of employment and Denmark as a national space. In the first example the entire negotiation about the Colombian versus the Danish pre-school follows directly from a talk about the candidate's previous work experience, which is thereby potentially challenged or undermined with reference to cultural differences. In the

Orchard example, the candidate's professional qualifications and experience are de-emphasized as the employer produces extended descriptions of what he will benefit from the internship, namely the 'ways' and practices of farming and trading at the Orchard and in Denmark in general. In both of these examples, specific professional skills, qualifications and experiences are contrasted with more abstract and general practices, 'ways' and 'systems'. Here the former is backgrounded and the latter is foregrounded instead. The foregrounding of nationality as an index for culture makes it difficult for the candidate to represent themselves as competent, experienced and professional, since the practices, norms and ways that are associated with the Danish context are only defined in abstract, general terms, if at all. As such, they become difficult for the candidate to relate and respond to, as well as agree or disagree with. In other cases, such as Extract 14 (The first encounter), nationality is not made relevant in relation to a discussion of the candidate's work experiences but is rather made an explicit topic of discussion, where the candidate is invited to share their experiences with Danes and Danish ways, norms and practices.

As shown by all the examples, the orientation towards nationality involves the application of the contrary repertoires of 'Culture as barrier' and 'Culture as resource' to either problematize or positively valorize the background of the candidate. What is shown also, however, is how both repertoires are in fact fuelled by the same ideological basis, namely a nationalistic ideology of cultural difference and opposition, which means that the application of both repertoires entails a foregrounding of difference rather than sameness.

In all cases, the implication is that the experiences, norms and practices of the candidates, vis-à-vis their cultural membership, must be adapted to the reality of a Danish work context. The candidates are constructed as workplace interns *and* cultural interns, and the experience they have from working within the same or similar professions in their home countries is more often treated as a disadvantage than an advantage. In Goffman's (1963) terms, the nationality of the candidates becomes a stigma that the candidates need to handle interactionally in order to pass as competent and suitable candidates in relation to a 'Danish' normativity defined by the employers. This finding is confirmed in a more recent study by Kirilova, who illuminates the implicit favouring of candidates that align with not only institutional discourse but also particular cultural ideologies naturalized within a Danish context.

It is clear from the analysis that the consequences for the future development of these kinds of interactions are highly dependent on the participation and the co-construction of the candidate, the employer and the consultant. In Extract 10 (Colombia), the extensive and elaborated participation of the candidate allows the candidate to challenge the notion of culture as a barrier by emphasizing cultural similarity rather than difference. In the orchard example, however, the participation of the candidate is minimal and the candidate is at no point engaging with the employer's construction of the practices of farming and trading as something nationally and 'culturally' specific. This is not to say that in this example there is no co-construction taking place. Both of these examples show the co-construction of cultural membership, but in the second example the co-construction of the candidate consists only of affirmative and acknowledging utterances, and the topical development and the distribution of turns is to a much greater extent given over to and left in the hands of the employer.

All of the examples analyzed so far show that membership categories related to nationality are interactional achievements that are informed by and interrelated with the participants' orientations towards other membership categories related to the participation framework and the speech situation of the internship interview. Furthermore, I have aimed to exemplify how the establishment and orientation towards the category of a given nationality illuminate a pattern of understanding 'culture' as a system of thought, values and action. Thus, constructions of nationality seem to index culture, which is only sometimes explicitly stated as in the case of Extract 11 (Tradition). Often the linking of nationality and culture is implicitly achieved through the association of nationality with particular 'ways' and 'systems' of thought and action. Finally, I demonstrated how categories related to nationality are in the internship interview context constituted through processes of difference and deferral from the membership category 'Danish' and that the internship candidate is excluded from this category but in various ways encouraged to acquire the actions, behaviour and values associated with the category.

Notes

(1) See Appendix 4 for an overview of the number of orientations towards nationality, language and religion in the various interviews.
(2) This extract has previously been presented and analyzed in Tranekjær, 2011.
(3) The notion of topical glide was originally introduced by Adelswärd (Adelswärd, 1988) and has been used by Roberts and Campbell in their study of job interviews in Britain. It describes the gradual rather than sudden shift from one topic to another and is, according to Adelswärd, more likely to occur in interactions where the participants share an understanding of the interview structure and aspects of social identity (Roberts & Campbell, 2006: 163).

5 Do You Understand? The Issue of Language

Language as a Means for and an Object of Negotiation

In any kind of interaction, participants make inferences about each other based on not only what is spoken but also how it is spoken, the language used (English, Danish, Arabic etc.), prosodic features (intonation, stress, rhythm) and paralinguistic features (back-channelling, vowel lengthening, voice quality etc.) (Gumperz, 1982a, 1982b; Akinnaso & Seabrook Ajirotutu, 1982; Roberts & Campbell, 2006). Language resources, and the way they are applied, display aspects of who people are and who they wish to be in a particular context. Language is in this way a central aspect of the cultural performances through which individuals mark their memberships and non-memberships of various categories. Similarly, language behaviour and speech style is a central interpretative resource as interlocutors determine and establish the category memberships of one another.

In the internship interviews, the candidates do not have the choice of speaking their native languages. All of the candidates were able to manage and complete the internship interviews in Danish, but they all spoke with varying degrees of proficiency and with particular features in their pronunciation that revealed that Danish was not their first language. As they interacted verbally with the other participants, certain aspects became visible (or in fact audible) deviations in relation to particular norms of language practice. The language practice of the candidates, and the other participants for that matter, were in this sense understood, recognized and interpreted on the basis of norms and ideologies of language at play within the particular situational context and the broader cultural context as a whole. Cultural common sense and the ideologies of language influencing this common sense in other words provided the boundaries for normativity and deviance in relation to language practice, which made the candidates visible as 'deviants'. What will be examined in this chapter is the concrete manifestation of such boundaries of normativity and deviance in relation to language practice and how the participants navigate within and sometimes across the boundaries of the expected and undesired language practice. As already stated, the candidates were all unable to 'pass' as native speakers of Danish, and in relation to this category they can be called deviants. The notion of passing has been discussed by Goffman (1963) within a sociological context and is furthermore widely used within and beyond the context of cultural studies in relation to race, gender, religion and sexuality (Jameelah, 2011; Alexander, 2004; Khanna & Johnson, 2010; Speer, 2009; Speer & Green, 2007). The notion of passing is very useful in highlighting the boundaries of normativity that are manifested when our practices make us push against or cross the determining limits of social categories. In other words, it brings attention to the 'slips that show and tell' (Britzman *et al.*, 1993) that we are constantly navigating in the liminality of different category memberships. As the internship candidates engage in interaction in Danish, a range of possible categories related to language become potentially relevant for them such as 'second-language speaker', 'second-language learner' and 'foreign-language speaker'. These language-related category memberships are established, negotiated and challenged during these interviews. This is so, partly because the negotiation of language membership is involved in the ordinary business of sense-making and partly because the evaluation of the candidate involves an assessment of the candidate's language abilities.

What this chapter examines is not only boundaries of normativity related to language behaviour within a Danish institutional context, but also the specific expectations of language proficiency within the context of the internship, as formulated and negotiated during the internship interview. What are the expectations of second-language speakers or second-language learners and how are such categories understood, negotiated and organized in relation to each other? When do the candidates manage to 'pass' as second-language speakers and when are they rather seen as learners? When are such categories even made relevant and when are they left unnoticed on behalf of other category memberships such as 'teacher', 'mother' and so on? And finally, how are they oriented to when they are noticed and made relevant, and with what consequences? Answering some of these questions illuminates the challenges that the candidates faced within the context of the internship interview but they also give an indication of some of the challenges they meet in their interactions with native-speaking Danes in society as a whole.

In all of the internship interviews, the language background and competence were made relevant by one or more of the participants. In the majority of cases, it was either the employer or the employee who brought it up. In these instances language was either made relevant because the participants in some way questioned the candidate's level of understanding or because they directly topicalized the candidate's language background. Both of these types of orientations towards language membership entailed a membership categorization of the candidates as non-native speakers and it involved solving 'the problem' of sub-categorizing the candidate as a specific type of non-native speaker. The meaning of the category non-native speaker is fluid and polysemic since it can imply varying degrees of competence, proficiency, experience and practice with a non-native language. Hence, when the participants negotiated the candidates' non-nativeness, they also negotiated the distinction between the related categories of 'second-language learner' and 'second-language speaker', just as they negotiated the candidates' affiliation with one or the other. This chapter examines how such categories are given meaning, distinguished and organized through the implicit and explicit formulation of certain rules that allow for the association or disassociation of the candidates from the various language-related categories involved.

The orientation towards the non-nativeness of the candidates was in some cases potentially related to the behaviour of the candidate that was at times minimal or oriented to as non-standard by the other participants. In other cases it was related to the question of the candidate's perceived or experienced ability to undertake the tasks required by him or her as part of the internship. In both cases it was clear that the negotiation of membership categories related to language was a high-stakes business since it was focused around ensuring a sufficient level of language proficiency for carrying out the interview and the internship. The categories native-speaker, non-native speaker, second-language speaker and second-language learner were in this sense valorized by the participants so that the category of 'second-language speaker' rather than 'second-language learner' was desirable, sought and defended.

'Do You Understand?' Co-constructing (Lack of) Understanding and Proficiency

The first group of examples are cases where the category of second-language speaker is made relevant as the other participants assess the candidate's linguistic competence and proficiency as a Danish speaker.

They do so in various ways by asking the candidate about their level of understanding, which projects a response from the candidate and, to varying degree, creates a disruption in the interaction which has to be dealt with in order for the interaction to proceed again. As we saw in Chapter 4, the orientation towards language foregrounds the otherness of the candidate who then has to defend not only their level of language proficiency but also their legitimacy as future workers. As will be shown, the level of disruption and the response from the candidate is related to the way that the question of understanding is raised. Furthermore it is related to whether the question is more or less embedded within the ongoing topical development.

Implicit Orientation to Language through Checking Understanding

While I will argue in this chapter that any kind of orientation towards language and proficiency in the internship interviews entails an othering of the candidate, I will show in this section how the more embedded types of topicalizations minimize the challenge of the candidate. In this respect the gatekeeping effects of embedded topicalizations of language can be said to be less pronounced. However, as I will also show, the less embedded and more explicit inquiries about understanding provide a better opportunity for the candidate to challenge the othering than the more embedded cases. While the gatekeeping processes are thus more pronounced and explicit in such cases they are also potentially less damaging to the migrant. I will begin by presenting examples of the most embedded form of questioning and finish with the least embedded kind.

The first example shows one of the most embedded types of inquiry about the candidate's level of understanding. The interviewee is a female candidate from Morocco who has been in Denmark for 18 years, where she has mostly worked in hotel kitchens. She is now being interviewed for an internship as an assistant cook in a government funded project for homeless people in Copenhagen.

The extract is taken from the middle of the interview. Previously in the interview the employee has welcomed the candidate and has given an elaborate description of the workplace and the work routines that the candidate will be taking part in, namely the preparing of food for the homeless. During this initial part of the interaction, the employer has indirectly addressed the candidate by using the pronoun 'you' but has not directly requested or invited a response. Nevertheless the candidate displayed understanding throughout the employer's and the employee's descriptions by means of minimal responses such as 'yes', 'mm', 'mhm' and by asking clarifying questions once in a while.

At this point in the interview, CO has just explained the importance of having a serious content and purpose for the internship, and HO has responded by explaining how they see the internship developing from smaller tasks to larger tasks.

Extract 16 Do you understand?

```
23          ..      -
24   EM:    [altså] vi har jo af erfaring (.) altså- lægger vi småt ud fordi
25          [that is] we have from experience (.) I mean- we begin small because
26
27          altså- [vi har jo erfaring for at .hh
28          I mean-[we have experienced that .hh
29
30  (CO:)              [(            )]
31   CO:            °ja°=
32                  °yea°=
33
34   EM:    =at det andet de:t altså hvis vi lægger for hårdt ud fra
35          =that the other i:t that is if we start off too hard from
36
37          starten så- så: det tit det vælter ik
38          the beginning then- the:n often it falls over right
39
40   CO:    ja
41          yes
42
43   HO:    mm
44          mm
45
46   EM:    °altså°
47          °that is°
48
49   CO:    Er du med (.) forstå- forstår du
50          Do you follow (.) do you- do you understand
51
52   IN:    ja
53          yes
54
55   CO:    ja
56          yes
```

The formatting of the question in line 49 is direct in the sense that it is explicitly inviting and projecting a response from the candidate. However, it is embedded in the sense that it is formatted as a general inquiry of understanding that could refer to the content or the gist of what the employer is saying rather than to the language as such. The wording 'do you follow' and 'do you understand' could in other words be found in conversations between native speakers of Danish where there was no question of a shared level of proficiency. These two questions do not point to the previous speech as a potential problem, but more generally inquire whether the candidate follows what is going on and being discussed. The embedded formatting and the wording of the question in this way do not make the category of non-native speaker relevant and do not initiate a negotiation of the categories second-language learner or second-language speaker. It is merely in light of the specific contextual circumstances that the question can be heard and interpreted as an inquiry about linguistic proficiency and it is only on the basis of this context that it can be said to make the linguistic background and (lack of) competence of the candidate relevant.

However, the fact that the question is posed by the job consultant and not the previous speaker, EM, reveals that this is something other than a regular checking of understanding found in native-speaking interactions, since the job consultant is hereby addressing a need to actively include the candidate in the ongoing activity of the interaction. The fact that it is the job consultant and not the employer or the employee who inquires about the understanding of the candidate can be said to illustrate the way that an orientation towards membership categories related to the speech situation interrelate with orientations towards other membership categories. As mentioned in Chapter 1, the role of the job consultant in relation to providing job counselling, setting up the interview and taking part in the interview influences the participation framework and the speech situation. This is seen in the way they themselves and the other participants orient to and construct their role as mediators between the different parties and as a spokesperson for the candidate. This orientation can be said to manifest in the act of checking or making sure that the candidate follows what is going on and thereby inviting her to respond and participate.

Although the job consultant is in this way bringing to the fore not only the category membership of 'candidate' but also the category membership of 'second-language speaker', her formatting does not project any further topicalization nor any defence or account from the candidate. The candidate is allowed to answer positively in a minimal way with no need for a follow-up explanation or account from the candidate or even for an explanation or justification from the job consultant for having asked the question. And yet the topicalization of language and understanding reveals an orientation towards the context as a situation in which the language of the candidate is potentially an issue and a problem. In Extract 9 (repeated from Chapter 2), this orientation becomes considerably more apparent and explicit.

Here the formatting of the question varies slightly from the previous one in that the question is less embedded in the ongoing interactional exchange. In contrast to the previous example, where the candidate had been markedly absent in the immediately previous turns, in this example, the candidate is responsive to the employer's utterances. Extract 9 is taken from the very beginning of the interview, where HO welcomed IN and asked about the training programme that the candidate was participating in. The extract begins with HO describing his experience with this training programme.

Extract 9 Do you understand what I'm saying? *(repeated extract)*

```
13   CO:    Du kender det godt ik os stig
14          You do know it right Stig
15   (0.4)
16   CO:    Det s- det det det grundforløb der| på skolen
17          That s- that that that basic course there| in the school
18
19   HO:    .hh Jeg [kender] jo: jeg kender lidt til det
20          .hh I   [know  ] yes: I know a little about it
21   CO:            [ja]
22                  [yes]
23
24   HO:    jeg [kender] det jeg [kender] det ikke vældigt godt
25          I   [know  ] it I don't[know]  it very well
26   CO:        [ja]                [ja]
27            [yes]               [yes]
28   (.)
29   IN:    o:[kay
30          o:[kay
31   HO:      [men øh jeg kender lidt til det
32            [but eh I know  a little about it
33
34   IN:    °ja°
35          °yes°
36
37   HO:    ja
38          yes
39   (0.5)
40   HO:    øh og når jeg siger jeg kender lidt til det så er det fordi
41          øøh .hhh jeg kend- jeg har sådan set studieordningen og f- og
42          v- kender sådan teorien i det kan man sige ik
43
44          Eh and when I say I know a little about it then it is because ehh
45          .hhh I know- I have you know seen the study description and f- and
46          v- know sort of the theory of it you could say right
47
48   IN:    °o:[kay
49          °o:[kay
50   HO:       [.hh øh [og] så har vi e- en øh en øh: en i praktik
51          [.hh eh [and] then we have s- someone eh someone eh: as an intern
52   IN:            [nå]
53                  [oh]
54
55   HO:    her øh som .hh som er på det særlige grundforløb
56          here eh who .hh who is doing the special basiccourse
57   IN:    °Nå [°kay°
58          °Oh [right°
59   HO:        [så]
60            [so]
61
62   HO:    me[n det] men det [de- det] den erf- det den erfaring
63          bu[t that] but that [th- that] is the expe- that's the experience
64   IN:      [det godt]        [heh. he.]
65            [that's good]     [heh. he.]
66
67   HO:    jeg har med  det så det jo ikke meget
68          I have with  it so that (you know) is not much
69
70   IN:    °ja°
71          °yes°
72   (.)
73   HO:    .hh [nej] .hh er det svært f- øh kan du forstå
74          .hh [no] .hh is it difficult f- eh can you understand
75   IN:        [°kay]
76            [right]
77
78   HO:    hvad jeg siger
79          what I am saying
80
81   IN:    £JA|AA£
82          £YE|ES£
83
84   HO:    >£Det godt£<
85          >£That's good£<
86
87   IN:    h[hundrede procent heh. heh. he. jah.][heh. heh. .hhhh]
88          h[hundred percent heh. heh. he. jah. ][heh. heh. .hhhh]
89   HO:    [heh. heh. he. he. he.                ]
90          [heh. heh. he. he. he.                ]
91
92   CO:                                          [Laika er god til dansk]
93                                                [Laika is good at Danish]
```

In this example the linguistic competence and thereby background of IN is made relevant by HO in line 73 where he shows that he interprets IN's previous responses as a display of not understanding. Hereby he simultaneously dissociates IN from the category native-speaker and potentially makes the categories 'second-language speaker' and 'second-language learner' relevant. These categories and IN's affiliation with either of them is thus turned into an object of negotiation which has to be resolved.

Looking at IN's responses, they seem fairly minimal, and although they cannot generally be said to be non-responsive or show direct displays of non-understanding, there are aspects about some of her utterances that could be indicating problems of understanding. As we see, her responses in lines 29, 34, 48 and 57 are thus all formatted either in low voice or with a lengthening of the first vowel (o::), which gives off a hesitant or withheld impression, which is accentuated by the fact that she does not take the floor and respond more elaboratively rather than minimally whenever an opportunity presents itself (most clearly in lines 39 and 57).

This minimally responsive behaviour can be said to prompt HO to elaborate on his knowledge about the programme after the 0.5 second pause in line 39, despite the fact that his knowledge is clearly neither central nor substantial. Again, IN responds minimally to HO's account of his (lack of) knowledge in line 48 with another 'o::kay' and then in line 52 she produces an 'oh', which would normally work as an acknowledgement or a change of state token that would prompt HO to continue. The placement is, however, a little off; it is slightly delayed as a response to the previous utterance, and slightly early to relate to the ongoing utterance, considering that HO has not yet supplied any additional information but merely taken an in-breath and said 'eh'. In light of her previous responses this could contribute to indicating a problem of understanding.

Similarly we see how IN misses HO's more explicit attempts to close the topic and renounce the floor in 59, where he overlaps the second half of IN's response 'nå 'kay' (oh okay) with a 'so', which indicates that HO has finished his turn and is giving the floor to the other participants. While IN orients to this closing by saying 'that's good', this response is once again minimal and again slightly delayed as a positive response to HO's description of previous interns.

The final sign of a problem in understanding is found in line 70 where IN says 'ja' in low voice as a response to HO's assessment of his own (lack of) knowledge, 'so that is not so much'. While IN's previous responses can be said to be ambiguous as displays of non-understanding, this final yes is a less ambiguous display of language difficulty because the previous utterance by HO in line 67 has projected a confirmation with negative, not a positive, polarity. HO responds to and repairs this mistake in line 73 by supplying the right response, 'no', at the beginning of his next utterance, immediately following an in-breath.

When analyzing IN's responses one by one, it is clear that aspects of them seem to display problems of understanding and this contributes to furnishing the interactional context for making the categories 'second-language learner' and 'second-language speaker' potentially relevant. However, I would argue that HO's inquiry about IN's (lack of) understanding cannot merely be considered a result of her responses. The low voice and minimal responses, for example, can in this case also be interpreted as a normal degree of hesitation and withholding within the context of the situation. In a context such as an internship interview IN is likely to orient towards her role as interviewee and internship candidate and towards HO's role as interviewer and potential employer.

IN's responses can, in other words, be seen as an orientation towards the contextual circumstances and the speech event, rather than merely a product and result of her language behaviour. If these contextual circumstances had been different, her physical appearance had been 'ethnically Danish' and her pronunciation flawless, her actual contributions might have allowed her to 'pass' as a native speaker, but the sum of these makes this passing impossible. The ambiguity about understanding is in other words brought along (Roberts & Sarangi, 1999c) and is already 'hanging in the air' (Day, 1998) on account of IN's transportable identity (Zimmerman, 1998) as non-Danish.

Regardless of whether we as 'outsiders' and analysts interpret IN's previous responses and back-channelling as weak or standard, HO illustrates by his utterance in line 73 that he interprets her actions as a display of not understanding. Moreover, he chooses to solve this problem by asking IN directly if it is difficult for her to understand him, which categorizes IN as 'second-language learner' rather than 'second-language speaker'. This question can be seen as highly challenging, especially considering that IN's previous contributions are in fact ambiguous and do not clearly display lack of understanding. If IN had been a native-speaker of Danish, it seems unlikely that this approach would have been used by HO, however ambiguous and weak IN's responses might have been. My suggestion is that HO uses the contextual knowledge locally available to him, such as IN's speech features, her appearance, his knowledge about the purpose of the internship and previous utterances, to make the category second-language speaker relevant. Thereby HO can be seen to account for and co-construct IN's previous actions as non-standard and problematic in terms of language skills.

Similarities and Differences in the Effects of Addressing (Lack of) Understanding

Returning to the differences in the formatting and the embedding of the question 'Do you understand?' in the two examples, they seem to result in a different uptake of the question. In the second extract, the candidate responds very emphatically in line 81 to the implied suggestion that she does not understand what HO has been saying, thereby displaying that she has understood the question as an implied negative assessment, which has to be countered or proven wrong. In her response she orients to the asymmetry that the question entails in the sense that by using emphasis and loud voice she is being assertive, rather than merely responsive. This can be interpreted as a criticism of the preceding question and projects that some sort of excuse, account or explanation for HO's question is to follow. At the same time, the assertiveness is done in a smile voice, which mitigates the implied criticism and rejection. Although HO does not explicitly respond by giving an excuse or account, he orients to the assertiveness and the rejection by giving a quick satisfied third turn response in line 84, also in smile voice. Hereby he is at once diminishing the negative thrust of his previous question and closing the topic on a good note.

In the first extract, on the other hand, the candidate orients to the question in line 52 as if it was merely about making sure that she follows the conversational content while being in no way emphatically marked. This is also illustrated by the following response by CO in line 55, who merely acknowledges that IN has understood rather than, as in the second extract, supporting IN by giving an account. After IN's confirmation that she has understood, IN continues in line 58 by describing what she is and is not able to do during the internship, thereby addressing what was initially mentioned by HO before CO's question. In other words, she not only claims understanding in response to HO's question, but also displays understanding by returning to the topic of discussion, namely the amount and complexity of the tasks of the internship and the expectations and concerns of HO and EM.

Although there are differences in the formatting and the uptake of the question 'do you understand', the two examples are similar in the way the question 'do you understand' makes the linguistic competence and thereby potentially also the background of the candidate relevant. In this way the topicalization of language presents a problem similar to the one presented in Chapter 4 – namely that the otherness of the candidates is foregrounded as a lack, which takes away attention from their work-related competences and social resources. Where the previous chapter showed the workings of the repertoire 'culture as barrier', these examples illuminate the workings of a similar repertoire, namely 'language as barrier', that have similar gatekeeping effects.

Another similarity between the two examples is the way the category second-language speaker is brought up in the general topical development of the interaction as a temporary check-up on the candidate's understanding of what is going on linguistically or topically. Even though the orientation towards language skills in the first example is slightly more embedded than in the second example, both extracts show how language is made relevant in relation to an interactionally embedded establishment of the candidate's level of linguistic proficiency and competence. This allows the candidates to respond to and potentially challenge the assumed problem of understanding while avoiding a prolonged topicalization of language. This will be clearer when looking at the next example, Extract 17.

While the contributions of the two candidates in the first two examples can be said to come off as weak or at least very minimal, this does not fully explain why the employer and the job consultant choose to inquire about the level of understanding. In both cases, there are aspects about the situation of this inquiry that reveal the influence of the internship interview as a specific speech situation and the broader context in which this speech situation is embedded. As discussed in Chapter 1, the speech situation is characterized by having been set up by a job consultant as part of a job-counselling programme for people with an ethnic minority background. Although we cannot say for sure how the internship or the interview was arranged and described between the job consultant and the employer prior to the interview, it is possible that the employer had been informed about the background of the candidate prior to the interview and that the issue of language may have already been mentioned or discussed. This prior knowledge can be said to have evoked a range of interpretative repertoires for the ones doing the interview which in turn can be said to have influenced the interpretations and the actions of the employer as well as the job consultant. This should be taken into consideration when trying to answer the question of 'why that now' with respect to the employer's question to the candidate in the first example.

Extract 17 makes it very clear that the specificity of the context in particular ways provides an orientation towards the language background and proficiency of the candidate. This example shows one of the least embedded ways of questioning the understanding of the candidate and thereby completes the continuum of embeddedness described in the beginning.

Extract 17 Intro 2

```
13
14   HO:    Men øøhm [ja] men velkommen hertil↓
15          But eehm [yes] but welcome here↓
16
17   EM:             [ja]
18                   [yes]
19          (0.3)
20   IN:    Tak skal du hah. .hh
21          Thank you hah. .hh
22          (0.2)
23   HO:    Og jeg vil da starte med at sige til dig hvis der er- jeg
24          siger noget du ikke forstår
25
26          And I will begin by saying to you if there is I
27          say something you don't understand
28          (0.6)
29   HO:    Så skal du sige det til mig ikke↑
30          Then you must tell me right↑
31
32          (0.5)
33   HO:    Med det samme der er ingen grund til vi fortsætter
34          Right away there is no reason for us to continue
35          (0.4)
36   HO:    og du så e:h (sound of a click)
37          and you then e:h
38          (0.6)
39   HO:    ikke forstår hvad det er jeg    [siger]
40          not understanc what it is I am  [saying
41
42   IN:                                    [okay-]
43                                          [okay-]
44          (0.7)
45  (IN:)   (okay)
46
```

Compared to the previous two examples, this extract shows a completely non-embedded inquiry about understanding which is non-ambiguous in its orientation towards the category of second-language speaker. The difference in this example from the previous two is that the inquiry about understanding is in fact not formatted as a question but rather as an invitation to confirm a statement, namely 'If there is something you don't understand you must tell me right away, okay?' This formatting is a very indirect way of asking a question, which only invites a very minimal response, which is perhaps part of the reason why, as we can see, IN does not reply at all. This lack of response makes HO elaborate on her statement with a new statement that specifies that she is concerned about the candidate's lack of proficiency rather than her ability to 'follow'. After yet another long pause, which indicates the ambiguity of what response is expected and appropriate, the candidate finally responds with a minimal okay.

Thus, it can be said that this extract shows an example of a very explicit and non-embedded way of orienting to an assumed lack of proficiency of the candidate. Even though this assumed problem of language is explicitly formulated, the indirectness of the question, however, does not allow the candidate much of a chance to respond to or challenge the presumed problem of understanding. On the other hand, a positive aspect of this indirectness is that the topicalization of language membership does not result in a prolonged negotiation about the language proficiency of the candidate as we saw in the previous examples. This unfortunately also means that the candidate is categorized as non-native speaker before having much of a chance to establish herself as a member of the category second-language speaker. This is in marked contrast to the first example where the candidate manages to strongly refute the suggested categorization as second-language learner and securely affiliate herself with the category second-language speaker. In this sense, this example shows how an assumed language problem can be strongly raised without being actually addressed and resolved.

Explicit Topicalizations of Language – Evaluating and Regulating Practice

The following examples of orientations towards language are different from the previous ones in the sense that they do not directly address or check the linguistic competence, proficiency and understanding of the candidate. Rather, they seem to make the negotiation of the categories 'second-language speaker' and 'second-language learner' relevant as a topic in its own right. Again, this negotiation is based on the implicit assessment and evaluation of the candidate as a non-native speaker, which is either inferred from the candidate's language performance or from knowledge of the specific context of the internship interview. The contexts in which this orientation or topicalization occur seem to be more marginal points in the interaction where the central aspects of the internship have already been discussed and where the participants have moved on to discuss the details of the future internship and summarize what the internship will involve, offer and require. The subsequent examples show how this type of orientation towards language not only involves an evaluation of the candidates' language background and competence as non-native speakers of Danish. It also involves the prescription by the employers of a particular type of language behaviour and language practice as interns and non-native speakers in general. In other words, the employers use the context of the internship and the negotiation of language-related categories as a platform to express their expectations and understandings of second-language learning within and beyond the context of the internship.

The first example, Extract 12, was previously presented in Chapter 4, where I showed that a cultural contrast was established between the candidate and the other participants as the candidate was categorized as an 'other' in relation to the category Danish and an outsider to 'Danish ways'. Here, the analysis will focus on the aspects of the categorization processes that have to do with language, although these are intimately linked with the orientation towards nationality, as I have already covered in the previous chapter.

Extract 12 **Danish** *(repeated)*

```
73    HO:    Men jeg kan give dig en fornemmelse af (0.6) hvad der sker
74           But I can  give you  a sense      of (0.6) what happens
75           (0.8)
76    HO:    Hvad det er vi lægger vægt på og hvordan vi gerne vil (0.2) øøh
77           ha' vores produkter
78
79           what it  is we  emphasize     and how we would like to have (0.2)
80           eeh our products
81
82    IN:    mm=
83    HO:    =øøh vores butiksform
84           =eeh our way of the store
85    (0.6)
86    HO:    Du kommer i kontakt
87           You will be in contact
88    (0.2)
89    IN:    jae=
90           Yea=
91
92    HO:    =hvis du kommer ind til mig i butikken her så har du kontakt
93           med nogle [kunder] nogle der taler dansk
94
95           =if you come with me in the store here you have contact
96           with some [clients] some that speak Danish
97
98    IN:              [ja]
99                     [yes]
100   (0.4)
101   IN:    ja=
102          yes=
```

In Extract 12 the linguistic competence and background of the candidate is not made relevant in the same direct way as in the previous examples and not in relation to a question of understanding. Instead, it is introduced as a side-remark in line 92 during a discussion of what the candidate can learn or experience during the internship. The category of second-language learner is introduced here as a specific dimension of the internship and not as an issue of understanding related to the ongoing interaction as such.

The category of second-language learner is not, as in the two previous examples, made relevant directly through an inquiry about understanding, but is rather introduced indirectly by means of the *consistency rule* described by Sacks. By describing 'the clients' as 'some that speak Danish' she is establishing the category of 'Danish speakers', and by characterizing IN as someone who will be in contact with members of this group she reveals an orientation towards IN as an outsider to or a non-member of this category. IN is in this way affiliated with an alternative category of 'foreign-language speaker' which is made available as part of the MCD 'language speakers' that HO is inferring the category 'Danish speakers' from. HO is in other words using a conceptual distinction between the categories of 'Danish speakers' and 'foreign-language speakers' as a basis for formulating what IN will gain from the internship. By making it relevant that the customers in the store would be people who speak Danish, 'Danish speakers', she highlights that the central output from having contact with the clients is language learning through language contact. The orientation towards IN as a 'foreign-language speaker' in this sense involves a categorization of him as a 'second-language learner'. When looking at the interaction in terms of the distribution of turns and the contributions of the participants, there are a couple of factors which can be said to contribute to this orientation towards language.

As in Extract 16 (Do you understand?), the distribution of turns was highly asymmetrical in the sense that the employer and the employee respectively were the ones dominating the interaction by giving elaborate descriptions of the workplace and the tasks that will constitute the internship. In this sense they oriented to and co-constructed the speech event as primarily an informative and instructional event rather than an interview and thereby gave the candidate little opportunity or encouragement to participate and contribute. During these two interviews the candidate was asked very few direct questions, and the few questions that were in fact asked were often closed questions that did not require or encourage much elaboration. Consequently, the contribution and the participation of the candidates were in both cases minimal, but more so in Extract 12 (Danish) than in Extract 16 (Do you understand?). As we can see, the candidate's contributions in Extract 12 (Danish) consist mostly of 'mm' and 'yes', whereas in Extract 9 (Do you understand what I'm saying?), the candidate uses 'okay' and 'yes'.

In Extract 16 (Do you understand?) the employer's interpretation of the candidate's participation is based on very few turns, since the question 'do you understand' is posed right at the beginning of the interaction. In this latest example, Extract 12 (Danish), however, the category of second-language speaker is made relevant right at the end of the interaction, and any interpretation or inference that the employer might have made as a basis for introducing this category is therefore based on a much longer period of participation by the candidate. When looking at the candidate's contribution previous to the extract, there seems to be a fair basis for evaluating it as minimal, even to an extent where it could be interpreted as non-standard. In other words, it seems likely that the employer oriented to IN as a 'second-language learner' because his contributions were too minimal to allow him to 'pass' as a 'second-language speaker'.

It should be said, though, that this interview is different from the others in that it consists of a tour around the orchard from beginning to end, and the main activity taking place is therefore that of the employer introducing the orchard and describing the work routines. Consequently, the candidate can be said to have merely oriented to this introductory and descriptive format of the interaction by acknowledging what he is being shown with acknowledgement tokens that are perhaps minimal but nevertheless appropriate. The candidate not only shows orientation to the tour guiding format, but at times also attempts to fulfil the minimal participatory potential of it by asking supplementary questions regarding the information he was given. However, in some of these cases the questions demonstrate a lack of understanding rather than understanding of what had been explained and shown. Extract 18, which takes place right at the beginning of the tour, is an example of this.

Extract 18 Plastic

```
11
12   HO:    o:g som du kan se der er gjort klar til vinteren
13          A:nd as you can see there has been made ready for winter
14   (0.9)
15   HO:    (klippet) ned
16          (cut)     down
17   (0.7)
18   IN:    mm
19   HO:    og lagt den lidt og blev ø::h lagt i sort
20          plastik for at beskytte
21   HO:    And laid it a little and was e::h laid in black
22          plastic to  protect
23   (0.8)
24   HO:    øh for sol og regn
25          eh for sun and rain
26   (1.0)
27   HO:    så det sådan når vi ska bru:ge (.) plastikket
28          til næste år så pakker vi det ud (0.3)
29          og trækker det på igen (.) og det er så for
30          [for]
31   HO:    So it is like that when we will ne:ed (.) the plastic
32          next year so we unpack it (0.3)
33          and pull it over again (.) and that is then to
34          [to]
35   IN:    [hvis jeg kommer: e:hm (0.8) vinter (0.2)
36          eh (0.7) (      )
37   IN:    [If I com:e e:hm (0.8) winter (0.2)
38          eh (0.7) (      )
39   (0.6)
40   HO:    ja
41          yes
42   (0.4)
43   HO:    Ikke om vinterer nej
44          Not in winter nc
45   (0.5)
46   IN:    ['nej·]
47          ['no·]
48   HO:    [til] sommer hhe. (0.2)
49          [in] summer hhe. (0.2)
50   IN:    til sommer okay=
51          in summer okay=
52   HO:    =til foråret. for at give dem va:rme
53          =in spring. to give them he:at
54   IN:    mm
55
```

In this extract HO explains and demonstrates the practice of covering up some of the crop, and the candidate initially responds to this in line 18 with 'mm'. After an elaboration by the employer of the function and management of the plastic used for this practice, IN asks a supplementary question in line 35, which demonstrates a misunderstanding of the time of the practice of covering. Instead he says 'if I come e:hm winter' followed by something unclear. This conjunctive construction projects either an affirmative or negative response from HO.

HO first responds to this in line 40 by supplying the continuer 'yes'. However, after a pause she provides a correction in line 43 'not in winter no', showing that she understands IN's utterance as a formulation or summary of what she had previously explained, and corrects this formulation while identifying the season as the problem source. IN responds to this repair initiation with 'no', spoken in low voice. This 'no' is overlapped by HO, who now provides the right answer 'in summer' in smile voice, which can be said to orient to the misunderstanding. IN acknowledges the misunderstanding in his next response by repeating and thereby aligning with HO, who then finally clarifies and elaborates on her previous correction by saying 'in spring to give them heat' in line 52. By giving this final elaboration HO supplies not only the right season but also points at the central aspect of the issue with the plastic.

The problem in this extract can be said to stem from, first, the indirect pointing to a practice by the first utterance in line 12, 'as you can see there has been made ready for winter', which does not specify what exactly IN is to notice, the plastic being put away or the plastic being ready to use for the covering up. This is made increasingly unclear by the following utterance in line 19, where HO talks about 'protecting' but not specifying whether it is the plastic or the crops that should be protected. In line 27, HO specifies that she is talking about the plastic, which should be ready for the covering next year, but at this point there is no specification of when the covering takes place. At this point then, it is unclear whether the crops are covered or uncovered during winter, and this is the issue IN can be said to be probing further with his utterance in line 35.

When looking at the contributions of HO, which are characterized by indirectness and a lack of specificity around the practice of covering up the crops and putting away the plastic, the probing utterance by IN in line 35 seems interactionally relevant and appropriate. Furthermore, the misunderstanding it displays appears less related to problems with understanding language and more related to problems with understanding a given explanation of a practice, which is not necessarily related to IN being a second-language speaker. However, this extract can, as first mentioned, be regarded as a situation in which the candidate shows problems with speaking Danish or with passing as a 'second-language speaker'. This is not only manifested in the misunderstanding as such. It is also indicated by the formulation that IN makes in line 35 which shows problems of understanding what HO has previously said and furthermore reveals problems with language formatting itself, since IN produces an incomplete conditional construction with part of the wording hardly understandable.

In this respect, the extract presents an example of a situation in the interaction where the category of 'second-language learner' is potentially made relevant by the participation of the candidate and thereby furnishes the conversational context for the specific topicalization that occurs later in the interview and was illustrated in Extract 12 (Danish) in Chapter 4. However, as already described in Chapter 2, many CA studies of second-language talk, multilingual encounters or native/non-native interactions (Gardner & Wagner, 2004; Mondada, 2004; Kasper & Ross, 2007; Fosgerau, 2007; Fosgerau, 2013; Svennevig, 2009, forthcoming, 2004) emphasize that the performance and proficiency of second-language speakers should not be understood in terms of the proficiency of the second-language speaker but should rather be considered an interactional phenomenon which is co-produced by the 'native'-speaker and the 'non-native' speaker. In the study by Brown (2003) as well as in the study by Kasper and Ross (2007) it is shown how interviewer behaviour is directly implicational for the construction of the candidates' proficiency, which was also argued in one of the earlier studies of gatekeeping by Bremer et al. (1996). A similar result is found by Christina Fogtmann Fosgerau, who has studied naturalization interviews between Danish police representatives and Danish second-language speakers applying for Danish citizenship. She argues that although the assessment of the applicants is related to their lexico-grammatic level of performance, the participation and behaviour of the applicants is highly related to and influenced by the interactional behaviour of the police representatives (Fosgerau, 2007: 290).

The mentioning of these studies in terms of the co-constructed nature of proficiency emphasizes the importance of studying the participation and behaviour of second-language speakers, and first-language speakers for that matter, as jointly constructed rather than as reflections of individual abilities and competences. As Gardner and Wagner state, 'an utterance is an interactional product, the construction of which is massively influenced by the "hearers", to the extent that these hearers can be seen as equal co-producers of the conversation' (2004: 2). This is not to suggest that the orientation of the employer towards the candidate from Somalia as a 'second-language learner' is not valid, but rather to emphasize the employer's role in generating or producing the minimal or non-standard behaviour of the candidate, which can be said to inspire this orientation. While this dimension of proficiency as co-constructed is beyond the scope of this book and will not be explored further, it is important to bear in mind in relation to the question of how, when and why categories related to language are made relevant and oriented to by the employers. The central point is that the employers and job consultants contribute to the 'passing' or 'non-passing' of the candidates by creating or preventing certain opportunities for language practice and language interaction.

To return to Extract 18, the categorization of the candidate as a 'second-language learner' and the assumptions made about the purpose and goal of the internship can be said to be influenced by interpretative repertoires of 'second-language speakers' and 'language learning' in general. First of all there is the interpretative repertoire of 'second-language learners' as 'isolated foreigners', which is closely linked to another repertoire related to language and immigration, namely 'learning through speaking'. In the example from the orchard, Extract 12 (Danish), these interrelated repertoires are reflected in the normative prescription of the employer that the internship candidate is to speak Danish, interact with Danish customers and learn about their 'ways'. In this example the utterance 'if you come with me in the store here you have contact with clients some who speak Danish' is based on the assumption that the internship candidate as a member of the category 'second-language speaker' is isolated from Danes or people who speak Danish. The establishment of the category 'second-language learner' can thus be said to be not only characterized by an exclusion from the category of 'Danish'. It is also informed by an interpretative repertoire about 'foreigners' in Denmark as isolated from 'Danes' and not speaking 'Danish'. This interpretative repertoire can be said to influence the interpretations of the candidate's contributions as non-standard.

The language evaluation and prescription expressed in all of the previous examples highlights how 'passing' and 'non-passing' as a 'Danish speaker' or a 'second-language speaker' is very much dependent on the category memberships that are 'brought about and brought along' (Roberts & Sarangi, 1999c). The language-related 'otherness' of the candidate is not only 'brought along' by speech features, level of proficiency and 'ethnic' physical appearance. It is also 'brought about' through the interactional co- production and achievement of particular language practices, influenced by the interpretative repertoires and cultural common sense available within the given situational context. As argued in Chapter 3 the interactional negotiations about categories and memberships are thus established on the basis of the interpretative repertoires which are available to and activated by the participants in the internship interview while faced with the particular properties and characteristics of the other participants. 'Passing' is in this sense made difficult not only because of individuals' inability to escape particular characteristics but also, and quite centrally, because of the repertoires and common sense understandings of such characteristics that have turned them into stigma over time. If particular linguistic and physical features were not automatically associated with 'otherness' and a lack of knowledge, ability and experience compared to 'Danish ways' then they could present less of a problem for the candidates. 'Passing' as 'Danish' or 'native-speaker' would in such a case no longer be central in order for the candidates to present themselves as able, competent workers.

In the next extract, Extract 19, the category of 'second-language learner', is once again addressed as a topic in its own right in relation to the expected language encounters that the future internship will entail. It is in this way similarly related to an indirect negotiation of the candidate's language abilities vis-à-vis the reality of the future internship. However, in this example, the emphasis is more on the issue of whether the candidate will be able to handle these language encounters with her current language resources, rather than on the benefits of engaging in and learning from them.

Extract 19 Can you read?

```
115
116    HO     Hvordan- har hvordan ville du have det hvis du skulle ud og købe ind for en kunde (.)
117           hvis du nu får en indkøbsseddel (.) kunden skriver hvad hvad hun gerne vil ha [(.)] eller
118
119           How wo- how would you feel if you had to go shop for a customer (.)
120           if you get a shopping list (.) the customer writes what she would like      [(.)] or
121    IN:                                                                                [ja]
122
123    HO:    man lige taler om (.) hvad der er på den
124           you talk about   (.) what is on it
125
126    IN:    .hja
127           .hyes
128    (.)
129
130    HO:    Det har du ikke sådan noget imod (.) at gå i ne:tto (.) eller i brugsen el- og handle for kunderne ik
131           you don't mind (.) going to ne:tto (.) or brugsen or- and shop for the customers right
132
133    IN:    .hja
134           .hyes
135
136    HO:    ja
137           yes
138
139    EM:    ka du læ[se]
140           can you [read]
141
142    IN:             [det ka ne-]
143                    [it can yo-]
144
145    HO:    ja=
146           yes=
147
148    EM:    =du kan godt læse ik
149           =you can read right
150
151    HO:    ja
152           yes
153
154    EM:    ja ja
155           yes yes
156
157    (0.3)
158
159    EM:    jeg spørger fordi vi har mange forskellige eh vi har et fint samarbejde med et andet firma som hedder Credo
160           'i Københavns kommune'
```

Extract 19 is taken from the beginning of the interview where the participants are talking about some of the tasks that the internship will involve. They have just talked about whether the candidate knows how to read a road map, which she will need in order to find the homes of the elderly. After establishing that she is able to do so, the employer raises the issue of shopping for the elderly. The extract begins with HO asking rather generally how the candidate would feel about shopping, but she quickly specifies her question in line 116, where she depicts a scenario where the candidate will receive a shopping list and the customer will explain what is on the list. The question is phrased in a very indirect manner 'how would you feel about ...' and the embedded question is concealed even further by the following rephrasing in the form of a described scenario. The candidate replies minimally with a '.hyes' in line 126 and HO then again elaborates on her question, this time emphasizing the actual shopping in a store rather than the shopping list aspect. Again she formats it not as a direct question but as a formulation that invites a negated confirmation. The correct answer to HO's indirect question should have been 'no' here but seeing as IN misunderstands the question or the formatting of it, witnessed by her answering with '.hyes', she manages to satisfy the request for confirmation but in the wrong way. HO apparently accepts her reply as satisfactory because she repeats IN's response in line 136 thereby potentially initiating a close. EM, however, continues probing the issue of proficiency and specifies the previously very implicit inquiry from HO by asking IN directly whether she can read. While the orientation towards the category 'second-language speaker' in HO's utterance is more ambiguous, EM's question leaves no doubt. She is explicitly affiliating IN with the category of 'Non-native speaker' and initiating a negotiation of what this category membership entails by trying to establish IN's reading skills in Danish. She is in this way elaborating on the shopping list issue that was introduced by HO rather than the more general issue of going to the store.

What is interesting here is that HO immediately and without any delay answers 'yes' on IN's behalf. This can be seen as having a dual function: on the one hand she displays that she has already received a satisfactory answer to this issue in the previous exchange; and on the other hand she confirms that EM's question constitutes a summary or a specification of her own previous question. EM does not fully accept HO's reply on IN's behalf as satisfactory because she restates her question in line 148, probably also due to the overlap of IN in line 142 that calls into question whether IN has heard the question at all. EM acknowledges the answer that HO has given because she changes the formatting of her previous question to a request for confirmation that projects a positive reply. Again, however, it is HO not IN who answers and this time with an emphasized 'yes'. In light of her previous 'yes' to the same question this can be said to present a topic-closing move which again suggests that HO is satisfied with the reply she received to her question earlier and is ready to move on to something else. Even though EM seems to recognize and accept HO's attempt to close, she nevertheless prolongs the orientation towards IN as a second-language speaker by producing an account for her question. We see this in the next part of the extract.

Extract 19 Can you read? *(continued)*

```
161
162         I ask because we have many different eh we have a good cooperation with another company called Credo
163         'in copenhagen municipality'
164
165   CO:   'det kender jeg godt'
166         'I know that'
167
168   EM:   jo så det dem der kommer vi havde s:eks eller syv efterhånden [(.)] dejlige piger [(.)] men det
169         yes so they come we had s:ix or seven now        [(.)] lovely girls [(.)] but it
170   HO:                                                    [ja]
171                                                          [yes]
172   CO:                                                                              [okay]
173                                                                                    [okay]
174   EM:   det var nogen piger som havde svært ved at læse |
175         it was some girls who had difficulty reading
176
177   CO:   mm
178
179   EM:   ja så så derfor spørger jeg det er vigtigt at du læser og forstår hvad står på indkøbssedlen
180         yes so so therefore I ask it is important that you read and understand what it says on the shopping list
181
182   IN:   .hja
183         .hyes
184
185   EM:   ja
186         yes
187
188   EM:   og en gang imellem det er også godt at spørge hvis der står bare
189         smør ja .hh i: eh der er mange ældre der mener at Kærgården det er
190         ikke smør
191
192         and sometimes it is also good to ask if it just says
193         butter yes .hh in: eh there are many elderly who think Kærgården that is
194         not butter
195   (0.4)
196   EM:   Det er margarine [o:g når de siger smø˚] så det de:t
197         it is margarine [a:nd when they say butter] then it i:t
198
199   IN:                    [.hh heh he]
200   ( )                   [heh he he]
201
```

In Extract 19 (continued) we see how EM (from lines 162–180) compares and affiliates IN with 'previous girls who had difficulty reading'. In line 179 EM makes a formulation or a summary of her point which once again returns to the issue of the shopping list that was introduced by HO. IN finally responds to EM's questioning in line 182, after a couple of acknowledgement tokens by CO in line 172 and 177. However, EM does not accept the closing of the topic and elaborates on the topicalization of language abilities even further in line 188 by adding a new dimension to the language issue, namely that with a more culturally specific meaning. With this she introduces another specific language competence the candidate will need for the internship besides the mere ability to read, which is the ability to understand or at least inquire about the culturally specific meanings of the items on the shopping list. The example she uses, namely butter, illustrates quite well that what EM is problematizing is IN's lack of knowledge regarding the historically and culturally specific meaning of particular items on the list that are associated with Danish heritage and pride.

Extract 19 Can you read? *(continued)*

```
202   HO:      så er det [rigtig Lurmærke rigtig lurmærkesmør]
203            then it is [real Lurmærke real Lurmærkebutter
204
205   EM:                [betyder det sådn- en ( )]
206                      [it means like- a ( )]
207   (.)
208
209   EM:      ja
210            yes
211
212   CO:      mm
213
214   EM:      sådan [en:] gammeldags dansk smør ik
215            like  [a:n] oldfashioned Danish butter right
216
217   CO:            [ja]
218                  [yes]
219
220            (.)
221   IN:      ja
222            yes
223
224   EM:      så det øh: (0.3) altid godt at spørge
225            sc it eh:  (0.3) always good to ask
226
227   IN:      ·k
228   EM:      øhm: sådan flere gange
229            (c.5)
230   IN:      .hja
231   (0.2)
```

In line 202 HO emphasizes the distinction between butter and margarine by naming a particular brand of Danish butter 'Lurmærke' and specifying this as an old-fashioned type of Danish butter. This particular kind of butter is thereby used to exemplify and underline the specific cultural meanings that IN is expected to understand or at least be sure to inquire about when shopping for the elderly. Thus the extract shows yet another example of how the orientation towards the category of 'second-language learner' involves a simultaneous categorization of the candidate as a non-member of the category 'Danish' who has to learn about Danish 'ways', or in this case Danish food customs regarding butter. Again, we see how interpretative repertoires are being applied in the interpretation of the candidate as a second-language learner, namely a conceptual linking of language and culture. This repertoire provides the premise for assuming that her potential lack of language proficiency implies a lack of cultural knowledge. Language and culture are in other words linked in ways that are similar to the linking of nationality and culture described in Chapter 4. Similar to Extract 10 (Colombia) and Extract 12 (Danish), the orientation towards the language background of the candidate involves the establishment of cultural differentiation which is formulated as something the candidate needs to overcome or handle as part of the internship. The categorization of the candidate as a 'second-language learner' in this way involves the evaluation of language competence and cultural difference as well as the prescription of certain practices of learning within the context of the internship related to language *and* culture.

Extract 8 is another example of the category of 'second-language learner' being addressed as a topic in its own right, and as in Extract 12 (Danish) it is related to an implicit assessment of the candidate's language competences as less than proficient, or non-standard. The language proficiency of the candidate is not, as in the previous example, raised as an actual question, but is assumed to be less than proficient or at a learner's level. The topicalization is, however, made directly rather than indirectly here. In this respect, it is similar to the first type of examples presented in this chapter. However, the topicalization of language in those examples was aimed at clarifying potential problems of understanding within the internship interview. This is not the case in Extract 8.

Extract 8 So you both have to learn Danish? *(repeated)*

```
13    EM:    Er din mand også fra I:ran, (very thouroughly prc
14           Is your husband also from I:ran
15
16    IN:    ja
17           yes
18
19    EM:    ja
20           yes
21
22    IN:    ja=
23           yes=
24
25    EM:    =[.tsk]
26           =[.tsk]
27
28    ( )    [.hja]
29           [.hjyeah]
30
31    EM:    Så skal I begge  [to lære £dansk£? =
32           So you both have [to learn £Danish£?=
33
34    IN:                     [han kommer (ja/her)=
35                            [he comes (yes/here)=
36
37    EM:    =[sk.ha]    [( )]=
38           =[sk.ha]    [( )]=
39
40    IN:    =[ja] ha ha [ha ]=
41           =[yes]ha ha [ha ]=
42
43    CO:    =[Nej han har ]boet her i mange år.
44           =[no he has  ] lived here ⁼or many years
45
46    IN:    =[ja::        ]
47           =[ye::s
48
49    EM:    Nå han har [boet her i mange år okay]
50           Oh he has  [lived here for many years okay]
51
52    (CO/IN:)            [ja (          ) også] boet [her]
53                       [yes(          ) also] lived [here]
54
55    EM:                                        [ja] ja
56                                               [yes] yes
57
58    IN:    .shll (makes a sort of slurping sound)
59           .shll
60
61    HO:    Så må i tale dansk hjemme,
62           So you must be speaking Danish at home,
63
64           (0.3)
65
66    IN:    °Nej°
67           °No°
68
69           (0.4)
70
71    HO:    Det skal i gøre (high pitch)
72           You have to
73
74           (0.2)
75
76    IN:    Persisk h. hi hi [hi (jheg skhal] thale mhed   pher[shisk)
77           Persian h. he he [he (i musth)  ] spheak whith Pher[shian)
78
```

```
78
79   HO:                    [ja:e           ]
80                          [ye:a
81   CO:                                         [Man taler nok
82                                               [One probably
83
84        [det sprog] man [har lettest ved ]
85        speaks [the language] one [is most comfortable with]
86
87   IN:      [JAAE hah.]        [DET SVÆRT for mig]
88            [JEAA hah.]        [IT IS HARD FOR ME]
89
90   HO:      Det gør man nok men man skal nok indimellem gøre det for at træne
91            ik?
92            One probably does but one should probably do it once in a while to
93            practice right?
94
95   IN:      Men øh min datter taler øh fi:nt dansk og også taler fint persisk.
96            But eh my daughter speaks eh go:od Danish and also speaks good
97            Persian.
98
99   EM:      ja det j[o g]odt
100           Well that [is go]od
101
102  HO:               [ja]
103               [yes]
```

In this extract, the category of 'second-language learner' is made relevant by EM in line 31, as an inference from the category 'Iranian'. Learning Danish is constructed as an activity which is bound to the category 'Iranian' and implies that the candidate does not know Danish, or at least that she needs to learn more. The implication of EM's utterance in line 31 is thus similar to the implication 'some that speak Danish' in Extract 12 (Danish) – namely that IN is a member of the category 'non-Danish speakers'. The function of these two utterances is furthermore similar in their normative suggestion that the candidate should speak and learn Danish.

In contrast to Extract 12 (Danish), the direct form of address projects and demands a response from the candidate or, as in this case, the job consultant, who comes to the defence of the candidate by stating in line 43 that her husband 'has lived here for many years'. This utterance counters the suggestion of EM that they both have to learn Danish by offering a countering implication, which is that since the husband has been here for many years he is no longer learning but in fact speaking Danish as a second language. This, however, only challenges the ascription of the husband and not the ascription of the candidate, who is also implied and included in EM's utterance 'so you both have to learn Danish', and the candidate remains categorized as a 'second-language learner' rather than a 'second-language speaker', i.e. as a not yet proficient Danish speaker.

The defence offered by the job consultant results in an extended topicalization of second-language speakers and language learning practices, which has to be closed before the interaction can go on. In Extract 12 (Danish), the indirectness of the way the category of 'second-language learner' was made relevant allowed for the interaction to go on without the candidate having to respond. The advantage of this is of course that it does not, as we can see when comparing the two examples, disrupt the interaction in the same way. On the other hand, the problem is that when the category of 'second-language learner' is made indirectly relevant, it is difficult for the candidate to respond to or confront this categorization and the assumptions and ascriptions it entails. Although one might say that IN does in fact respond in line 34, I would argue that this response is rather a follow-up response to the initial question of whether her husband is from Iran, since it is uttered in overlap with the part of EM's utterance in line 31 that adds the language dimension. Therefore it cannot as such be considered as a reply to the language issue. When perceived this way, the language issue is not responded to by IN, but only by CO in line 43.

Although the job consultant's defence is successful in the sense that her redefinition of the husband as a 'second-language speaker' rather than a 'second-language learner' is accepted by EM in line 49, the topic is not closed down by either of the participants. In line 61 HO renews the orientation towards the language practice of IN by asking the strongly suggestive question 'So you must be speaking Danish at home, which is formatted as an implication of the category "second-language speaker"' co-constructed by CO and EM immediately prior. HO's question addresses IN directly and its formatting is strongly projecting a positive answer. By uttering the following 'no' in line 66 in low voice, IN orients to her response as not preferred, but nevertheless she does not use the 0.4 seconds pause following her response as an opportunity to account for her negative reply. Thereby she does not mitigate the challenge that her 'no' entails to which HO responds by upgrading her initial suggestive question to the explicitly formulated demand 'You have to'.

Kjærbeck (2003), in a study of social service interactions, describes similar evaluative statements made by a social worker to a client, and she argues that they are illustrative of the achievement of a certain distribution of rights and power. This argument seems to be confirmed in this example, where HO's strong normative and directive statement shows an orientation towards a privileged right to prescribe a certain behaviour from the candidate. The power and position claimed by the employer in this example is, however, not confirmed and accepted by the other participants. Remarkably, the very strong normative proclamation does not make IN 'give in' and admit the wrongness of her behaviour. Nor does it push her to provide the account that was not given in line 69. Instead she merely provides a follow-up elaboration of her 'no' in line 66, namely that she speaks Persian at home, which is, however, by means of laughter, showing an awareness of the challenge this reply entails.

Once again, we see in line 81 how the job consultant orients to the delicacy of the situation and the problems of the internship candidate with defending her practices as a 'second-language speaker' by giving a defence on her behalf. CO generalizes the issue of language practice by using the indefinite pronoun 'one', which removes some of the specific attention on IN and turns the practice of 'speaking the language one is most comfortable with' into something general and normal. HO only partially accepts this defence and in line 90 incorporates the generalizing format and the partial agreement in yet another argument for speaking Danish at home, namely that 'one should do it to practice'. In line 95, IN attempts to justify her language practices and difficulties with Danish with the fact that her daughter speaks Danish well, thus supporting the shift in attention away from herself, which is first initiated by the job consultant. This is finally accepted by EM and HO, and the orientation towards IN's membership as a 'second-language learner' and the negotiation of what practice can or should be associated with this category is abandoned.

There are a range of interpretative resources brought into play when making sense of and negotiating the language practices and language membership of candidates. The categories brought forward in other words actualize and activate a range of common sense ideas that manifest themselves in the links established between categories and between categories and actions as well. When examining these in relation to the present example, the politicized context of migration immediately becomes apparent once again, even more so in this example than in the previous one. In this example we see how a number of inferences are made about the Iranian husband that reveal the naturalized assumption or idea of 'learning through speaking'. The husband is first categorized by the employer as a 'second-language learner' purely on the basis of his membership of the category Iranian but this is then challenged by the job consultant, who proposes the alternative category membership of 'second-language speaker', based on a foregrounding of the length of his residence in Denmark. Living in Denmark and speaking Danish is, in other words, assumed to entail learning how to speak Danish. In the same example, the interpretative repertoire 'learning through speaking' is even more clearly manifested in the contribution of the employer, who later in the exchange makes an account for the formulation in line 61 'so you speak Danish at home' and in line 71 'you have to' which emphasizes speaking as a means of practising and improving. This account, which is found in line 90, rejects a defence presented by the job consultant on the internship candidate's behalf after she has admitted in line 76 that she speaks Persian rather than Danish at home. As we see here 'learning through speaking' constitutes one of the interpretative repertoires used to negotiate and categorize the actions, behaviour and category membership of the internship candidate, which is linked to ideologies about second-language speakers formulated in this example and the previous one with the internship candidate from Somalia. These ideologies take for granted that second-language speakers should associate and speak with Danes, speak Danish in general and furthermore speak and practice Danish at home. While it is not possible within the context of this book to analyze and illustrate the manifestation of such ideologies in contexts beyond the internship interview, the following example from the Danish media debate is useful in illuminating the ideologies and traces of meaning manifested in this and other internship interviews. The following news headline is taken from one of the biggest newspapers in Denmark and it is a clear illustration of the discussion about migration, integration and language practice, which has been centrally placed in the media and public debates in Denmark for years.

DF: Indvandrere skal tale dansk hjemme	DF (Danish People's Party): Immigrants must speak Danish at home
Dansk er forudsætningen for integration, derfor skal indvandrerforældre ikke tale deres modersmål, men dansk i hjemmet, mener DF.	In DF's opinion, Danish is the basis for integration and for this reason immigrant parents should not speak their mother tongue, but Danish, at home.

SOURCE: POLITIKEN, 12. AUG. 2007 KL. 08.28,
HTTP://POLITIKEN.DK/INDLAND/ECE357022/DF-INDVANDRERE-SKAL-TALE-DANSK-HJEMME/

Examples such as this clearly show the kind of argument reproduced in Extract 8 and in this way exemplifies the point by Bakhtin about the historicity of words. It shows how the interdiscursivity analyzed and documented within and across the various internship interviews can be traced and charted within a broader discursive context.

The politicized public debate about migrants in Denmark, which has been led and informed to a large extent by the party Dansk Folkeparti (Danish People's Party) is not only manifested in the interpretative frameworks drawn upon within the context of the internship interviews. It is also reflected, I would argue, in the way that the particular speech situation of these internship interviews seems to allow for the topicalization of issues and categories that would otherwise be considered inappropriate, private or irrelevant to the overall purpose and goal of the speech situation. Whether the candidate speaks Danish or Persian at home is in other words hardly relevant for establishing the terms and possibilities of a future internship. The fact that the internships were specifically targeted at migrants makes a range of interpretative frameworks relevant and available that would not otherwise be relevant if the candidates were not 'ethnic Danes'. Furthermore, the limits for what can be discussed during these interactions seem to be influenced by the hybridity of the speech situation compared to, for example, a job-interview situation and ordinary everyday interactions. The imposition of prescribing a particular language behaviour of someone in the private realm of their own home is in this case made possible by the combination of a dominating ideology about the obligation of migrants to speak Danish at home and the fact that the speech situation is less formal than a job interview and yet more institutional and hierarchical than ordinary everyday interactions.

Extract 8 is in this sense a good example of how the local context of the speech situation interplays with the broader context of multiculturalist debate in the sense that participants' negotiations about the candidate's membership of the category 'second-language speaker' invokes an argument between naturalized yet conflictual common-sense assumptions or common places (Billig, 1996) about the language behaviour of migrants. We see these assumptions reflected in, first of all, the way the question 'so you both have to learn Danish' in line 31 is formatted as a natural and logical consequence of the fact that IN and her husband are from Iran. This can be heard as an expression of a particular position within the Danish debate on integration, namely that foreigners coming to Denmark must learn Danish, which is a position that is not only common sense (in an ideological sense of the word) but is a legislatively established fact. Second, we see them manifested in the response made by CO to this assumption, 'no he has lived here for many years', which expresses another and contrary commonsensical position, namely that if a person has lived in Denmark for many years their Danish skills are at a level that makes further formal teaching superfluous. The two utterances expressed by EM and CO can in this way be understood either from an strictly interactional perspective as verbal actions (a question which projects agreement) that project and respond to other actions (answer/rejection), but they can also be interpreted as utterances that represent positions in a culturally specific landscape of ideology and opinions. From this perspective the challenge or rejection by the job consultant does not merely serve a local interaction function of defending the candidate but also of countering a majority-defined idea about migrants that reproduces asymmetric relations of power between migrants and native Danes.

The perspective of interpretative repertoires and common sense illuminates some of the patterns in assumptions and understandings related to migrants, language, nationality and integration that are evoked and in effect during the internship interviews and tie in with the interactional actions and negotiations more specifically related to various goals of the speech situation. The planning and organization of the internship interview is, as illustrated, closely interwoven with a range of ideas and assumptions about the internship candidates' membership to the categories 'second-language speaker', 'second-language learner', 'Iranian' and not least their non-membership to the category 'Danish'. A more discursively oriented analysis in this way illuminates that what is, in some internship interviews, required of the candidate is not only a professional but also a linguistic and cultural development and integration.

Although Extract 8 shows a very normative and prescriptive dimension of how language can be directly topicalized during the internship interviews, it also shows how the orientation towards the language background of the candidates sometimes expresses an affiliative move on behalf of the employers. This is to argue that the employers orient to the language background and competence of the candidates in order to express interest in accommodating and potentially solving some of the language problems that candidates are assumed to have. This example and Extract 11 (Danish) can in this way be said to show interactional practices that express the good intentions and well-meaning suggestions of the employers. Extract 20 shows a similar case of how these direct topicalizations of language background can be seen as an affiliative move of the employers.

This extract is taken from the same interview as Extract 16 (Do you understand?), shown in the beginning of this chapter, but from the very beginning of the interview. Just before the start of the extract, IN has explained why she is interested in doing the internship and the extract begins with HO's reply to this.

Extract 20 But you speak Danish nicely

```
68    HO:     jamen det synes jeg da lyder fornuftigt
69            well I think that sounds reasonable
70
71    IN:     mm hhe.
72            mm hhe.
73
74    HO:     og du har boet her i Danmark øøh:
75            and you have lived here in Denmark eeh:
76
77    IN:     ni år
78            nine years
79
80    (0.2)
81    HO:     i ni år [ja]
82            nine years[yes]
83
84    IN:             [ja]
85                    [yes]
86
87
```

```
88   HO:    men du taler jo fint dansk
89          but you speak Danish nicely
90
91   IN:    åh .h ta[k he.]
92          oh .h th[anks he.]
93
94   HO:        [ja]
95             [yes]
96
97   CO:        [ja det rig]tigt
98             [yes that is ri]ght
99
100  IN:    ['ja']
101        ['yes']
102
103  HO:    [.hja↑] [det] synes jeg du gør↑
104        [.hja↑] [I] think you do↑
105
106  CO:        [.hja]
107           [.hyes]
108  (1.4)
109  IN:    okay
110        okay
111
112  HO:    Hva- hedder det hvordan har du det med ældre mennesker
113        well                how do you feel about elderly people
```

This example is similar to the previous one in the sense that the topicalization of language is made without any immediate logical link to the previous topic, namely IN's motivations for applying for the internship. Similar to the previous example it seems to be merely used as an interactional lubricant that both has a small-talk function and a getting-to-know-you function. However, in this example the orientation towards IN is markedly more positive as she is not categorized as a 'second-language learner' but as a 'second-language speaker' and is even complimented for her language skills. Nevertheless the topicalization of language background and language competence, as in the rest of the examples shown, introduces a strong evaluative element that, regardless of the good intentions most likely behind it, establishes the candidate as an 'other' and increases the asymmetry between the participants.

Good Migrant, Bad Migrant

In Chapter 4 I argued that interpretative repertoires were being drawn upon that linked notions of 'nationality' with the idea of 'culture' or a 'system of actions, beliefs and values'. Similarly, in this chapter I have shown how nationality is seen to imply a certain language membership and a certain language practice, and also how language membership and language proficiency is related to cultural membership. It is also clear how the orientations towards language are informed by naturalized versions of reality, or ideologies, regarding how the candidates should use, practice and learn Danish as a second language. These naturalizations give an impression of the interpretative frame of reference of native Danish speakers when faced with a multilingual reality. This gives an indication of the challenges or the evaluative premises that the candidates face within the context of the internship interviews – and perhaps in other places as well. When examining the claims and assumptions made by the employers, the employees and to some extent the job consultants as not only representatives of the labour market but also members of the Danish native-speaking majority, a pattern emerges that demands some attention here. Namely, the interpretations of the categorizations related to language are deeply influenced by broader structures of meaning and ideologies about ethnicity, integration and immigration.

Interpretative repertoires linked to categories such as 'second-language speaker' and 'second-language learner' can in this way be said to constitute the premise for the employers' expectations regarding the language proficiency and problems of the candidates. This was shown in the analysis of the first type of orientations towards language background with focus on embeddedness of the orientations. These repertoires however manifest themselves most clearly in the examples where language and linguistic membership are topicalized as issues in their own right. Here the arguments of job consultants, employers and candidates reflect the influence of contrary repertoires about non-native Danish speaking migrants living in Denmark that I will refer to as the contrary repertoires of 'good migrant' and 'bad migrant'. These repertoires are employed as resources of argumentation or 'common places' (Billig, 1996) in the local sense-making practices and they are informed and fuelled by other repertoires related to language learning that have already been described, e.g. 'learning through speaking'.

In Extract 8 (So you both have to learn Danish), for example, we see how the negotiations of EM, HO and CO about the practices and proficiency of the candidate involve the co-production of a positively valorized idea about migrants, the 'good migrant' repertoire, that describes migrants living in Denmark, learning Danish and speaking Danish at home. The formulation of and drawing from this repertoire involves a simultaneous construction of its opposite, namely the repertoire 'bad migrant' that describes migrants living in Denmark, not learning Danish and not speaking Danish at home. We also see the application of the good migrant 'repertoire' in Extract 19 (Can you read), though less explicitly formulated, in the valorized formulation of the assumption that the candidate reads, which is made relevant as a requirement of the job. The point that I wish to make in relation to this example is not that employers should not expect their workers to read: this is an understandable requirement in most jobs. What I wish to highlight, however, is that by asking the candidate whether she reads the employers show that while they *expect* her to read they do not *assume* that she reads. Their inferences about her as a member of the category 'migrant', in other words, involve a distinction between two different categories of migrants, 'literate migrants' and 'illiterate migrants', where the former is positively valorized and naturalized as the expected and desired norm in relation to the other. While the ideological positioning involved in this example is much more subtle than in Extract 8, the employers in this way implicitly make two opposite categories or subject positions available for the candidate, namely 'good migrant', who reads, and 'bad migrant', who does not.

Another example is Extract 20 (But you speak Danish nicely) where we see these repertoires being applied as the employer makes a positive evaluation of the candidate's language skills based on her nine years of residency in Denmark. Here the repertoire 'bad migrant' is used in the opposite way, however, as the employer formulates the positive evaluation of the candidate's language competence as if it was surprising considering her nine years of residency in Denmark. The formatting of her response *'but* you speak Danish nicely' (my emphasis) suggests exactly that one would expect otherwise. HO is in other words formulating her positive evaluation of IN against the backdrop of the interpretative repertoire of 'bad migrants' that do not speak Danish despite a long period of residency in Denmark. This constitutes the opposite position of the common sense from what was expressed by the job consultant in Extract 8 (So you both have to learn Danish) – namely 'no he has lived here for many years'. Together, these two alternative ways of drawing from this repertoire reveal the dilemmatic and controversial nature of common sense regarding migrants and language learning in Denmark.

The analysis of the interpretative repertoires in light of these examples shows how orientations towards the category second-language learner and second-language speaker are influenced by naturalized conceptions about nationality, migrants and foreignness. The conceptualized link between language and nationality or 'foreignness' is locally triggered by the context of the speech situation in the sense that the context provides for a certain interpretation of the internship candidates as migrants and second-language speakers of Danish. Furthermore, it is triggered by the specific language behaviour of the candidates, which, as I have argued, can be considered non-standard. Finally, one might argue that the internship candidates, and the other participants, carry with them certain transportable identities reflected in body traits, voice characteristics and religious symbols that make the category 'foreigner' potentially relevant for the participants and, following the described assumption of a direct link between nationality and language.

Some may find that the disassociation of the candidate with the category 'Danish' is in no way strange and that it is equally 'natural' that their association with categories related to nationalities other than 'Danish' is used as a basis for associating them with the category of second-language speakers. However, such membership categorizations are, as illustrated by the various examples in this chapter (Extracts 8, 19 and 20) and Chapter 4 (Extracts 12, 13, 16), intimately linked with ideology (Billig, 1996, 1991, 1999; Wetherell, 1998, 2005; Wetherell & Potter, 1988, 1992), and it is exactly the taken-for-granted nature of these categorizations that reveals their ideological nature. As described previously in Chapter 3, ideology is found in the taken-for-granted assumptions of a given time and place, whereby ideological challenging and critique involves the denaturalization and deconstruction of such assumptions.

It is in no way a given that being born in Iran or any other place implies non-membership of the category 'Danish' or membership of the category second-language speaker. It is quite possible for a person to be born in Iran, speak Danish as a first language and be 'Danish'. Similarly, it is not a given that a person having lived in Denmark for nine years does not speak Danish or that a person having lived in Denmark 'for many years' speaks Danish. Finally, it cannot be taken for granted that simply because a migrant has lived in Denmark for many years and speaks Danish as a second language well that he or she speaks Danish within the realm of the private home. These naturalized assumptions and expectations express ideological common-sense positions that are formulated and potentially challenged or confirmed as part of the participants' evaluative, decision-making and interviewing practices.

Summary

The analysis of how language is made relevant shows the varying ways in which language and membership categories related to language are made relevant and the different local contexts in which this occurs. I have identified two different types of orientations towards language, one which is related to the action of checking the understanding and proficiency of the internship candidate and one which is related to an actual topicalization of language membership and proficiency, involving the evaluation and prescription of particular language practice.

In the case of the first type of orientation, language is made relevant as the representatives of the workplace or the job consultant seek to establish or check whether the candidate understands and follows either the linguistic or topical development within the interaction. In the examples presented the embeddedness and the directness of the question leads to different degrees of interactional disruption and different responses from the candidates and job consultants. The analysis suggested that this form of checking or inquiring about the level of understanding of the candidate occurs at points in the interaction where the contributions of the candidate can be said to have been weak, minimal or non-standard in the immediately previous turns. However, I also argued how the contributions of the candidates did not unambiguously display problems of understanding. For this reason, I argued that the other participants' interpretations of the candidates and their contributions were influenced by their expectations and assumptions with respect to the context of the speech situation and their orientations towards the transportable identities or the visible and hearable 'otherness' of the candidates.

The second type of orientation towards language was related to topicalizations of language proficiency, language practice and language affiliation as an activity in itself. These topicalizations involved an assessment or negotiation of the internship candidate's language membership and language practice and was tied in with negotiations of language as a specific dimension of the internship. The examples shown, in other words, illuminated another dimension of the establishment of the category 'second-language learner' which was not related to specific issues of understanding. In the first example, the category 'second-language learner' was made relevant indirectly by introducing the category 'some who speak Danish'. In the other examples presented the category 'second-language learner' was addressed more directly, either through explicit inquiries about language abilities or the explicit topicalization of language learning.

In all cases, orientations towards language and membership categories related to language were established through a dissociation of the candidate from the category 'Danish' or 'Danish speaker' and they were in this way, I would argue, informed by an implicit assessment of the internship candidates' language performance. In the second type of orientation towards language, the actual performance of the candidates is, however, not addressed explicitly and this can be considered a paradox in light of the degree of explicitness and forwardness exhibited by the employers and employees in this second type of orientation. The cases examined and illustrated nevertheless show a pattern in the way that explicit orientations towards language performance and ability do not involve an explicit topicalization of the candidates' language-related category memberships and do not involve specific inquiries about language performance and ability. In all cases, however, the internship candidate's membership of the category second-language learner is either implicitly or explicitly assumed. What characterizes the cases where language is topicalized rather than being merely oriented to in relation to clarifying understanding is that the orientation towards language in these cases entails a normative suggestion or prescription of language behaviour. In the first of these cases, the indirectness of the orientation towards the category 'second-language speaker' allows the interaction to go on undisrupted but this at the same time makes it difficult for the internship candidate to respond to and contest the ascription and suggested behaviour. In other cases the internship candidate is invited to negotiate and respond to the categorization and the normative suggestions made but, as illustrated, this is a difficult and delicate task which ends up involving the job consultant and, ultimately, produces an extensive orientation towards and discussion of language.

As a whole, the various examples of orientations towards language and membership categories related to language illustrate how the orientation towards the specificity of the speech situation interrelates with orientations towards a broader cultural and linguistic context of meaning. This context makes certain actions and interpretations possible and available. As I have argued and illustrated, the actions and orientations of the participants draw on interpretative repertoires related to language, nationality and migration which is manifested in certain patterns of assumptions and meaning.

The internship interviews seemed to generally be informed by a conceptual linking of nationality and language on the one hand and residency and language learning on the other hand. These conceptual links or assumptions were more concretely manifested in the two repertoires 'good migrants' and 'bad migrants' that were used as a conceptual tool for the evaluation and categorization of the candidates and the prescription of particular language practices. 'Good migrants' and 'bad migrants' express opposite but equally meaningful commonplaces, that is, common-sense notions that were drawn from as part of argumentation. On the one hand they expressed the expectation that migrants interact with and speak with Danes and practice Danish in the private realm of the home. On the other hand they expressed the idea of migrants as isolated from Danes and not speaking Danish despite many years of residency.

Finally, I have aimed to show how common-sense notions and interpretative repertoires expressed in these examples tie in with broader ideologies of language, nationality and immigration, and also inform and influence the very 'local' negotiation and assessment of the internship candidate. In this sense, the negotiation of meaning of the category 'second-language speaker' taking place is illustrative of the ideological battles that characterize the controversial nature of common sense (Billig, 1996, 1991). What a microanalytical perspective on membership categorization processes contributes to the conceptualizations of Billig is how such common-sense dilemmas and ideological struggles are manifested in the concrete turn-by-turn negotiation of meaning around the categories second-language learner, second-language speaker, Danish speaker, Iranian, which takes place through concrete actions such as asking questions, making normative claims, suggesting behaviour and giving defences and accounts. What neither Billig nor MCA illuminate, however, is how the systematic drawing upon of particular common-sense repertoires in categorization processes produces valorized hierarchies between categories that produce an asymmetric relation between participants. In other words, how utterances and actions, including membership categorizations, not only reveal but also produce a particular discursive and social organization in which some categories and members are positioned unfavourably in relation to others.

6 Liquor, Pork and Scarfs – The Issue of Religion

Ideological Opinions and Arguments about Practicalities

In the previous two chapters I argued how membership categorization practices related to nationality and language reveal the implicit expectations of normative boundaries of behaviour that play into the evaluations of the internship candidates. In the case of nationality this was shown to occur as the participants discussed the competences and experiences of the candidates and in the case of language it occurred in relation to evaluations of language proficiency. The third and final pattern of membership categorization processes described in this book is found in the way religion, or more specifically Islam and particular practices associated with Muslims, is being oriented to as a potential source of conflict in relation to the future internship. These specific practices, namely wearing a scarf, dealing with pork and buying alcohol, are in various ways problematized in relation to certain tasks involved in different internships. Thus orientations towards religion present a barrier for the internship candidates since they call into question the candidates' abilities and compatibility in relation to the future internship.

This chapter will show how the argumentation about particular practices and categories reveal ideas, or common-sense (Billig, 1996) knowledge and repertoires, that bear close resemblance to the previously mentioned conceptualization of nationality – communities that determine a shared practice and thought or a specific 'way of life'. The process of associating the internship candidate with categories related to religion is thus related to dissociation from 'Danishness' and 'Danish ways'. I will show how the orientations towards the category 'Muslim' create an axis of differentiation, not between Islam as a religion and other religions such as Christianity, but rather between Islam as a culture and Danish culture. Islam is, in other words, constructed as a system of practices determining the behaviour of Muslims and this system of practices is considered conflictual and problematic in relation to common sense and common practices in Denmark.

There were only five cases of orientations towards religion in the internships recorded, which is markedly fewer than the number of orientations towards nationality and language. While it is impossible to say precisely why this is so, one can speculate that it is partly related to the amount of attention that the focus on Muslims has received in the media and public debates which has turned it into a delicate matter of controversy. Furthermore, some right wing party representatives in Denmark have contributed to radicalizing and polarizing debates about Muslims to an extent that makes it difficult for others to engage in nuanced discussions about Islam without unwillingly positioning oneself with the extreme right or the extreme left, the politically incorrect or the politically correct. The 'issue of Islam' is in other words dangerous territory in a Danish context when engaging in arguments with strangers, but at the same time it is something that most Danes are opinionated about. This provides a partial explanation for why religion is not raised as an issue more often in the internship interviews and, perhaps more importantly, why it is oriented to and treated the way it will be shown in this chapter. In all cases it is the employer or the employee addressing and evoking the category 'Muslim' and in all except one case it is related to a negotiation of the candidates' compatibility with a Danish workplace. In the following, I will show and compare two cases in which it is the employer and the employee respectively who make religion relevant as a potential work-related problem and compare these with the deviant case, where the workplace in question is an Islamic kindergarten. The similarities and differences between these three examples will prove to be particularly illustrative of the points I aim to make.

Negotiating religious communities and conflicts

The following two examples show how religion is topicalized as the employers address assumed conflicts between the practices involved in the internship and the practices commonly associated with Muslims. The negotiation of these potential work-related conflicts in this way involve the categorization of the candidate as a member of a particular religious community which is linked to a range of particular practices, preferences and 'ways'. The challenge of the candidate is hereby two-fold in the sense that they have to simultaneously defend their ability to solve the work-related 'problem' raised and account for the implications of their membership of the Muslim community they are associated with. The examples furthermore show how the problematization of the candidate's religious membership is treated as a sensitive issue that involves the dissociation of the candidate from 'Danish ways' and how this sensitivity contributes to extending the topicalization of religion beyond what is necessary to solve the practical work-related 'problem' raised. Finally, it will be shown how the job consultant plays a central role in assisting with solving the specific 'problem' at hand as well as accounting for the religiousness of the candidate.

The first example is from an interview with a candidate from Somalia, who is being interviewed for an internship at a residential home. The exchange occurs approximately 12 minutes into the interaction. Prior to the extract the participants were talking about the candidate's motivations for doing the internship; the employer has presented the residential home and described the tasks that the candidate will be involved in. Immediately before the beginning of the extract, the job consultant provided a long description of some of the things that would be valuable for the candidate to learn about and take part in while doing the internship, which the employer interrupted with a request for the candidate to present herself. The extract begins with the end of this presentation by the candidate. The candidate has been formatting her presentation as a list,[1] providing information such as her Somalian origin, her age, her parental status and her occupational goals. The first line of the extract continues this listing, which is now focused on personality traits.

Extract 21 The scarf

```
234   IN:   Jeg er meget tålmodig o:g jeg ⌊er⌋ tenlig
235         I am   very  patient   a:nd I  ⌊∠m⌋ friendly
236   HO:                          ⌊ja⌋
237                                 ⌊yes]
238   (0.2)
239   HO:   .hja  [.hhh
240         .hyeah[.hhh
241   IN:         [og jeg er god til at [samarbejde med]
242         [and I am good at at [cooperating with]
243   HO:                              [Nadia nu jeg nødt til at spørge dig]=
244                                     [Nadia now I have to  ask    you]=
245
246         =fordi jeg kan jo se du har beklædning på og når  det  [er]
247         =because I can see that you are wearing a clothing  and [when]
248   IN:                                                          [·ja·]
249                                                               [·yes·]
250   HO:   man går rundt og har meget med hygiejne at gøre
251         one is walking around dealing a lot with hygiene
252
253   IN:   ja
254         yes
255   (0.2)
256   HO:   .h øøhm (0.5) hvordan havde du tænkt dig at øøh være klædt der
257         .h eehm (0.5) how were you planning on eeh being dressed then
258
259         altså vi har jo hvide kitler vi har på .hh
260         I mean we have white uniforms that we wear .hh
261
262   HO:   [og] du skal  nok   have   noget   mindre  ned over dig
263         [and] you will probably need something smaller over you
264   IN:   [ja]
265         [yes]
266
267   IN:   ja jeg har l- en lille tørklæde.
268         yes I have s- a small scarf.
269
270   HO:   Det har du.=
271         You do.=
272
273   IN:   =ja=
```

```
274              =yes=
275
276    CO:       [så det]   [er godt (forberedt)]
277              [so that]  [is well (prepared) ]
278    (HO:)     [(       )]
279              [(       )]
280    IN:                  [jeg skal   af den  store ]=
281                         [I will get rid of the big]=
282    HO:       =ja
283              =yes
284
285    IN:       [ja]
286              [yes]
287    HO:       [nå] men det er fint nej [men] jeg ville spørge dig fo[rdi jeg
288              [well] that is fine  no [but] i wanted to ask  you be[cause I
289    IN:                                     [.hh]                    [jahh=
290                                            [.hh]                    [yeahh=
291
292    HO:       ved jo ] at øh   [i har jeres: øh:] forskellige måder hvordan det
293              do know] that eh [you have you:r eh.] various ways in which it
294    IN:       =hh  ]           [det godt spørgsmål ja ]
295              =hh  ]           [it's a good question yes]
296
297    HO:       er [at  det er  vigtigt ] for jer at [på]klædnin[gen]
298              is [that it is important] to you that[the]   clo[thing]
299    IN:       [ja hhh.]                            [ja]      [ja]
300              [yes hhh.]                           [yes]     [yes]
301
302    HO:       skal være [ik?]
303              should be [right?]
304    IN:                 [det rig]tigt
305                        [that's ri]ght
306
307    IN:       [ja jeg har et lille tørklæde]
308              [yes I  have a small scarf]
309    HO:       [.hh jeg ved også at jeg bliver nødt] til at sige dig omkring netop
310              [.hh I also know that I will       have] to say to you about
311
312              hygiejnen altså [der] kan vi simpelthen ikke have noget
313              hygiene I mean  [there] we can simply   not have anything
314
```

There are four things especially worth noting in this extract: first of all, by interrupting in line 243, HO diverts the topic of the presentation from the personality traits that IN has offered in lines 234 and 241 and focuses on the topic of IN's clothing. As Roberts and Campbell describe, such listing of traits without anchoring or exemplifying these in relation to particular practices can be found unconvincing (2006), which might account for this interruption. In any case HO shows with her interruption that IN is not supplying the kind of information HO is after. HO does not format her inquiry about IN's clothing as a direct question, but as a question embedded in a declarative statement of a need, namely 'now I have to ask you'. This constitutes a preface that works to pre-empt an account for the posing of the question and to mitigate HO's responsibility for the actual question, which follows in line 256, namely 'how were you planning on being dressed then'. As previously described in Chapter 4, prefaces can have a range of functions such as the projection of an extended turn of talk (Heritage, 2006; Schegloff, 1980, 1982; Kjærbeck, 1998), the initiation of a topic shift (Kjærbeck, 1998) and the mitigation of a less preferred or a disaffiliative action (Heritage, 1984). These functions can all be said to be in effect in the present example – the introduction of the issue of the scarf by HO represents not only a topic shift and a mitigation of a disaffiliative action, but also the beginning of an extended unit of talk, which is allowed to continue until HO marks the completion of the issue of the scarf much later in the interaction. I will return to this later in the analysis.

The second point that should be noted is that HO orients to the sensitivity of the issue of religion by refraining from explicitly mentioning religion. She does this by avoiding the use of the religious term for the scarf that IN is wearing, namely 'hijab', as well as the word 'scarf', which is the term normally used in public debates about the style of dress of Muslim women. Instead she uses the word *'beklædning'* ('garment'), which can be said to be a more neutral, though slightly awkward, term that could just as easily refer to IN's pants or overcoat rather than her headdress. In this way she avoids turning the issue into a religious one but, as will be shown, ends up doing this anyway.

Through the account for asking the question that HO provides in line 250, prior to the actual question, HO further avoids the explicit topicalization of religion by presenting the issue of IN's clothing as one related to a matter of hygiene. Hereby, she frames the question as being strictly work related. Thus, HO goes to a lot of trouble to make the question appear neutral, practical and work related, but at the same time she orients in various ways to the sensitivity of it: by formatting the question in a very indirect way, by emphasizing her obligation to pose it in the first place and by avoiding the use of terms such as hijab or scarf that both carry a heavy connotational meaning in a Danish context.

Third, it is important to note how the 'problem' of the scarf is immediately acknowledged and solved by IN in line 267. A lot of quite intricate inferential and interpretative processes can be said to be involved in this response, which demonstrates the substantial communicative competence of IN (Gumperz, 1982a). It also shows her ability to decode the above-mentioned mitigated and indirect question presented by HO as well as the implicit common-sense criticism of the scarf that this question entails. Not only does IN manage to infer that HO is referring to the scarf with the term *'beklædning'*, but also she manages to infer from the proposition made by HO in line 262 *'og du skal nok have noget mindre ned over dig'* ('and you will probably need to have something smaller over you') that the problem is the size of the scarf. IN thus tunes into what is explicitly and implicitly communicated to her within the context of the speech situation and, more specifically, the context of the utterance by HO. Furthermore she seems to orient to a broader ideological context within Denmark informed by public debates about Muslim scarfs.

The final thing to take note of is that the issue of the scarf is continually renewed by HO in lines 287 and 309 through a series of accounts for why the scarf is a problem and why she has brought it up. This is despite the fact that the problem is already potentially solved in line 270 where HO gives a satisfied third turn response. These accounts make it clear that HO's topicalization of religion is based on certain conceptualizations and expectations with respect to Muslims that represent a barrier to the candidate and have to be challenged or defended.

The first account that HO provides for having asked the question is particularly interesting, since it does not, contrary to the account provided in advance in line 250 and the account provided in line 309, focus on the issue of hygiene but on the commonsensical knowledge of Muslim practices of dressing. HO accounts for posing the question by referring to her knowledge of the importance of the scarf for Muslim women while the practical issue of what clothes are convenient in relation to work is backgrounded. Thereby the question is legitimized or explained as a courtesy to IN and an attempt to establish and meet her needs. Again the words Muslim, Islam, hijab or even scarf are not explicitly used, but through the continuing use of the personal plural pronoun 'I' ('You') and the previous context of IN's mentioning of the scarf, the category of Muslim women is constructed and attributed with specific category-bound activities, namely dressing in a specific way and having specific feelings invested in doing so, while IN is associated with this category by being addressed as a member of the category. We see here how the negotiation of a particular practical work-issue and the category 'Muslims' are interrelated.

The categorization of IN is, in other words, done by combining the semiotic, social and interpretative resources available within the immediate speech situation, such as the headdress that IN is wearing, the distribution of roles and rights of the participants and culturally established ideas about Muslim practices and dispositions. HO thus draws on an interpretative repertoire about Muslim women, which is used as an interactional resource for the interactional establishment and negotiation of the candidate and the future internship. IN confirms HO's categorization of her and the construction of the category 'You' by saying 'it's a good question yes' in line 294, by giving acknowledgement tokens in line 299 and finally by saying 'that's right' in line 304.

The second account that HO provides in lines 309 to 313 focuses on the issue of hygiene, like the first account provided in lines 243 to 250, which seeks to legitimize the question on the basis of practical concerns related to the internship rather than social considerations towards the practices and orientations of Muslims. As opposed to the account emphasizing the social considerateness of HO, the two accounts addressing the issue of hygiene are both formatted in a way that mitigates the responsibility of

HO by framing bringing up the issue as an obligation. Thus, HO seems to orient towards two opposing norms or beliefs – on the one hand, the idea that people should adjust and accommodate their individual practices to the framework provided by institutionalized public establishments and regulations such as those constituted by and constituting the context of a residential home, and on the other hand, the idea that people have the right to have and practice different religions. The hyper-accountability that HO displays in the extract may be viewed as a manifestation of and orientation towards the contrary and dilemmatic nature of common sense regarding the individual's rights and practices in relation to the demands of society.

Through the accounts that HO provides, she orients to different positions in a social, cultural and ideological dilemma and an ongoing public argumentation. IN shows understanding and alignment with the various positions that HO presents, but nevertheless continues to dismiss the issue as a problem by repeating in line 307 that she will be using a small scarf. In other words, IN manages to present a compromise to the dilemma that HO indirectly describes and orients to. Although HO accepts this solution right away, she makes the discussion of the scarf carry on for over a minute by continuing to present a total of five different accounts for addressing the scarf, three of which appear within this extract and two of which appear just after. This forces the candidate into a difficult and prolonged position of defence and rebuttal that not only diverts the focus of the interaction away from the presentation of self that was initially requested by HO, but also poses an increasing and perhaps unnecessary linguistic, social and interactional challenge for the candidate.

One can argue that HO is doing both parties a favour in addressing this delicate topic and allowing IN an opportunity to state her position in this regard. The immediate and relevant response by IN seems to support this argument in the sense that she is able to use the opportunity given to voice her opinion in a way that accommodates the interests of HO and presents herself as willing to make compromises for the sake of fitting in. However, the continual renewal of the relevance of the issue of the scarf, and thereby the relevance of the category 'Muslim', is problematic for both the internship candidate and the employer who both struggle to close the topic and move on to other discussions.

The job consultant contributes by attempting to alleviate the situation and diminish the problem with the scarf. First, she supports the initial response by IN in line 276 by saying 'so that is well prepared', which actually suggests the conclusion to be drawn by HO. Later, in the following part of the exchange, she prompts IN to show HO the small scarf that she plans on using and illustrates how IN plans to wear it.

Extract 21 The Scarf *(continued)*

```
336   CO:   =Nadia du har jo dit lille tørklæde med,=
337         =Nadia you did bring your small scarf,=
338
339   IN:   =ja
340         =yes
341
342   CO:   [s- ]Nadia har sagt hun vil sætte den under uniformen så også
343         [s- ]Nadia has said she will put it under her uniform so also
344   HO:   [ja]
345         [yes]
346
347   CO:   [(flytte) den ind her]
348         [(move) it in here]
349   HO:   [jamen lige [præcis] ]
350         [yes well   [exactly]]
351   IN:              [ja]
352                    [yes]
353   CO:   [og så]
354         [and then]
355   HO:   [ ja ]
356         [ yes ]
357
358   CO:   j[a og så den vej ind      ]
359       y[es and then that way in   ]
360   IN:   [jeg er klar over det her.]
361       [I   am aware of it heh.]
362
363   CO:   [bagved]
364         [behind]
365   HO:   [ja]
366         [yes]
```

Thus, the job consultant takes part in the interactional work of IN to solve the issue. However, neither her initial pre-closing move, 'so it is well prepared', nor her demonstration of how the scarf will be worn contributes to the closing or abandoning of the topic. Rather it prolongs the issue further since HO is apparently not ready to abandon or close the topic and instead provides three more accounts following this sequence.

The two extracts shown so far from this exchange illustrate the influence of the participation framework and the distribution of rights to talk and control the interaction. Although at various moments throughout this exchange, HO gives satisfied third turn responses to the rebuttals and solutions offered by IN and CO, HO is the only one being granted and claiming the right to move on to a new topic. Hence, IN and CO continually acknowledge, respond to and meet the problems and accounts raised by HO, but leave it up to HO to decide when the problem is properly solved and when she is ready to move on to something else. In the following and final part of the exchange, we also see this interrelation of the distribution of roles and rights and the dynamics of the specific ongoing activity of negotiating the problem with the scarf.

Extract 21 The Scarf *(continued)*

```
389   HO:    [et ældre menneske]så skal du šku ku mærke og de [skal] ku mærke dig
390          [an older person] then you must feel them and they [must] feel you
391   ( )    [(               )]
392   IN:                                                              [ja]
393                                                                    [yes]
394   HO:    [også ik]
395          [also right]
396   IN:    [ja det rig]tigt ja
397          [yes that's ] right yes
398
399   IN:    jeg klar om det.
400          I am aware of that.
401
402   HO:    ['ja']
403          ['yes']
404   CO:    [og] især også sådan altså at man er på arbejde når man har [sådan
405          [and] especially also that one is at work when one is wearing [kind
406   HO:                                                                 [ja]
407                                                                      [yes]
408          lidt sådan lidt and-[andre tøj på]=
409          of a bit sort of dif[ferent clothes]-
410   IN:                        [ja det rigtigt]=
411                              [yes that's right]=
412   HO:    =ja
413          =yes
414
415   IN:    Man kan [ik'] arbejde og så [man] har e[t stort ]  tør[klæde]
416          One can [not] work and then [one] is we[ring a big] sca[rf]
417   (HO/CO:)        [('ja')]              [('ja')]   [('nej''.hja')] [(.hja)]
418                   [(yes)]               [(yes)]    [(no  .hyea)] [(.hyea)]
419   (0.3)
420   (HO/CO:)mm=
421          mm=
422   HO:    =.h[hh vi har vi har jo udover øøh]
423          =.h[hh we have we do have besides eeh]
424   IN:       [Man skal have en lille]
425          [one should have a small]
```

Here, in line 389, we see the final account provided by HO during the negotiation of the scarf, which is focused on the need of the elders to feel the candidate and vice versa, which again is acknowledged and confirmed by IN. Once again, HO gives a satisfied third turn response in line 402, but does not follow this up with a clear topic-closer or the initiation of a new topic, so CO and IN, one after the other, each make another attempt to ease and accommodate the concerns of HO by providing two additional accounts for why a smaller scarf would be a good idea.

The first account by CO suggests that a change of clothes in general has a symbolic function of indicating a change from a private to a professional context. This is confirmed by both IN, in overlap, and HO in the next turn. The account offered next by IN has a slightly different emphasis on the impracticality of working in a big scarf and this is supported with acknowledgement tokens from HO. The greatness in number and the placement of these acknowledgement tokens suggest that HO is at this point bringing the topic to a close, which she then finally does explicitly in line 422 by introducing a new topic.

IN, however, does not pick up on the fact that HO is finally moving on to something new, but rather anticipates that HO's utterance is still on the matter of the scarf, which is clear from the fact that she, in overlap, makes yet another conclusive response to the subject namely *'man skal have en lille'*, 'one needs a small'. Considering that this utterance overlaps almost entirely with the topic initiation by HO, IN's utterance seems more like a delayed elaboration than a display of misunderstanding of HO's turn. In any case, the central point here is that the topic is finally abandoned and that the participants orient to HO as having the right to initiate and close the topic.

This first example of religious categorization of the candidate shows how religion is not topicalized and negotiated directly. Rather it is oriented to indirectly through the negotiations of the extent to which a specific form of practice, in this case a specific way of dressing, constitutes a potential problem for the tasks involved in the future internship. The implicitness in the topicalization of religion and the repertoires invoked as part of this topicalization illuminate how the immediate discussion and negotiation of a specific religious practice reflects a controversial and delicate dilemma between two contrary common-sense positions. Namely, on the one hand the right of individuals to practice their religion and on the other the right and necessity of institutions to regulate and restrict religious practices and behaviours to the extent that these collide with the institutional rules and practices.

The Interactional Manifestation of the Controversial Nature of Religion

The previous example clearly shows how the orientation towards the controversial and dilemmatic nature of the issue of religion has clear interactional consequences in the sense that the topicalization of the scarf is prolonged way beyond the solving of the issue raised by the employer. The elaborate work of the employer put into handling the issue of the scarf in the 'right' way can be seen as an attempt to mitigate the employer's imposition and power in addressing this issue. However, this affiliative or accommodating strategy leads to an overemphasis on the issue of the scarf which is counterproductive to the solving of the issue and presents an extra challenge for the candidate. The example in this way shows how the candidate's performance as a suitable internship candidate is not merely dependent on her willingness to accommodate and change her way of dressing and her ability to communicate this willingness. It also, and perhaps even more so, depends on the employer's conceptualizations of the issue of religion and her way of handling it interactionally. We see here, in other words, a good example of how the employer, as previously described in Chapter 2, has a triple gatekeeping function. First of all, her power and ability to decide whether or not the candidate will be offered the internship. Second, her power and right to decide which topics are to be addressed during the interview and when they have been sufficiently covered. Third, to reproduce a particular meaning of the category 'Muslims' as people who are determined and limited by their religious practices and who stand in an oppositional relationship to Danes. These three gatekeeping functions are related and mutually reinforce one another.

In the next example, Extract 22, we see a similar situation in which a question is being asked about a potential conflict between a specific religious practice and a work-related task. Again, this conflict is immediately solved by the candidate and yet the issue is elaborated and expanded into an extended discussion of religion that forces the candidate and the job consultant into a position of defence and rebuttal.

The example is taken from an interview with a candidate from Afghanistan for an internship at a home help company. The extract occurs about five minutes into the interview, where the participants have talked about the experience that the candidate has with similar kinds of work and after the employer and the employee have talked about some of the things that the candidate needs to know and do in the job. Immediately prior to the exchange the employee has asked whether the candidate is able to read from a shopping list and established that this will not be a problem.

Extract 22 Liquor and pork

```
144   EM:    og du har heller ikke noget imod at ehm: du
145          har ikke noget religiøse sådn- begrænsninger i forhold til at .h
146          købe nogen varer vel?
147
148          And you don't mind either ehm: you don't have any
149          religious kind of- limitations in relation to buying some groceries
150          right?
151   (0.2)
152   IN:    mm nej
153          mm no
154
155   EM:    nej det godt
156          no that's good
157   (0.3)
158   EM:    Fordi vi havde nogen piger som sagt nej til at købe øhm: (0.4) .h
159          spiritus 'for eksempel' >de ville ik de må- de- de måtte< ikke
160          røre ved dem [(ja)]
161
162          Because we had some girls who said no to buying ehm: (0.4) .h
163          liquor for example >they would not they co- they- they could< not
164          touch them [(yes)]
165
166   CO:                [helle]r ikke flas[ker]
167                      [not ] bottles eit[ther]
168   IN:                                  [heh.]
169   (0.6)
170   HO:    nej=
171          no=
172   EM:    ='n[ej']
173          ='n[no']
174   HO:       [n]ej
175       [n]o]
```

```
176  HO:   vi har ogs- haft pro[blemer med] svinekød=
177        we have als- had pro[blems with] pork=
178  EM:              [og de:]
179                   [and they:]
180  EM:   =ja: og [svine]kød de ville heller ikke købe nogen pøl[ser]
181        =yes: and[por]k they would not buy any sausages    ei[ther]
182  CO:           [okay]
183                [okay]
184  HO:                                                         [nej]
185                                                              [no]
186  EM:   eller svinekød eller sådan noget det det kan vi ikke bruge til
187        noget
188
189        or pork or that kind of thing that that is of no use to us
190  (0.5)
191  EM:   Med alt vores respekt for forskellige: øh: religi[øse:]
192        with all our respect for different: eh:    relig[ious:]
193  HO:                                                    [religioner]
194                                                         [religions]
195  EM:   sådan øh: religioner o- så videre .h det kan vi ikke bruge til
196        noget fordi [vi] kan ikke (0.4) byde vores kunder på at nå nu nu
197
198        like eh: religions an- so on .h that is of no use to us
199        because [we] can not (0.4) tell our clients that oh now now
200  IN:           [.hja]
201                [.hja]
202  EM:   kommer den hjemmehjælper så skal [du] spise oksekød det det kan vi
203        this homehelper is coming so [you] must eat beef that that we can
204  IN:                                   [n-]
205
206  EM:   desværre ikke
207        unfortunately not do
```

As opposed to the previous extract, the question from the employer is in this extract posed quite directly and it specifically projects a negative response as a preferred answer, which is received from IN in line 152. There is some indication of hesitation and word-search displayed by the dispreferred format of the 'ehm:' in line 144 and the '*sådn-*' ('kind of') in line 145, but contrary to the previous example, religion is explicitly topicalized and attributed with specific dispositions and limitations regarding certain groceries.

The formatting in the first part of this example is however quite similar to the one in the previous example in the sense that we have a slightly hesitant question that topicalizes religion, associates the candidate with this religion and presents a potential disagreement between the activities attributed to this religion and the activities involved in the internship. This question is then responded to by the candidate in a way which dismisses and solves the suggested conflict which leads to a satisfied third turn response from the person having asked the question in the first place.

The final similarity is that this does not close the topic and lead the employer or the employee to move on to a different topic but rather it is followed up by the employer producing an account for the question and for the assessment in line 155, which is an elaboration of the proposed conflict. Here EM focuses the account on previous experiences with girls that would not buy liquor. There is an interesting self-repair here, where EM repairs '*ville ikke*' ('would not') into '*måtte ikke*' ('could not'), which highlights that the girls' saying no to buying liquor was not a matter of choice but rather of dictation or prescription. Similarly to Extract 8 in Chapter 5, this self-repair can be understood in relation to a broader cultural context of ideologies and common-sense understandings regarding Muslim women. From this perspective, emphasizing the girls' Muslim practice as dictated rather than chosen can be seen as a reproduction of a common-sense position often voiced in the debate on Muslim women and integration – namely that Muslim women are oppressed by their religious background, and often more specifically, their fanatic husbands. Furthermore, the denial of buying alcohol is changed into a lack of allowance to even touch alcohol ('røre') in line 160 which constitutes an upgrade and what Pomerantz calls an extreme case formulation (1986), that serves to legitimize the claim that EM makes, which in this case makes her question seem commonsensical.

After a confirmation from both EM and HO in lines 170, 172 and 174 to the question posed by CO in line 166 'not bottles either', HO takes the opportunity to further expand the legitimizing description of previous experience just offered by EM in line 176. She does so by describing in more general terms how 'they have also had problems with pork', which attributes another form of behaviour to the previously established category of Muslim girls, namely not eating or dealing with pork. EM overlaps this utterance with what seems to be a continuation of her previous more specific description of the situation with the girls, but she gives up and restarts this description in line 180 after HO has finished, now formatting it as a response to HO's contribution and incorporating the issue of pork into her description of how the girls would not buy sausages. EM finishes this description by making an evaluation in lines 186 and 195 of this type of behaviour, namely 'det kan vi ikke bruge til noget' ('that is of no use to us'), which finally explicitly establishes the argumentative thrust of the original question posed, namely that if IN were to have problems with buying either pork or liquor then she would not be useful for them as an intern. In line 191, EM makes a disclaimer for this statement and emphasizes that it is not a matter of having a lack of respect for religion as such but merely a practical question of offering the clients a certain service.

EM and HO in other words cooperate here in describing a problem with the behaviour of certain Muslim members of staff which works to legitimize and account for inquiring about the candidate's preferences and position regarding shopping for the clients. Furthermore it works to normatively prescribe a specific behaviour, which the candidate is forced to position herself in relation to. In the continuation of Extract 22 we will see

how IN responds to the categorization of Muslims and Muslim behaviour
that HO and EM have made and associated IN with.

Extract 22 Liquor and pork (continued)

```
208    (0.2)                          -
209    IN:       Fordi: jeg har også arbejdet i Rigshospitalet
210              because: I have also worked in Rigshospitalet
211    (0.2)
212    EM:       mja
213              mja
214    (.)
215    IN:       I opvask og ogs- i køkkenhjælp
216              In dishwashing and also- in kitchen help
217
218    EM:       ja
219              yes
220
221    IN:       men jeg har også hakket svinekød
222              but I have also chopped pork
223
224    EM:       okay
225              okay
226
227    IN:       men jeg har ikke [spist]
228              but I have not [eaten]
229
230    EM:                       [du har] ikke noget problem
231                              [you have] no problem
232    IN:       nej
233              no
234
235    EM:       nej nej
236              no no
237
238    IN:       For jeg har også muslim↑ men jeg ↑ikke spiser
239              Because I have also Muslim↑ but I ↑not eat
240    (0.2)
241    EM:       ja=
242              yes=
243
244    IN:       =bare jeg skærer svinekød=
245              =just I cut pork=
246
247    EM:       =ja
248              =yes
249
250    IN:       også jeg hakker den
251              also I chop it
252
253    EM:       ja
254              yes
255    (0.5)
256    IN:       også jeg (0.4) lægger på plads
257              also I (0.4) put it in place
258
259    EM:       ja (.) ja selvfølgelig ja
260              yes (.) yes of course yes
261
262    IN:       alt muligt
263              all kinds of things
264    (0.2)
265    EM:       selvfølgelig ja
266              of course yes
267    (0.4)
268    EM:       .hja det godt
269              .yhes that's good
```

Here we see how IN formats her defence as a continuation or elaboration of her previous defence. By beginning her utterance with the word *'fordi'* ('because') followed by a description of her previous work at Rigshospitalet, she offers her handling of pork in the past as proof that her religion is not in the way of the job. In lines 227 and 238–244, she dissociates herself from the category established by EM and HO of Muslim women, who do not eat, handle or buy pork. EM responds positively to IN's description of her previous experience with handling pork and does not take the floor or close the topic until IN indicates that her description is over by saying *'alt muligt'* ('all kinds of things') in line 262. At this point EM gives a final indication that she has understood IN's description, namely *'selvfølgelig ja'* ('yes of course'), which constructs IN's utterance as commonsensical and accepts it as a valid and satisfactory reply to the concern raised. Finally, in line 268, after another pause, which gives IN the opportunity for supplementary comments, EM indicates a closing of the topic by saying *'.hja det godt'* ('.hyes that's good').

Juggling with Crystal - The Counterproductive Actions of the Job Consultant

In the previous example we saw how the job consultant contributed to the immediate solving of the issue by supporting the candidate's response in saying 'so that is well prepared'. Here the job consultant enters the exchange at a slightly different position, namely in line 166 after the account provided by the employer, and rather than contributing to a quick solving of the issue she contributes to prolonging the orientation towards religion started in line 158 by probing that account and thereby inviting an elaboration from the employee. The orientation towards and discussion of religion begins with a narrative about the other Muslim girls that used to work at the company and did not want to buy alcohol and as we shall see in the following part of the analysis it does not end till much later when HO gives a where HO gives a satisfied conclusive remark 'yes well that is then sort of all right' and moves on to another topic.

Although the actions of the job consultant here contribute to opening up the topic of religion rather than closing it, the contribution of the job consultant does implicitly support the defensive or dismissive thrust of the response from the candidate, since her utterance *'heller ikke flasker'* ('not bottles either') works to make the choice and position of the girls extraordinary. In other words, she constructs this group of Muslim girls as distinct and different from the candidate and associates the former with a more extreme or radical behaviour, which makes the candidate's position seem more aligned with the common sense that EM has established by her initial question. As mentioned previously, the job consultant contributes in a different way in the beginning of the sequence than the job consultant in the previous example and, as shown, this can be said to contribute to an elaboration rather than a closing of the topic. While EM is indicating a closing of the topic in line 155, CO takes the floor, rather than allowing for either EM or HO to change the topic, and makes a comment that again opens up or prolongs the topic of pork.

Extract 22 Liquor and Pork *(continued)*

```
268   CO:    men [så] længe man ikke spiser den=
269          but [as] long as one does not eat it=
270   EM:        [så]
271            [so]
272   IN:    =nej=
273          =no=
274
275   CO:    =så så bliver man ikke syg af den=
276          =then then one does not get sick from it=
277
278   EM:    =nej=
279          =no=
280
281   CO:    =fordi der er også mange danskere der ikke sp- spiser svinekød
282          =because there are also many Danes that don't eat- eat pork
283
284   EM:    nej rigtigt
285          no right
286
287   CO:    og det er netop på grund af hygiejne heh. [heh. heh.]
288          and that is exactly because of hygiene heh.[heh. heh.]
289   HO:                                              [heh. heh.]
290                                                   [heh. heh.]
```

CO's comment has the function of in some ways summarizing the gist of what they have been negotiating, namely the difference between not eating pork and not handling pork. Furthermore, it has the function of downgrading the seriousness of the matter by introducing yet another reason for not eating pork, namely the diseases and bad hygiene that pork is often associated with. This is more explicitly turned into a joking format in lines 281 to 287 where CO delivers the punchline and signals this with laughter. The humorous remark has two consequences. On the one hand CO's comment in this way contributes to the closing of the topic by summarizing the issue of not eating pork and turns it into a joking matter, which draws attention away from the seriousness with which the subject was previously dealt and furthermore normalizes IN's behaviour by making 'eating pork' seem commonsensical. In this sense, it has a supportive function in relation to the candidate. On the other hand, the comment potentially opens up and prolongs the topic by sequentially inviting a response from EM and HO, which is counterproductive to refocusing the interaction on the competences and qualities of the candidate, which was the ongoing activity before the issue of pork and liquor was initiated.

In this specific case the job consultant's attempt to downgrade the topicalization of religion is partially successful in the sense that she manages to generate some laughter from HO and the exchange later moves into a more general discussion of other reasons why some people choose not to eat pork, such as animal welfare and so on. Nevertheless the action of the job consultant is potentially problematic for the candidate since it, as mentioned, postpones a final closing of the topic and diverts attention away from the subject of the internship and the competences of the candidate. The fact that the topic is not closed and replaced with another enables the following return to the original topic of religious practices.

Extract 22 Liquor and Pork *(continued)*

```
293   .
294   .
295   .
296   EM:   Så så så (.) køber de ikke (.) svinekød mere
297         so so so (.) they don't buy (.) pork anymore
298
299   HO:   og for eksempel vil de ikke købe for eksempel to øl eller
300         sådan noget lignende de kan ikke tage to øl ik altså
301
302         and for example they will not buy for example two beers or
303         something like that they can not ake two beers right
304
305   CO:   ne:j
306         no:
307
308   HO:   fordi man ikke drikker det behø- derfor kan man jo godt købe
309         to øl med to øl med til en kunde ik
310
311         because one does not drink it need- one can still buy
312         two beers for two beers for a client right
313
314   CO:   [det jo] det
315         [that's] right
316
317   IN:   [.hja]
318         [.hyes]
319
320   HO:   ja
321         yes
322
```

While the general discussion about eating pork for other reasons than religion has been omitted from this extract, we see how EM's summarizing comment in line 296, which is about people who have stopped buying pork for animal welfare reasons, is used as a stepping stone for HO to return to the issue of not wanting to buy alcohol, which initiated the topicalization of religion. The topical development of the discussion of religious practices in relation to certain groceries is in this way not only influenced by the sequential context and the participation framework but by a lexical development in the formulation of the issue. HO in other words uses the resource of '*køber de ikke svinekød*' to reactivate the category of Muslims and the category-bound behaviour of not wanting to buy alcohol, although the category made relevant by EM just previous to this extract is in fact not 'Muslims' but 'animal welfare conscious consumers'.

During this long exchange circling around the issue of practices in relation to liquor and pork, the category 'Muslim' is in this way continually relevant and 'hanging in the air' (Day, 1998), although not explicitly at all times, and HO's reintroduction of the issue of buying alcohol shows this. The summarizing comment previously made in line 268 by the job consultant thus turns out to have counterproductive consequences since the candidate is now again faced with a highly normatively laden statement about Muslim practices, which she has to position herself in relation to and counter.

Facilitated Opposition to 'Religion at Work'

What is clear from Extract 22, and made mostly explicit in the following and final extract, is how the orientation towards religion as a relevant category in the internship interview involves a differentiation between Danish and non-Danish 'ways' of acting and being. Religion is made relevant in relation to a normative prescription of certain behaviours, positions and preferences, which are outlined and defined as different from and in conflict with those characterized and established as common sense within a Danish context. While this differentiation has in the extracts shown so far been subtle and implicit, it is now formulated explicitly as part of a defence produced by the job consultant.

Extract 22 Liquor and Pork *(continued)*

```
323   CO:   Men jeg tror Zabia de:t sådan som er mit indtryk hun e:r (.) .h
324         ligeså Muslim som de fleste danskere er kristne
325
326         but I think Zabia tha:t as far as I understand she i:s (.) .h
327         as much Muslim as most Danes are Christian
328   (0.2)
329   EM:   ja:
330         ye:s
331   (0.5)
332   EM:   så du:
333         so you:
334
335   CO:   såh. håh. håh. [håh heh. håh. håh. håh. [.heh]
336         soh. heh. heh. [heh heh. heh. heh. heh. [.heh]
337   EM:                  [ja]                      [ja ja]
338                        [yes]                     [yes yes]
339   CO:   man er det men øh (0.3) men man er ikke følsom med det
340         one is it but eh (0.3) but one is not sensitive about it
341   (0.2)
342   EM:   ˚ne:j˚
343         ˚no:˚
344   (1.0)
345   CO:   ja men det jo sådan set det udmærket
346         yes but that is then sort of all right
```

In the previous example, Extract 21 (The Scarf), lines 336 and 342, I showed how the job consultant had prepared for the topicalization of religion and how she facilitated a display of accommodation to the demands of the workplace and the employer. In this final part of Extract 22 we see a similar situation, where the job consultant co-constructs a defence by speaking on the candidate's behalf in a way which dismisses the problem and represents the candidate as accommodating and flexible in her religious practice. CO's claim about IN's religiousness in line 323 thus works to diminish the relevance of the category of Muslims or at least downplays the assumed implications for her practices as an intern on account of it being similar to Danish 'ways' of being Christian. Although EM immediately displays understanding and confirmation of this comparison in line 329, CO elaborates and explains what is meant by it in 339, namely that IN belongs to a specific religious group but that she is not 'sensitive' about the implications of this membership with respect to the practices it entails. After another quiet display of understanding and acknowledgement from EM and a one second pause indicating that none of the other participants has anything to add, CO decides that the issue is now finally settled and closes the topic by making the summarizing and evaluating statement in line 345 and in the following turn moving on to the topic of the internship agreement.

From the job consultant's utterance in line 281, *'fordi der er også mange danskere der ikke sp- spiser svinekød'* ('because there are also many Danes that don't eat- eat pork') it is clear that the category 'Danes' is made relevant as a commonsensical opposite to the previously established category of 'Muslims'. According to the description of MCDs presented by Sacks this shows that the participants orient to a social organization in which the category 'Muslim' not only makes sense as part of the MCD 'religious orientations' but is also given sense in relation to the MCD nationalities. Or in other words, the fact that the category 'Danes' is made relevant and evoked in opposition to the category 'Muslims' reveals that the people considered as members of the latter are not considered as members of the former. The example thereby shows that a logic of differentiation and deferral is at work, which makes being Muslim equal to being non-Danish and makes being Danish equal to being non-Muslim. This logic has the implication that, as the candidate is associated with the category 'Muslim', she is simultaneously dissociated from the category 'Danes'. Her suitability for the future internship seems to be questioned on the grounds of not only her membership of the category 'Muslim' but also her non-membership of the category 'Danes'.

What is apparent when considering the first two examples is a pattern in the way different religious practices are considered problematic and conflictual in relation to the practices and routines of a particular workplace. What the analysis shows is that what is being negotiated is not only whether the internship candidates in question will adapt to or perform a specific work-related practice but also a *general* and *potential* conflict between a religious practice and a workplace culture and requirements.

As illustrated in Extracts 21 (The scarf) and 22 (Liquor and pork), religion is topicalized by the employer or the employee inquiring about the position and behaviour of the internship candidate with regard to a specific religious practice, which is then presented as problematic in relation to a specific practice in the workplace. The actual topicalization is in this way informed by the assumption that a given religious practice is conflictual with a given work practice, which is an assumption that is informed by the employers' previous experience and general understanding. What both examples reveal, however, is that the potential conflict foreseen by the employer is not solved or dismissed by the internship candidate's accommodation or agreement with the particular problem raised but is rather re-established and reproduced by the employer or the employee presenting additional assumptions and concerns. I would argue that this reveals how the employer does not merely use previous experience of a religion-related conflict to address and solve a specific issue but rather draws on and formulates an entire interpretative repertoire of religious practices as conflictual with certain work practices. This repertoire, which I will call 'religion at work', is characterized by the conflation and generalization of a range of practices as incompatible with religion.

In the first example, Extract 21 (The scarf), the participants co-construct the problem with the scarf as related to 'hygiene', 'physical interaction' and 'being professional', and these very different dimensions of work-related practices are conflated and oriented to as different sides of the same coin. In Extract 22 (Liquor and pork), the participants refer to problems in relation to 'buying liquor', 'pork' in general, 'buying sausages', 'pork and that kind of thing', 'chopping pork', 'eating pork', 'cutting pork' and 'buying two beers' and these are all constructed as synonymous examples of the same thing, namely a conflict between religious practices and work-related practices. What is clear from both extracts is that the employers elaborate work to communicate, and account for, common sense ideas about Islam as a problem in the workplace overshadows the attempts of the candidates and the consultants to accommodate to the specific issues raised. The topicalization of religion in itself, in this sense, becomes more of a problem than the religious practice, which is addressed.

The Opposite Case – Accommodating to Muslim Workplace Rules

The third example of orientations towards religion is similar to the previous two in the sense that what is being negotiated is the compatibility of the candidate with certain 'ways' and practices of a workplace. There are various differences, however, in how this negotiation plays out and how the candidate is positioned in relation to the other participants as part of this negotiation. These differences can to a large extent be explained by the fact that in this example the workplace in question is a Muslim kindergarten and the candidate is a woman from Bosnia who is not visibly 'marked' and identifiable as Muslim in the sense that she does not wear a scarf. Whereas the previous two examples showed a problematization of the Muslim candidates' compatibility with a non-Muslim working context, this example shows the presentation of a Muslim work context and the negotiation of how the candidate's behaviour, practices and preferences should relate to this. While the issue of compatibility between the candidate and the workplace is again a central part of the negotiation, it will be clear that there are distinct differences to the other two examples with respect to the distribution of roles and rights between the participants and not least the power relations and asymmetry of the interaction.

The following example involves two partially separated topicalizations of religion, found in two different extracts. The first is initiated by the employer in relation to a presentation of the workplace and the particular religiously defined rules and regulations of an Islamic kindergarten. The second is initiated by the candidate as a re-topicalization of religion which consists of a presentation of the candidate's relationship with Islam and Muslim codes of conduct.

The first extract is taken from the beginning of the interaction and begins at a point where HO starts her presentation of the workplace. As we will see, religion is topicalized and emphasized right from the beginning as part of this presentation.

Extract 23 **A religious institution**

```
13      HO:      vores børn er kun børn af muslimske familier
14               Our children are only children of muslim families
15      (0.3)
16      HO:      .hh .tsk hvoraf størstedelen er meget religiøse familier
17               .hh .tsk whereof the majority are very religious families
18      (0.2)
19      HO:      .hh .tsk det her det en puljeinstitution og er skabt a:f forældre,
20               .hh .tsk this is a private institution and is created by: parents,
21      (1.2)
22      HO:      .tsk hvor vi selvfølgelig nu er en almindelig børnehave
23               .tsk where we of course now are an ordinary kindergarten
24      (0.3)
25      HO:      men (.) vi får driftstilskud fra Københavns Kommune .hh .tsk
26               men ellers er det meget forældrene
27
28               but (.) we get financial support from Copenhagen Municipality .hh .tsk
29               but otherwise it is a lot the parents
30
31      (IN/CO:)hmm
32
33      (0.2)
34      HO:      som lægger retningslinjerne for hvordan vi arbejder her i
```

```
35            institutionen
36            that set the guidelines for how we work here in
37            the institution
38
39    CO:     [okay]
40            [okay]
41
42    IN:     [okay] væ::re klar at følge lovene .heh.
43            [okay] be:: ready to follow the laws
44    (0.5)
45    HO:     Det jo så det vi arbejder selvfølgelig også efter pædagogisk
46            perspektivplan læreplaner og serviceloven så så meget forskellighed
47            er der heller ikke
48
49            It is so that we work of course also after pedagogic
50            perspective plan learning plans and servicelaw so so much difference
51            there is not either
52    (0.3)
53    HO:     men der er noget forskellighed
54            but there are some differences
55
56    CO:     mm
57            mm
58    (0.7)
59    HO:     altså vi prøver at gribe de muslimske familier på den måde at vi for
60            eksempel vegetarer
61
62            that is we try to embrace the muslim families in the way that we for
63            example are vegetarian
64    (0.4)
65    IN:     de-
66            they-
67
68    HO:     Her i børnehaven bliver børnene bespist (0.2) det vil sige de får
69            [mad] her i børnehaven .hh
70
71            Here in the kindergarten children are fed (0.2) that means they are
72            [food] here in the kindergarten .hh
73
74    IN:     [ja]
75            [yes]
76
77    HO:     det gør personalet også
78            the staff also
79
80    IN:     også
81            also
82
83    HO:     man kan ikke tage sin egen mad med
84            one cannot bring ones own food
85
86    IN:     okay
87            okay
88
89    HO:     udefra ind i Mosaik vi spiser allesammen det samme
90            from outside into Mosaik we all eat the same
91
92    IN:     det sammen
93            the same
94
95    HO:     .h og det er m·nus kød
96            .h and that is minus meet
97
98    (0.4)
99
100   HO:     .hh her er ingen rygning ingen alkohol
101           .hh here is no smoking no alcohol
102   (0.2)
103
104   HO:     .hh her er ingen mænd på toiletterne
105           .hh here are no men in bathrooms
106   (0.2)
107   HO:     .h og her er en dresscode som betyder at ens tøj når her ned til
108           .h and here is a dresscode that means that your clothes reach down to here
109
110           .hhh og ned over knæene (.) og ingen bare maver så det skal du
111           .hhh and down over the knees (.) and no bare stomachs so that you have to
112
113           huske (.) Naya du skal ikke komme her [med bar mave]
114           remember (.)  Naya you can not come here [with bare stomach]
115
116   CO:                                           [ha ha ha ha ha]
117                                                 [ha ha ha ha ha]
118
119   IN:     og jeg køb[te] meget speci[elt] [tøj(klæ]de)
120           and I boug[ght· very spec[ial] [scar(f)]
121
122   HO:               [.tsk]          [JA] [beklager]
123               [.tsk]          [YES] [sorry]
124
125   HO:     beklager
126           sorry
127   (0.2)
128   IN:     AAAH
129
130   HO:     ja
131           yes
132
133   CO:     he he [he] he he [he]
134           he he [he] he he [he]
```

The main difference between this extract and the previous two is that religion is not topicalized as part of a problematization of Muslim practices. Muslims are categorized as part of a 'we' that includes the workplace and the employer, and Muslim practices are presented as the normative framework which the candidate is to relate and adapt to. With respect to the former, we see how HO uses the term 'our children' in line 13 and links them to the category of 'children of Muslim families'. Knowing that HO is a leading member of staff in a kindergarten, 'our children' should be heard as the children in the kindergarten, and not any children she might have of her own, who are thereby collectively described as Muslim children. The choice of the wording 'our children' as opposed to for example 'the children here', 'the children in this kindergarten' or even 'Mosaik's children' contributes to emphasizing a close affiliation between HO and the children, since it is a formatting that could just as easily have been used to describe a family relation where HO would represent 'the mother'. The relation between HO and the 'Muslim children' is in this way established as personal, close, intimate and invested in the same way as one would expect the relation between the categories 'mother', 'father' and 'children' within the MCD 'Family'. Besides representing herself as 'mother', HO furthermore constitutes herself as an institutional representative that mediates between the demands of the 'very religious families' and 'the municipality of Copenhagen'.

There are, in other words, two complimentary goals involved in the presentation that HO makes – namely the portrayal of herself as the loyal, sympathetic and sensitive caretaker of 'the Muslim children' and the responsible manager of an 'ordinary' Danish kindergarten, funded by the municipality. From lines 19 to 34 we see this contrast that is established between on the one hand a 'parental we' that has established the kindergarten and determined the rules of conduct, and on the other hand an 'institutional we' that is financed by and reports to the municipality of Copenhagen. IN picks up on this dilemma or contrast between the demands of the parents and the municipal demands faced by 'ordinary' kindergartens, as she responds in line 42 'okay be ready to follow the laws'. This leads to an elaboration by HO in line 45 of how they live up to the regular requirements and rules of municipal kindergartens, namely by following particular pedagogic plans of learning and the relevant legislative framework called 'Serviceloven' ('service law' in English). This elaboration is formatted as an account to IN's response, which HO apparently hears as an inquiry about the extent to which the differences of the kindergarten challenges the boundaries of the ordinary and acceptable. In line 53 HO concludes this accounting format by summarizing and underlining her previous emphasis on difference, although in a somewhat moderated form, namely 'but there are some differences'. The orientation towards religion and the presentation of the kindergarten as Muslim is in this sense focused on striking a balance between 'the ordinary' and 'the different'. This is achieved by minimizing the difference from the category 'Muslim, which is in marked contrast to what was found in the other two examples, especially in Extract 22 (Liquor and pork).

In line 59, HO begins her unpacking of what the differences actually are and framing them as attempts to 'embrace the Muslim families'. In other words, HO provides a list of various 'different' practices that are compatible with the category 'Muslim' and present these practices as something shared by all, including HO herself. The first 'difference' presented is 'we are for example vegetarian', which once again establishes a category of 'we' that closely affiliates HO with the kindergarten, the Muslim children and the Muslim families. Furthermore, by formulating it as 'we are vegetarian' rather than for example 'we don't serve meat', HO is affiliating herself, the kindergarten, the Muslim children and the Muslim families with a non-religious category of people making a particular dietary choice of not eating meat. Again this is in contrast with the emphasis on problems with buying pork in the previous example, which is immediately and almost exclusively interpretable as a religious, and more specifically Muslim, 'difference'. In that example, we saw how HO explicitly distanced herself and the practices of the elderly from practices bound to the category 'Muslim', whereas here HO constructs a 'we' that includes herself, the Muslim children and the Muslim families in the shared practice of not eating meat.

Nevertheless, there is an important similarity between this example and the previous one. Namely, the orientation towards religion is designed in a way that implicitly prescribes a certain type of behaviour from the candidate. The key element here is not what the children eat but the fact that the staff eat the same as the children and that the candidate has to accept not eating meat for this reason as well. We see this from line 68 to 89 where HO summarizes the dietary rules, 'the children are fed' ... 'the staff also' ... 'one cannot bring one's own food' ... 'we all eat the same' ... 'and that is minus meat'. 'One cannot bring one's own food' is thus an indirect, and a very 'matter-of-fact', way of stating that the candidate has to eat the same as the children when undertaking the internship. This is similar to the way that buying alcohol and pork was presented as non-optional in the previous example. However, in the current example there is much more emphasis put on outlining the workplace rules of conduct than on enquiring about assumed problems that the candidate may have with such rules. This again minimizes the problematizing element found in the previous example. One could argue of course that, as a consequence, the candidate in the present example is not given as much of a chance to relate and respond to the rules presented since she is not explicitly asked whether these prescribed rules of conduct present a problem for her. They are merely presented as 'rules of the house' that the candidate has to accept as part of the internship. Nevertheless the candidate does manage to meaningfully respond in relevant places such as line 80 where she shows understanding by repeating HO's 'also' and in line 86 where she positively acknowledges with an 'okay' that one cannot bring one's own food. In line 98 there is a 0.4 second pause where IN is given a chance to respond to what is the central part of HO's first rule, namely the 'minus meat' part. Since she does not take this opportunity, HO continues her list of rules from line 100 to line 110 where HO then explicitly invites IN to respond to and accept what is presented so far.

The items on the list involve 'no smoking', 'no alcohol', 'no men in bathrooms' and 'a dresscode' and they are again presented with small pauses in lines 102 and 106, which provides the opportunity for response. The final item, namely dresscode, is however immediately elaborated on in a more precise description of how to dress with which the candidate is explicitly, yet indirectly, encouraged to agree in lines 110–114: 'so that you have to remember Naya you can not come here with bare stomach'. Although this is clearly an invitation for a response from the candidate, the suggestion that IN might turn up for work wearing clothes that reveal her stomach can be heard as a joke since IN is a mature woman and not a young girl.

The fact that HO addresses the issue of dresscode in this joking manner minimizes the prescriptive element of HO's utterance while minimizing the pressure on IN to respond and accept explicitly. She is in this way put less 'on the spot' so to speak, which is in contrast with the previous two examples, as well as examples shown in Chapters 4 and 5 e.g. Extract 8 (So you both have to learn Danish?). The joking format is immediately acknowledged by both CO, who responds with laughter in overlap, and IN, who contributes to the joke by adding that she has bought a 'very special scarf'. HO overlaps this response with a 'yes' and a 'sorry' which works to underline the joking format since it repeats the suggestion that this is something IN would actually do and acknowledges CO's laughter as appropriate. It also indicates that IN was not expected to respond in any serious manner to what had been said since the overlap shows disregard or a lack of interest in IN's response. HO repeats her declaration of regret in line 125 after IN has finished her turn, which shows that IN's mentioning of the 'special scarf' is not heard as a serious contribution and IN continues the joke by also expressing regret. CO then once again contributes with laughter that displays her hearing of the exchange as a cooperative joke. What is highlighted by this joking exchange is a marked difference in the way that religion is not topicalized as an assumed conflict between the candidate and the workplace. Furthermore, it emphasizes how religion is neither treated as a sensitive issue, as we saw in the first example, or as a controversial problem, as we saw in the second example. The category 'Muslim' is merely presented as the common denominator for a set of rules and practices to be followed by the internship candidate as a future member of staff. While these rules and practices are definitely raised and presented for the candidate to respond to and accept, there are no assumptions made about potential problems that the candidate may have with following them and the candidate is not explicitly challenged or inquired about her willingness or ability to comply. This results in a cooperative and pleasant negotiation about the implications and requirements of the future internship. In the following part of the same interview, we see how the topic is slightly extended by the candidate through an elaboration of the joke about the dresscode of the kindergarten, but is then brought to a close by HO with an account of the rules and prescriptions previously presented.

Extract 23 **A religious institution** *(continued)*

```
135         - -      - -
136  IN:    [en]      [en [(    )]
137         [a]       [a]
138  HO:              [desværre]
139              [sorry]
140
141  IN:    [en kort (  ) og]   en mini [nel]e[del]
142         [a short (  ) and]  a mini [skirt]
143
144  HO:    [desværre det kan du ikke ja][jae]
145         [sorry you cannot yes [yeah]
146
147  CO:                         [nej] men den tager du
148                              [no] but you can wear that
149         på imorgen [i stedet for]
150         tomorrow   [in stead]
151
152  HO:              [det går ikke]
153              [that does not work]
154  IN:    h:ie
155         h:ie
156
157  HO:    [nej]
158         [no]
159
160  CO:    [he ]he he [he]
161         [he ]he he [he]
162
163  HO:              [det] [(   )] ikke et pro[blem] for os men det kan
164              [it]  [(   )] not a prob[blem] for us but it can
165
166  IN:              [(ja )]          [(ja)]
167              [(yes)]          [(yes)]
168
169  HO:    være [et] pro[blem] for [no:gen og derfor] [er] det noget vi altid
170         be   [a]  prob[blem] for [so:me and therefore] [it] is something we always
171
172  IN:    [ja]
173         [yes]
174
175  CO:              [ja]      [(for de ældre)]
176              [yes]     [(for the elderly)]
177
178  IN:                                      [ja]
179
179  HO:    [for]tæller [at] at sådan er det her i Mosaik fordi at vi ønsker at
```

(Continued)

```
180          [tell]      [that] that this is how it is here in Mosaik because we want
181
182   IN:    [ja]        [(følgelig)]
183          [yes]       [course]
184
185   HO:    vores forældre skal føle [sig] rigtig t[rygge]
186          our parents to feel       really s[afe]
187
188   IN:                [ja]             [ja selvfø]lgelig
189                      [yes]            [yes of course
190
191   HO:    det her er for mange familier det første skridt .hh i en
192          integrationsproces .h så derfor er det så vigtigt .hh
193          at vi møder familierne uden at virke skræmmende (.) så det er nogen
194          små bitte reguleringer som gør at ø:h (.) .h mange mange mennesker
195          søger til Mosaik og vi har en lang lang venteliste
196
197
198          this is for many families the first step .hh in an
199          integrationsproces .h so therefore it is so important .hh
200          that we meet the families without seeming intimidating (.) so it is some
201          small tiny regulations that make e:h .h many many people
202          seek Mosaik and we have a long long waiting list.
20?
```

From lines 135 to line 160 we see the mentioned elaboration and closing of the joking exchange, which involves adding the item of 'miniskirt' to the potential inappropriate items of clothing that the candidate may have otherwise considered wearing. This is once again followed by laughter from CO, which emphasizes the joking nature of the utterance, and repeated rejections by HO, who thereby maintains her role as interviewer and employer while not interrupting the joking exchange. From lines 163 to 181, HO exercises her right as interviewer to close a topic and also change the tone of the exchange to something more serious as she produces a closing account for the reasoning behind the rules and restrictions she has presented.

This account is similar to the accounts found in the previous two examples in the sense that it constitutes a form of reasoning for the rules and practices of the workplace, but is markedly different since it does not follow from a previous controversial or sensitive prescriptive utterance made towards the candidate. At this point the practices and compatibility of the candidate have not been seriously addressed or questioned as in the previous two examples so the account produced here does not have a mitigating function. Rather it constitutes a closing move where HO reasserts her role as interviewer and representative of the kindergarten. In other words, she returns to the previous presentation format and restates her representative role for the Muslim families' needs and feelings of security.

HO closes her presentation by legitimating the rules of Mosaik as facilitating measures in an integration process. This part of her presentation shows very clearly how the negotiation of particular practices and rules within the context of the internship interview is embedded in and influenced by a wider context of ideology and public debate about religion and integration. It also underlines an important distinction in the orientation towards religion found in this example compared with the other two, namely that religiously based differences in practices and rules of conduct are minimized and de-emphasized as 'slight adjustments' rather than problematized.

What is noticeable about this example in relation to the previous two is how the orientation towards religion is much less focused on the religiousness of the candidate. In the first two examples the candidates are immediately categorized as Muslim and it is the implications of this membership in relation to the practices and rules of the workplace which is the topic of negotiation. In this last example, however, religion is topicalized almost strictly in relation to a presentation of the workplace and the candidate's membership or non-membership of the category 'Muslim' is not addressed or assumed in the formatting of this presentation. The only reference made to the practices and behaviour of the candidate is the joking statement made about bare stomachs and miniskirts, which would be equally meaningful if they were uttered to a Muslim or a non-Muslim woman in her twenties applying for an internship as a kindergarten teacher since it would be equally inappropriate clothing in both instances.

This non-orientation towards the candidate's religiousness is, as mentioned, made possible by the fact that she is not visibly marked as 'Muslim' and her relation to this category is therefore ambiguous. In fact, it might well be that this ambiguity is part of the reason for the employer's lack of orientation towards her religiousness. The advantage of the lack of orientation towards the religiousness of the candidate is that the employer manages to present and prescribe the particular rules of conduct within the workplace without problematizing the candidate's ability to comply with these and without emphasizing her potential 'otherness' in relation to the other participants. The interaction could in this sense have continued with other topics than religion after this initial presentation by the employer. However, the candidate herself chooses to renew the relevance of the category 'Muslim' in relation to a presentation of her own category membership. This happens after a short negotiation between the employer and the job consultant about the difference between public and private kindergartens. As we will be clear from the following and final part of the example from this interview, this negotiation of religiousness by the candidate is similar to the previous two examples in the sense that it constitutes a defence that highlights an accommodating position towards the rules and demands of the workplace presented by the employer. There is a marked difference however in the way that the category 'Muslim' and the implications of this membership are explicitly rather than implicitly negotiated.

Extract 23 A religious institution *(continued)*

```
203   .
206   % sequence in which they discuss the nature of the institution, whether it
207   is private or public
208   .
209   .
210   (5.48 min)
211   IN:    Du det har ik problem med: eh- m- på mig ti:l eh: tø:j e:lle:r
212          You have not problem wi:th eh- w- on me to: eh: clothes o:r
213
214          jeg eh:
215          ih eh:
216   (0.6)
217   IN:    kender mange der muslimske £(     )£ [fordi jeg er] selv muslim .h
218          know many that muslim £(       )£   [because I am] myself muslim .h
219
220   (HO/CO):                                   [mm           ]
221   IN:    og jeg bor også i: hh. (0.6) de:n muslimsk £kvarter£
222          and I also live i:n hh. (0.6) the: muslim neighbourhood
223
224   HO:    ja
225          yes
226
227   CO:    ja
228          yes
229
230   IN:    hvor jeg må også ik gå uden (0.7) øh- (0.5)
231          where I also am not allowed to go without (0.7) eh- (0.5)
232
233   HO:    ærme
234          sleeve
235
236   IN:    arme [eller]
237          arms [or]
238
239   HO:         [ja o]kay
240               [yes o]kay
241
242   IN:    m he he [shor.hhorts] eller >mini< MEN mine øjne er (.) .hh s ik
243          m he he [shor.hhorts] or >mini< BUT my eyes is (.) .hh s not
244
245
246   HO:              [ja]
247              [yes]
248
249   IN:    behøver den
250          needs it
251
252   HO:    nej
253          no
254
255   IN:    slags tøj [.hh] de var 1- rang [til] efter [mig] he he [he he he]
256          kind of clothes [.hh] they were 1- rang [for] after [me] he he [he he he]
257
258   HO:              [nej]            [mm]      [mm]
259              [no]             [mm]      [mm]
260   CO:                                             [he he he]
261                                                   [he he he]
262
263   (1.5)
264
265   CO:    men er du selv muslim
266          but are you muslim yourself
267   (0.7)
268   IN:    ja↑=
269          yes↑=
270
271   CO:    =ja nå men de:t [var da ikke sikkert he he he]
272          =yes oh but tha:t [was not certain right he he he]
273
274   IN:                   [he he he he he he [he he he he]
275                   [he he he he he he [he he he he]
276
277   HO:                                     [det kan man jo ikke lige se
278                                           [it is not immediately apparent right
279
280   IN:    he he [he
281          he he [he
282
283   HO:         [på] [andre] mennesker [hvilken] religion de [tilhører]
284          [in] [other] people      [what ]  religion they [belong to]
285
286   ( )               [( )]         [( )]
287   IN:                                           [he he [he] he he
288   CO:                                                  [nej]
289                                                         [no]
290   (1.4)
291
```

We see here how the candidate herself raises the potential 'problem' or conflict between her own practices and the religiously defined rules of conduct at the workplace – this was raised by the employers in the previous two examples but not raised explicitly by the employer in this example. Here, IN does this by emphasizing that the employer will not have a problem with her with respect to the dresscode of the workplace and then legitimizing this claim in lines 217–221 by affiliating herself with the category 'Muslim' in three different ways, by saying 'I know many Muslims', 'I am myself Muslim' and 'I live in Muslim neighbourhood'. She then elaborates on the implications of this affiliation by describing that similar rules of conduct to those in the kindergarten apply to her neighbourhood and explaining how she is used to following them. Finally, she gives her own perspective and position with respect to those rules, stating that she finds them unnecessary. CO apparently misses IN's 'because I am Muslim myself' in line 217 because after a long pause she explicitly requests a clarification of IN's membership of the category 'Muslim' – 'but are you Muslim yourself' in line 265. After a relatively long break, IN responds positively to this question with emphasis and raised pitch in line 268, which is very similar to the response found in relation to language proficiency in the previous chapter, Extract 9 (Do you understand what I'm saying?). In this example, as in Extract 9, the strong emphasis seems to strongly reject the alternative option, namely that she is not a Muslim, and the implicit assertion that what she has previously said could be heard to imply the opposite. That said, the strong rejection can be heard as part of an argumentation for coherence between her previously uttered opinions and the category 'Muslim'. CO immediately accepts IN's response in a 'yes oh' format which is a change of state token similar to the one found and described in Chapter 4 on nationality, Extract 10 (Colombia). Here, much as in Extract 10, it displays an element of surprise or a change in perception which is possibly related to the fact that, as mentioned, the candidate does not wear a religious scarf and is thereby not visibly signifiable as a Muslim woman. This is confirmed in the following utterance by CO 'that was not certain right' and not least HO's overlapped response in line 277 'it is not immediately apparent right in other people what religion they belong to'. Both CO and HO hereby confirm the aforementioned potential ambiguity about the religious membership of IN, an ambiguity that would most probably not have been addressed or solved if IN had not reopened the topic of religion. This confirms that the orientation towards religion is not focused on the identification and problematization of the religiousness of the candidate and the implications of this vis-à-vis the rules of the future workplace. This was the case in the previous two examples. Rather, in this example the topic of religion and the category 'Muslim' is made relevant in relation to a presentation of a workplace with rules and regulations that deviate from the norm of public kindergartens and not least in relation to a clarification of whether these rules of conduct can be accepted by the candidate, regardless of her own religious orientation.

This difference has consequences with respect to the distribution of power between the participants, which can be said to manifest in the markedly different tone in the final example compared to the previous two. In the first two examples, the candidates were immediately attributed to a category which the other participants and the future clients were not members of. This membership was assumed to have certain implications that were problematized in relation to the future internship and for this reason the candidates were put in a position where their practices and preferences as 'Muslim' were to be accounted for and defended. Simultaneously, the fact that the employers in the first two examples spoke as representatives of the non-Muslim majority in Denmark immediately turned the problematization of the candidates' religiousness into a delicate and sensitive matter which influenced the interactional dynamic of both interactions. In the third example, the employer and the workplace were immediately affiliated with the category 'Muslim' as part of a presentation of a set of rules and regulations that were different from and in opposition to those of a normal Danish kindergarten. The employer thus immediately placed herself in a position where she was the one to defend certain practices and preferences as an implication of the religious foundation of the kindergarten. This made the issue of the candidate's compatibility with and acceptance of the rules of the workplace much less of a sensitive issue, since the demands made by the employer were not those of a majority member to a minority member. This difference was, as shown, manifested in a joking atmosphere between the participants and in a more equal distribution of roles between the participants with the employer being less accusatory and the candidate and the job consultant less defensive.

While the central issue in all three examples is to establish a possible 'fit' between the candidate and the workplace, the candidate is in the third example not immediately positioned as the deviant 'other'. She is therefore not in the same way as in the first two examples defending her membership of the category 'Muslim' as such but merely accounting for her willingness to accept the presented rules of the future workplace and thereby her position with respect to practices and preferences of 'Muslims'. The gatekeeping involved in the first two examples can in this way be said to have been reinforced in comparison with the third example in the sense that the candidates in the first two examples defend and account for not only their ability and willingness to comply with particular demands and rules of the future workplace, but also their membership of the category 'Muslim' as such. This double gatekeeping role of the employer is not in effect in the third example since the employer and the workplace are not representatives of the majority and norm of Danish society and the candidate is not visibly deviant. This central difference highlights how the consequences of orientations towards religion are clearly dependent on not only the religiousness of the candidates but on the extent to which the norms and rules of the workplace are presented as 'the ways' of the majority.

Religion as a Barrier for Co-membership – The Linking of Religion and Culture

In Chapter 4, I argued that orientations towards nationality are informed by a conceptual link between nationality and culture in the internship interviews, manifested in the way that national membership was formulated as implying a particular 'system of thought' and 'way of life' of its members. Looking at the examples analyzed so far of orientations towards religion, the same thing can be said to be in effect. What was very clearly pronounced in the orientation towards religion was the unspecified formulation of and reference to a religious community as an absolute and coherent system of actions, beliefs and values that was assumed to dictate the actions, beliefs and values of its members. As argued in relation to nationality, this presented a barrier for the candidates in their attempts to present themselves as competent and suitable candidates for the future internship since religious membership and religious practices became something to be accounted for and defended.

In the first example, the conceptual linking of religion and culture was manifested in the following formulation by the employer: 'I know that you have your various ways in which it is important to you that the clothing should be,' which was confirmed by the internship candidate. The employer and the candidate in this way co-construct the category of 'Muslims' and associate it with a specific set of values in relation to clothing. This construction is based on the assumption that a religious affiliation implies a certain set of values and actions, and that this is shared by all its members. In the second example, Extract 22 (Liquor and pork) the understanding of religion as a community of a shared set of values and practices is manifested slightly differently.

Here, the employee's questions regarding the candidate's willingness to buy certain banned groceries, framed in a way as to avoid previous problematic experiences with Muslim employees, establish a category of people with religiously grounded limitations, practices and beliefs. Similar to the first extract, however, is the formulated assumption that religious prescriptions and rules are considered to determine individual practice and preference, which was for instance expressed in the repair of the utterance 'they would not' to 'they could not touch them' (line 158) which highlights the inability of the individual to make choices based on their own will.

However, the negotiations also reflect the manifestation of the opposite assumption that religious prescriptions can be interpreted and bent by the individual, such as the formulation in line 308 'because one does not drink it one can still buy two beers for a client', 'not bottles either' in line 166 and the distinction made by the internship candidate between 'not eating and not cutting pork'. The linking of religion and culture can in this way be said to be mediated by two different repertoires that are used in the distinction between different members of the category 'Muslims' – namely 'moderate Muslims' and 'radical Muslims'. These repertoires were also found in Extract 23 (Religious institutions) where the internship candidate expressed her own interpretations of the dresscode prescribed by the Muslim community she considered herself being part of. These repertoires are similar to the repertoires 'good migrant' and 'bad migrant' described in the previous chapter, except for the fact that the normative valorization of 'moderate Muslims' and 'radical Muslims' is in this case not only established by the employers, as was the case in relation to language. The valorized repertoires of 'moderate Muslims' and 'radical Muslims' are also applied by the Muslim candidates themselves as part of their accounts and defences for how their individual religiousness is compatible with the demands and rules of the future workplace.

The distinction between two ways of 'being' or 'practising' ones religion can be seen as a way for the participants to deal with a conceptual dilemma between two contrary ideological positions regarding the relation between the individual and society. What is being negotiated in Extract 21 (The scarf) and Extract 22 (Liquor and pork) is how and whether the internship candidates' religious practices and beliefs are compatible with the practices of a particular workplace and the needs, interests and behaviour of the Danish clients being served. This negotiation is informed by a dilemma between two contrary but equally commonsensical principles or 'common-places' of modern society: on the one hand, there is the individual right to have and practice religion, which is legally constituted through the Declaration of Human Rights. On the other hand, there are the democratic principles of the modern nation-state that comprise a range of rules that define and limit the exercising of such individual rights for the purpose of serving a common good. The negotiation of whether and how the internship candidate's religious affiliation can be combined with a work-related context reflects the dilemma that these oppositional principles present.

In the first example, Extract 21 (The Scarf), the dilemma between 'individual rights' and 'the interests of the community' is reflected in the employer's utterance in line 292: 'I know that you have your various ways in which it is important to you that the clothing should be.' This is formatted as a disclaimer for the demands presented to the internship candidate. In the second example, these contrary commonplaces are reflected in EM's statement in lines 191 to 206 where she concludes that regardless of all their respect for different religious practices they cannot tell their clients to change their food preferences. EM hereby uses both the commonplace of 'individual right' and 'the interests of the community' to construct two different solutions to the conflict between 'religious practices' and 'work-related practices', namely to either accommodate and respect the practice of the Muslim employee or the practice of the client and position herself in relation to the two.

The analysis of the repertoires and commonplaces present in the topicalization of religion shows how the negotiation of categories such as 'Muslims' and Muslim practices entails a negotiation of the category 'Danish' and Danish practices. While the consistency rule accounts for how the mentioning of one category makes other categories within the MCD that this category belongs to relevant, it does not explain how orientations towards 'Muslims' entails orientations towards 'Danes'. This link between categories can however be explained through the logic of culture which is manifested in the topicalization of nationality as well as religion. The conceptualization of religious membership as a cultural membership with implications for an individuals' 'ways' of thought and behaviour implies that the association of the internship candidate with 'Muslims' involves a naturalized disassociation from 'Danes' and thereby, following the same logic, from 'Christians' or 'Protestants'. This dissociation is obviously problematic for the candidate since it presents them with a double gatekeeping situation where they are to simultaneously defend their position as future interns and their co-membership of the 'community' of the Danish majority. As it appears from not only this chapter but also the previous two chapters, the internship and the internship interview involve both simultaneously.

Summary

This chapter showed how categories related to religion are made relevant in relation to an inquiry and negotiation about whether a specific form of practice, such as wearing a hijab or buying alcohol, constitutes a potential problem for the tasks involved in the future internship. In the first example, this practice of wearing a hijab was carefully dissociated with religion by the use of neutral terms and by associating the issue of clothing with hygiene, personal contact and professionalism. In the second example, the practice of buying alcohol was explicitly associated with religion and linked to previous problems with other employees, but again a specific reference to Islam or Muslims was avoided and merely implied through the practices described.

The first two examples are very similar in the way the topicalization is initiated by a question from the employer or the employee about a specific practice which is responded to and potentially resolved by the internship candidate and accepted by the person who asked the question. In both cases, this does not close the topic, which is instead renewed and pursued at great length, driven by a range of different accounts supplied by the employer or the employee. The third example deviates markedly from this, since the orientation towards religion is rather made as part of the employer's presentation of the workplace, which in this case is a Muslim kindergarten. While the implication is the same, namely that the candidate has to adapt to the rules, regulations and normativities of the particular workplace, the religious dimension of this normativity is made explicit. In the first two examples, on the other hand, religiousness only becomes an issue related to the category membership of 'the other', while the implicit religiousness of the majority defined norm of the workplace is made invisible or non-existing. The norm of the workplace is in this way merely implicitly formulated through the deviance of the candidate. This was not the case in the third example.

What is confirmed in all three examples, however, is the previously mentioned role of the job consultant as a defender and advocate of the internship candidate, although the three examples show different ways of managing this role. In the first case, the job consultant immediately contributes to the solving of the issue by emphasizing that the issue of clothing was well prepared, whereas in the second example, the job consultant more implicitly supports the defence of the internship candidate by dissociating the candidate from more radical Muslims and associating her with Danes. She does this, however, by probing the descriptions of Muslim practices co-constructed by the employer and the employee, which leads to a prolonging of the topic. Furthermore, she uses humour as a resource, which on the one hand alleviates some of the tension and moves the attention away from the internship candidate, but on the other hand, once again prolongs the topic. Finally, she also uses the defence technique used by the job consultant in the first example, namely giving a more direct and explicit account or statement about the practice and values of the internship candidate, which counters the claims presented by the employer and the employee. The third example again deviates from the first two since the situation does not in the same way call for a defence but rather the support of the job consultant in co-constructing the joking format and tone in relation to the presentation of dresscode demands.

In the first two examples, the use of accounts by the employer is predominant and seems to have the function of legitimizing the topicalization of religion in the first place, as well as indirectly formulating a normatively prescribed behaviour that the internship candidate has to respond to and ultimately accept. These accounts produce extended negotiations about religion in both examples and present the internship candidate as well as the job consultant with various positions, claims and understandings that they have to respond to and refute in order to adequately close the topic. These extended sequences of claims and defences obviously take time and attention away from the competences and abilities of the internship candidate and delay any decisions and planning made with regard to the internship per se. This tendency is similar to what was observed and described in relation to the topicalization of language in Chapter 5. Again, we see a marked difference in the third example, where the employers' expectations about the accommodation of the candidate are not formulated on the basis of an assumed incompatibility between the practices of the candidate and the workplace. The assumptions of difference expressed are to a much larger extent related to the deviation of the workplace in relation to the surrounding society as a whole. Since the workplace and the employer in this way are also representatives of 'the other', there is less of an imposition to account for than in the cases where the employers represent the majority. Again, this confirms how the asymmetries (re)produced within the internship interview are not merely of an institutional nature. However, the employer still produces an account for the particular rules and regulations of the workplace in question but this account seems to rather be legitimizing a deviating set of rules and practices from those of an 'ordinary' Danish kindergarten.

As in the previous two chapters, the analysis of orientations towards religion shows how the participants' orientations towards the participation framework and the distribution of rights associated with this interrelates with the orientations towards broader social categories such as being Muslim. Thus, it was once again demonstrated that the job consultant often acted in defence and spoke on behalf of the internship candidate, and that HO is frequently the one granted with the right to initiate and terminate the orientation towards the internship candidates' membership of a specific religious community. Such orientation towards the participation framework, much as described in Chapter 2, informs and enables the orientations towards and negotiations of broader categories such as Muslims.

The negotiation, assessment and acceptance of the internship candidates depend in this way not only on the candidates' willingness to accommodate and change their practices, but also on the extent to which the other participants facilitate and accept their formulation of this willingness. Thus, as described previously, the employer has a triple gatekeeping function which is manifested in their power to determine the outcome of the interview, in their right to decide which topics are to be addressed during the interview and when they have been sufficiently covered and in their ability to establishing the normative framework for passing and non-passing in relation to the workplace and the category 'Danish' more generally.

These gatekeeping functions are intimately related, which is clear in the way that particular issues such as wearing a religious scarf or buying alcohol are negotiated to a length that exceeds what is projected by the original question posed by the employer and the following answer given by the candidate. Not to say that this is in itself extraordinary, but merely to suggest that these issues could potentially have been abandoned sooner, which would have allowed for an earlier return to other topics of relevance.

The negotiations about the meaning of the category 'Muslims' described within all three examples reveal the centrality of the various practices, beliefs and understandings associated with, and bound to, specific categories. In the first example, the various accounts offered by the employer reproduced opposing commonplaces related to, on the one hand, the rights of the individual to have and practice a certain belief, and on the other, the rights of a community to decide and prescribe a certain practice. The hyper-accountability illustrated in this example can in this way be seen as an orientation towards the dilemma of accommodating conflicting interests and concerns, which is realized by using conventional interactional strategies and resources. In the second example, the negotiations and accounts of the participants reflected a conceptual link between 'being Danish' and 'being Christian', which was associated with a range of specific practices that were constructed as commonsensical. These were distinguished from and disassociated with Muslims and Muslim practices, which were established as somewhat illogical in comparison to Danish practices. The negotiation of Muslims and Muslim practices involved the constitution of and reference to 'a coherent and absolute system of beliefs and practices', which manifested a conceptual link between 'religion' and 'culture' that is similar to the link between 'nationality' and 'culture' described in Chapter 4. Finally, the third example again differs since the negotiation about the category 'Muslim' and Muslim practices is not focused on the employer's attempts to secure and justify the demands and rules of a 'Danish' workplace but rather her attempts at presenting a 'Muslim' kindergarten in a way that strikes a proper balance between its particularity and ordinariness in relation to 'normal' Danish kindergartens. This has consequences in the sense that differences between the category 'Muslim' and the category 'Danish' are minimized rather than emphasized and the ambiguity of the candidate's affiliation with either one or the other becomes less of a high stakes issue.

While there are in this way differences in the realizations of categories and the interactional consequences of this, all of the examples presented in this analysis illuminate how the negotiation of specific categories and category-bound actions is informed by and draws on a dilemmatic common sense that offers conflictual ideological positions regarding issues of migration, language, religion, learning and culture. The negotiation about candidates is in this way simultaneously a negotiation about ideas and ideologies.

Note

(1) Roberts (Roberts & Campbell, 2006) describes how the choice of such a listing format is a more prevalent feature of presentations made by born-abroad candidates, and how this format can contribute to giving the impression that the candidates' answers have been taught or tutored and hereby make the born-abroad candidates seem less independent and competent.

7 Gatekeeping – The Power of Categories

> *We can get stuck in institutions by being stuck to a category.*
> *That is not to say that we cannot, or do not, value the work of these categories.*
> *But we can be constrained even by the categories we love.*
> (Sara Ahmed, 2012: 13)

The Power of Categories

This chapter will pull together the central ideas and findings presented in the previous theoretical and analytical chapters. There are three central arguments that I make in this book – one theoretical, one methodological and one empirical – all of which are related to the power of categories. I will present these one by one and finish on some broader reflections on their implications.

The central theoretical argument I have outlined deals with redefining the potential and scope of the term 'gatekeeping', in contrast to how it has been predominantly defined and used in previous studies within the field of interactional sociolinguistics, as it has been limited to its emphasis on institutionality, communicative style and discriminatory selection processes. While previous gatekeeping studies very clearly show discriminatory processes in the selection, evaluation and treatment of interviewees, clients or candidates, they do not deal with the turn-by-turn complexity of the category work involved in making inferences about candidates. Thus, I have argued that it is this category work that forms the locus of gatekeeping processes which then manifest more specifically in institutional processes of selection/evaluation/service provision. Part of the reason for the lack of attention paid to showing how participants establish and negotiate various categories as part of their attempts to establish understanding and affiliation has been due to the emphasis put on measuring the outcome of differences in communicative style or linguistic behaviour. While gatekeeping processes certainly involve inferences about communicative style and linguistic difference, they are to an equal extent found in relation to orientations towards a range of other features, traits and actions related to an individual.

This book has argued that gatekeeping processes are found in any kind of encounter, and in the implicit processes of differentiation and otherness that take place as categories, memberships and non-memberships are established interactionally. Such processes of differentiation will naturally have larger consequences in institutional encounters where asymmetric distribution of power between the participants implies that the categorizations of some will have concrete, and sometimes far-reaching, consequences for others. The participation framework of the internship interview thus intertwines with and supports processes of gatekeeping, but this is only on the level of decision making and assessment. The gatekeeping processes described in this book are in this sense not primarily related to the employers' participant status as decision makers, but to the patterns of categorization related to nationality, language and religion which positioned the candidates in an inferior position to the other participants. In this way I have argued that by addressing gatekeeping as first and foremost an institutional phenomenon, we are merely scratching the surface of it. Gatekeeping processes cannot be described just through a characterization of linguistic behaviour or communicative style and feedback interviews. Rather, it must be illuminated through an investigation of the power inherent in processes of categorization. In this way, I have aimed to address the power of categories (rather than the power of individuals) to position, qualify, disqualify and sanction individuals in institutional (and non-institutional) encounters.

This brings me to the second argument presented in this book, which deals with methodology – namely, that the study of the microdynamics of categorization processes is essential for our understanding of how gatekeeping processes work. Membership categorization analysis reveals how the orientations and inferences of interactants (re)produce hierarchical relations of difference between categories on the basis of common-sense knowledge and ideology. While the role of categories, memberships and non-memberships is highlighted by the vast majority of gatekeeping studies, they are often used as a point of departure for the study of communicative differences, or they are considered in relation to interlocutors' abilities to achieve affiliation or co-membership through (or in spite of) their linguistic and communicative behaviours. Within the field of interactional sociolinguistics or linguistic anthropology, the meaning of categories and differences related to language, ethnicity, race, class, profession and so on, are often applied to account for differences in linguistic behaviour or the success/failure in achieving trust, affiliation or co-membership.

However, none of these gatekeeping studies seeks to highlight interactional processes during which interactants can be seen to orient to, establish and negotiate the relevance and meaning of categories, as well as address how hierarchization and power are effectuated and reproduced through such processes. I have argued in this book that Conversation Analysis, and Membership Categorization Analysis specifically, provides a tool for such illumination and yet, while many CA studies have already provided convincing accounts of the category work involved as interlocutors make sense of and interpret one another in the turn-by-turn development of interaction, only very few engage with issues of power, ideology and gatekeeping (Saft & Ohara, 2003; Speer & Parsons, 2006, 2007; Speer, 2009; Speer & Green, 2007). It is therefore important to draw attention to and understand processes of categorization as deeply embedded in and informed by the cultural and ideological context of common sense within which they occur, while being a rich source of knowledge about not only inferential processes but also context-specific norms, expectations and assumptions. These include assumptions and expectations about categories, members and difference. Difference is in this sense something which is at once established and negotiated in interaction but it is also something which is inherent in the meaning attributed to particular categories. Establishing the meaning of 'Danish' thus involves ideas about what is not 'Danish' or what is different from 'Danish'. This book has proposed and shown the power of categories in illuminating the patterns of common sense and ideology that (re)produce oppressive patterns of meaning and processes of power. I have argued that such patterns and processes present the actual *gates* that migrants face and which are more fundamental to gatekeeping processes than the *gatekeepers* themselves.

Following this line of thought, the empirical argument presented in this book is related to the description of the 'gates' that internship candidates face within the context of the internship interview. I have shown in the analysis chapters how the negotiation, establishment and orientation towards categories related to nationality, language and religion are prevalent within the internship interviews and how this orientation systematically involves the (re)production of hierarchization and power-asymmetry between the candidates and other participants. While there was no actual selection process taking place during the internship interviews, the participants oriented to the interaction as a high-stakes, evaluative encounter where the employer had the role of evaluating and interviewing the candidate with regard to the future internship. This institutional asymmetry at once enables and reinforces the gatekeeping aspects of categorization processes.

What is found in the cases where the participants orient to categories related to nationality as well as religion is that a specific 'way' of doing things within a Danish context is compared to and distinguished from another way of doing things – the 'way' of the candidate. A system of relations is thereby established between the category 'Danish' and a range of other categories such as 'Colombian' and 'Muslim', to name a few. 'Danish' is thus characterized as the normative basis which the other categories are compared with and distinguished from. Furthermore, the behaviours, characteristics and practices attributed to these 'other' categories are described and evaluated as inferior, illogical and unreasonable in comparison to 'Danish ways'. This was found not only in the words and formulations used to describe the practices associated with, for example, the category 'Muslim' and the category 'Colombian', but also in the implicit and explicit expression of the expectation that the candidate should learn and adapt to the 'Danish way'. The 'otherness' of the candidate with respect to nationality or religion is thus seemingly considered as a barrier for the integration into a professional context and the previous work experience of the candidate is also devalued and disregarded on the grounds of its difference from 'Danish' work-related practices and values.

Gatekeeping processes related to orientations towards language can be seen slightly differently in this regard, as they do not involve the establishment and opposition of different 'ways' or the uneven distribution of rights, knowledge and status compared to participants associated with such ways. Rather, they are constituted in the orientation towards the language behaviour and language features of some candidates as 'non-standard' as well as the implicit and explicit association of candidates with the category 'second-language speaker', both of which are established by the norms and deviances with respect to language behaviour and language membership. This was found in the checking of the candidate's understanding, in the suggestion that the candidate meet and talk with Danes and in the assumed link between being from Iran, or simply another country, and having to learn Danish. In all cases, the language of the candidate is oriented to as deviant and as something that potentially presents a barrier in the internship interview and the internship to follow.

To sum up, a social relation of power is in all categorizations established between the participants in which the 'Danishness' of some of the participants and the 'otherness' of the candidate involves an uneven distribution of knowledge, rights and status. In Chapter 4, such relations of power were manifested in relation to a negotiation of the rule-governed Colombian kindergarten system compared to the norm-governed Danish one and in the employer's characterization of a specific system of values and practices related to producing and selling crops at a Danish orchard. In Chapter 5, it was reflected in the positive valorization of speaking Danish well, in the encouragements made to meet Danes who speak Danish and in the normative suggestions and prescriptions made regarding the language behaviour of the candidate in her private home. In Chapter 6, it was identified in the negotiation of 'Muslim' practices and values in relation to 'Danish ways', where the former was established as problematic or incompatible with the latter. These examples in various ways show the establishment of a system of relations between normative categories and practices versus deviant categories and practices; the candidate is immediately associated with the latter, and the other participants are associated with the former.

The Interrelation of Categories

I have illustrated how categories and repertoires are fundamentally intertwined and related. From the three individual analytical chapters it was clear how negotiations of categories related to language involved negotiations of categories related to nationality, and categorizations related to religion involved categorizations related to nationality. This interrelatedness of various categories is a fundamental premise for processes of meaning and social organization that involve the temporary establishment, as well as the continual renegotiation and redefinition, of categories and actions. Recently, within Cultural Studies, and more specifically among critical feminist theorists, there has been a lot of discussion around the concept of *intersectionality*, which is useful to describe the interactional interrelatedness of categories. The concept has been used to highlight the intersection and intertwining of various social categories and processes of subjectification (Carbin & Tornhill, 2004; Lykke, 2003; Collins, 1998). It has primarily been employed to describe the crossings of social categories such as gender, race and class on a broader discursive, sociological and structural level. Moreover, it has been reworked on a post-structuralist and social constructionist basis to be used on a subject level to describe situational processes of identity (Staunæs, 2003). Similarly to this, the analysis in this book shows how the intersection of categories within an interaction can be described as a result of the participants negotiating, establishing and inquiring into the social and discursive order that is available to them as participants in a particular speech situation and a broader cultural and social context. The intersection of categories involved relates not only to the fact that orientations towards language involve orientations towards nationality and so forth, but also to the interrelation of institutional and non-institutional categories, or situational and transportable identities. This interrelation leads to a reinforcement of the gatekeeping effects in the sense that the interactional performance of situational identities, such as candidate or kindergarten teacher, is challenged by being oriented to as an 'other'. Gatekeeping, in other words, unfolds as migrants are systematically categorized in ways that limit their cultural performance by differentiating them from and subordinating them to majority-defined categories.

The interrelation of categories in sense-making practices has consequences for how individuals are able and expected to act and perform as members of particular categories. What I mean by this is that the association with certain categories facilitates or limits possible association with other categories. While the links between categories are in some cases naturalized to the extent that they are taken for granted, for instance, the link between the categories 'doctor' and 'educated', other links are more dilemmatic or controversial and yet equally meaningful and commonsensical. Examples of such links come to mind when we (honestly) consider our own assumptions and expectations about categories such as 'lawyer', 'bus driver' or 'nurse' and the way they are individually more or less likely to be associated to categories such as 'white', 'black', 'male', 'old', 'young' etc. The establishment and negotiation of not only categories, but also the organization of categories in relation to one another, reveal the culturally and contextually specific workings of ideology and power. The working of ideology in processes of language is not a new idea. It was formulated clearly long ago by thinkers such as Gramsci (1971) and Volosinov (1973) among others and it has since then been a central perspective within Linguistic Anthropology (Ahearn, 2012; Blommaert, 1999), Discourse Analysis (Fairclough, 2001; Blackledge, 2005; Wodak, 1989) and Discursive Psychology (Wetherell & Potter, 1992; Billig, 1991) and has more recently even been addressed by researchers within Conversation Analysis (Saft & Ohara, 2003; Speer, 2005). However, there has been a tendency to either emphasize how language practice is shaped by language ideologies or how the construction and negotiation of particular categories, such as race or gender, are enabled and limited by ideologies. This book, on the other hand, proposes the need to investigate how ideologies play a central role in establishing hierarchical and asymmetric relations between interlocutors in interaction on account of the way they shape ideas, conceptualizations and expectations of categories and individuals. In other words, I suggest that the workings of ideology in processes of categorization constitute the main dynamic of gatekeeping processes. While language ideologies are a central part of this,

this book shows that the real power of categories and ideologies lies in the interrelation of language ideologies and other ideologies related to, for example, culture, nationality, religion, migration, welfare state etc. When investigating how ideas and expectations about categories, memberships and non-memberships manifest themselves in interaction, we illuminate how such ideas and expectations establish boundaries and barriers for the 'being' and 'doing' of individuals.

The Reproduction of Difference and Exclusion

The gatekeeping processes found in the internship interview are especially informed by meanings and common-sense understandings related to nationality, language and religion, and more broadly by various positions related to immigration and integration. These are manifested in the normative claims made by the employers and employees and in the expectation or demand of certain behaviours such as knowing how to dance, speaking Danish at home or cutting pork. What is being negotiated and evaluated is the behaviour of the candidate not merely as an interviewee or a future intern, but also as a migrant, a foreigner and a second-language speaker in general.

The processes of gatekeeping that reveal themselves in the internship interview have repercussions and implications beyond the context of the speech situation in the sense that they reflect and inform gatekeeping processes in other contexts and in society more broadly speaking. If we take it that the assumptions, categorizations and social relations of power manifested in the internship interview represent and are informed by common sense within a Danish context, then this implies a more widespread conceptualization of a discrepancy between the category 'Danish' and categories such as 'second-language speaker' and 'Muslim' in Denmark. The more far-reaching consequences of processes of 'othering' related to migrants in Denmark have been witnessed in studies of other job-related gatekeeping encounters as well, for example Marta Kirilova's (2013) and Dennis Day's (1998, 1999) studies of workplace interactions. As described previously in Chapter 4, Day refers to such 'othering' processes as 'ethnification' (1998). He defines this as 'processes through which people distinguish an individual or collection of individuals as a member or members respectively of an ethnic group'. While Day describes how ascriptions to specific ethnic groups, such as Pakistani or Swedes, present a problem for the person being categorized, I would argue that any systematic categorization of a person in relation to one particular membership category, in place of other categories, is problematic in the sense that it can potentially restrict processes of meaning and categorization, as well as a wide range of possible interactional developments.

The analysis provided in this book of the internship interviews discloses the gatekeeping effect of such systematic foregrounding of some category memberships over others. People can be ascribed to various different categories in various different contexts, and by foregrounding and orienting to certain categories, behaviours or meanings others are backgrounded and silenced. While all interactions, including the internship interviews, offer many possibilities of categorization in relation to the age, the gender, the hair colour, the occupation and the educational background of the participants, the categorizations made reveal patterns in the foregrounding of some categories and the backgrounding of others. Such patterns should be investigated and questioned, since they inform and reveal the structures of meaning and common sense that constitute our membership knowledge and in this way potentially constitute a barrier for alternative categorizations and meanings. Although the selection of categories and the organization of them in relation to other categories is informed by individuals' membership knowledge and the common sense of a given time and place, such common sense is, as described in Chapter 3, controversial and thereby offers the possibility of alternative categorizations and meanings. As Billig describes, common sense contains the seeds for change (Billig, 1991).

Can Categories and Inequalities be Challenged?

What has been stated about the processes of gatekeeping in internship interviews seems to imply that gatekeeping is a simple process of category attribution in which the candidate is passively associated with a particular category by the other participants, especially by the employer and the employee. This is, however, not the case. Gatekeeping is not an individual act, but a joint co-construction of a system of relations between categories which involves the production and reproduction of social relations of power. Membership categories and the development of interactions are negotiated and co-constructed, but it is the participation framework that grants certain rights to the employer, the gatekeeper, with respect to initiating and closing topics, controlling the development of the interaction and making decisions about the internship. Although these rights are also co-constructed, they affect the negotiation of membership categories and the topical development.

As my analysis has shown, processes of gatekeeping can be challenged and in some cases the candidate ends up being associated with a category that is established as less different from the 'Danish' category than first assumed. This was the case in Extract 22 (Liquor and pork), Extract 10 (Colombia) and Extract 21 (The scarf). In all of the examples, the job consultant and the candidate managed to renegotiate the assumptions and categorizations of the employers and employees. In Extract 12 (Danish), these assumptions and categorizations were, however, left unchallenged and not negotiated by the candidate. It was furthermore evident in relation to the orientations towards language, such as in Extracts 8, 9 and 38, where the presumptions of the employers and employees about the language proficiency and the language behaviour of the candidates were challenged by the candidate as well as the job consultants.

The result of these negotiations of and challenges to the categorizations made by the employers and employees is fortunately a more nuanced and complex axis of differentiation between the categories 'Danish culture' and 'other cultures,' or between 'Danish speaker' and 'non-Danish speaker'. This involved the establishment of temporary liminal positions for the candidates, who are momentarily attributed with actions, practices and values similar to, although not equal to, those associated with the normative 'Danish culture'. This was clear in Extract 22 (Liquor and pork), Extract 10 (Colombia) and Extract 21 (Scarf), where the negotiation of the categories 'Colombia' and 'Muslim' in comparison to 'Danish' created a way of acting and behaving for the candidate within the realms of the attributed category membership that was considered compatible with 'Danish' ways. It was furthermore clear in Extract 8 (So you both have to learn Danish) that the suggested categorization of IN as 'second-language learner' was negotiated and changed to 'second-language speaker'. With this, the processes of gatekeeping in the internship interviews involved not only the distinction of 'Danishness' from 'otherness', but also the establishment of a scale of varying degrees of 'otherness' where some candidates were established as more sensible and compatible with 'Danish ways' than others.

The Institutional Reinforcement of Asymmetry

As suggested in the presentation of the broader context of the internship interview, one might argue that the continual orientation towards the 'otherness' and 'non-Danishness' of the internship candidates with respect to nationality, language and religion is related to the establishment and context of the speech situation. Although it was not possible to systematically examine the processes of planning and establishing the internship interviews that preceded them, it is likely that this process influenced the participants' mutual expectations to the speech situation. The internship candidates were all, except for one, participants in job-counselling programmes that focused on people who were born abroad and spoke Danish as a second language, but the criteria of referral to these programmes was neither clearly nor unanimously defined as related to the nationality, language or religion of the participants. Rather, what seemed to explain the referral of the internship candidates to these specific job-counselling programmes was the general and underlying assumption that being a migrant or a refugee naturally implied certain difficulties in getting a job – an assumption that is arguably supported by Danish statistics (see Chapter 1).

This referral of the candidates to the specific job-counselling programmes for migrants, as well as the assumptions behind this referral, could in one way be said to have worked to the advantage of the candidates in the sense that it has provided them with an opportunity to enter the Danish labour market. On the other hand, this referral has consequences for the ways in which the migrant is understood and treated throughout the job counselling, the interview and potentially the subsequent internship. In other words, what happens when the categories that are used to provide a special opportunity or grant a particular service simultaneously work to maintain a migrant's subordinate position in relation to other categories and individuals within society? The 'othering' which forms the premise of the counselling can be seen to manifest in the arrangement and development of the speech situation and in the categorization processes within the interaction as we have seen in the examples analyzed in this book. The internship interview, or more broadly speaking the job counselling programmes, that the candidates participate in are part of an initiative aimed at migrants for the sake of securing them a place within the labour market, and yet the institutional categorization of them as a particular target group with particular challenges has repercussions for the way they are being oriented to in the internship interview and potentially also the internship. This problematic is accentuated or reinforced by the fact that many of these internships never lead directly to paid employment.

Consider Extract 21 (Scarf), where the woman wearing a hijab is associated with the category Muslim and as a result is dissociated from the category 'Danish' and Danish practices and norms. One might argue that this orientation towards the 'otherness' of the woman is 'commonsensical' within the context of the speech situation since one of the goals of this interaction is to establish whether the internship candidate is capable of and suitable for an internship, and the issue of wearing a scarf might be a potential problem in this regard. One might also argue that the orientation towards the 'otherness' of the woman is commonsensical irrespective of any specific work-related problems with the scarf, because the scarf constitutes a religious symbol that displays an affiliation with a religious ideology that is different from Danish 'ways', practices and norms. These are the two logics of differentiation (re)presented by the employer in this specific example.

The purpose of this book is not to contest or evaluate the common sense expressed by the participants but to illuminate and describe what is and is not formulated and accepted as commonsensical within a given cultural, institutional and social context, as well as to address the hierarchization and power asymmetry involved in particular categorizations. The underlying hope and ambition has been to inspire and encourage reflection on the implications of such ideological status quo for the social organization and distribution of power in society. Is the logic of differentiation and dissociation between Muslims and Danes necessarily commonsensical, and what are its implications for the social organization and social distribution of power, rights and possibilities between the members of such categories? What does it say about Danish society and the Danish labour market that this logic of differentiation is formulated and accepted as commonsensical? How is the goal of integration through employment to be met if a large proportion of the people who are expected to integrate are Muslims and thereby commensensically considered incompatible with Danish work-related practices and norms? These questions have not been addressed explicitly in this book but they implicitly and forcefully present themselves from the findings I have presented and will hopefully inspire further discussion and reflection.

The internship interviews studied in this book provide a good example of some of the newly emerging types of encounters that seek to handle the challenges of multilingual superdiverse societies (Blommaert, 2013). The hybridity and complexity of this speech situation reveal the ambiguities related to not only the distribution of institutionally defined roles and rights but also to appropriate and legitimate handling of difference and 'otherness'. The amount of work that the employers in the internship interview put into making sense of the candidate in a way that formulates their expectations and concerns about difference in an appropriate and legitimate way reveals the dilemmas that hierarchized diversity creates. The internship interview as such, and not least the behaviour of the participants with respect to the topicalization of difference, can in this way be seen as a manifestation of the political and public debates about integration, Muslims, migration and not least of the surges of political correctness in relation to such issues.

While the implications of special counselling programmes and internships that are offered to migrants cannot be easily determined, it is important to stress that they cannot, and should not, be measured merely in terms of their success or failure in getting an internship nor in the success or failure in getting a job. If we accept the fact that the gatekeeping of migrants in employment processes, and elsewhere for that matter, consist in their subordination to a majority defined 'otherness', then passing 'through the gates' involves the ability to perform this 'otherness' in a way which accommodates the expectations and demands of a given workplace or institutional encounter. While such passing may result in the migrant being successful in terms of getting the job it also results in a reproduction of the ideologies and the hierarchization of categories that established the 'gates' in the first place. While the migrants may, in other words, benefit from and even appreciate how being accepted as an intern allows them to improve their language skills or to gain knowledge of the Danish labour market, the special job counselling programmes or the internship interviews do not help them in challenging the commonsensical and marginalizing views of them as cultural 'others' in the labour market and Danish society as a whole. As stated in the quote by Sara Ahmed in the beginning of this chapter: 'We can get stuck *in* institutions by being stuck *to* a category. That is not to say that we cannot, or do not, value the work of these categories. But we can be constrained even by the categories we love.' The proposition with which I wish to leave you at the end of this book does not entail viewing internships for migrants as a bad idea or employers and job consultants as ill-willed in their ways of trying to manage and conceptualize difference. Rather, I propose that in order for migrants to get 'unstuck', in institutional as well as non-institutional contexts and encounters, there is a need for researchers and other interactants alike to be more aware and critical of how the workings of ideology and common sense in processes of categorization contribute to upholding a cultural illusion of similarity and homogeneity where difference appears as fundamentally problematic.

8 Interactional Pitfalls and Pointers

The findings presented in this book with respect to gatekeeping processes involved in orientations toward nationality, language and religion should not be regarded as merely a deconstructive criticism of the way professionals deal with diversity in relation to employment. All of the employers, job consultants and employees were working towards the goal improving the job situation of the migrants and all were well-meaning and cooperative in their encounters with the migrants. The findings can however be used to shed light on some of the shared assumptions and ideologies that influence how professionals such as employers and job consultants interpret the migrants practices, experiences, attitudes and background. An increased knowledge of these assumptions, stereotypes and expectations that influence not only the professional's but also any layman's way of approaching and responding to diversity can enable a more nuanced and reflexive encounter with the complexities of reality. Furthermore, and perhaps more importantly, the findings presented provide insight into the consequences of addressing and topicalizing these assumptions in particular ways.

There is no doubt that when an employer is faced with a possible future intern or employee that they consider to have potential barriers with respect to nationality (or cultural 'ways'), language or religion, they need to address such concerns whether they are based on presumptions, experience or both. This book shows examples of how such concerns, presumptions and experiences are dealt with and addressed in real life and how this influences the interactional flow and development in particular ways. Hopefully, and most likely, the examples given illustrate interactional strategies and practices that are recognizable or common sense (for better or for worse) to most readers, professionals and laymen alike. And hopefully the book has given indications as to how we might address common-sense concerns and presumptions related to diversity in somewhat alternative ways and hereby avoid some of the negative consequences. The final chapter of this book will be dedicated to assisting this self-reflexive process among professionals and laymen alike and will apply the findings already presented to some preliminary suggestions of interactional pitfalls and pointers.

Raising the Issue of Language

Potential lack of understanding or misunderstanding is obviously something of concern to participants in any interaction and it needs to be addressed and resolved preferably as soon as the suspicion arises. In institutional interaction involving evaluation such as the internship it is of an even bigger concern to professionals, since they need to know that they are being understood and that the candidates will be able to undertake the tasks required as part of the internship.

In Chapter 5 I identified various ways of addressing this issue, some of which were highly embedded in the topical development and others that were not at all or less so. When we look at the responses to these topicalizations of language and their interactional consequences, some preliminary conclusions can be drawn that might be useful to professionals or others navigating in diverse language settings.

First of all, it was shown in Chapter 5 how in orientations towards language, the level of disruption and the response from the candidate were related to (a) the way that the question of understanding was raised and (b) the extent to which the questioning was embedded within the ongoing topical development.

To begin with the latter, I found that the more embedded the questions about understanding are, the less disruption they cause. This may seem a banal observation but it is most probably not something that the interactants consider when they find themselves wondering about the candidates' level of understanding and language proficiency generally. In any case, it raises a couple of things to consider when a person wants to address the issue of language while having to strike a suitable balance between acquiring the needed information and avoiding some of the negative consequences of doing so:

• While there might be an advantage in minimizing the directness of the inquiries about understanding, it is necessary to bear in mind that completely embedded questions might not resolve the issue of language at all since they do not invite a direct response.

• So, if you are unsure of whether the person understands you and want a clear response, you need to ask in a non-embedded manner, thereby giving the other person an explicit request for confirmation or response and allowing them the chance to unfold or express their level of understanding.

• If you simply wish to check that the other person is following what you are saying, language differences or not, but are not so much in doubt that you wish to jeopardize the ongoing flow, you can ask in a more embedded manner. This way, you avoid disrupting the direction and flow of the interaction and still provide a possibility for the other person to object or request an elaboration or clarification.

• If you choose to topicalize language proficiency or language background in a non-embedded manner, bear in mind that it will disrupt the topical flow of the interaction, sidetracking it from whatever other topics and issues were being currently discussed. Furthermore it will emphasize the other person's foreignness and will highlight as well as increase their inferior position in what is already an asymmetric relationship to majority members within as well as beyond the context of the interaction.

With respect to how the question about understanding is phrased, there are a couple of lessons to be learned from the findings in Chapter 7 as well. As shown, there are different ways of asking whether a person understands, some more specifically addressing assumed language difficulties than others. Such specification can be used strategically to different ends:

• The most general and non-specific way of formatting the question is 'forstår du?' which in English would correspond to 'do you understand?' or more likely 'do you see?' or simply 'you see?' or 'you know?' This format is also the one that is most easily embedded within the ongoing topical flow of an interaction since it does not necessarily invite an explicit or elaborate response from the other participants. It can therefore be met with a minimal acknowledgement token such as 'mm' or 'yes', hereby allowing the speaker to continue his or her turn and not least allowing the ongoing topic to continue.

• The general formatting of this question has another property that can be regarded as an advantage or a disadvantage depending on the intention of the speaker. I am thinking here of the inherent ambiguity of the question with respect to whether it addresses a possible language difficulty or merely a potential lack of clarity in the speaker's point or formulation. If a person wishes to check the understanding of the non-native speaker in a way that is the least obtrusive as possible, the general formatting allows the other person a chance to respond minimally without 'losing face'. In other words, it allows for checking potential language difficulties in a format that does not reveal that this is in fact what is being done and that avoids an explicit orientation towards the other as a non-native speaker. As stated earlier, the downside of this is that it also allows for potential misunderstandings to go on without being actually addressed. Then again, this unfortunately is an inherent condition of social interaction as shown by many theorists within the field of intercultural communication or interactional sociolinguistics. If the intention of the speaker is exactly this, namely an explicit clarification of potential language difficulties, then the general formatting might be at loss and might not be the optimal choice.

- The alternative formatting which was described and analyzed in Chapter 5 was the more specified question 'Forstår du hvad jeg siger?' or in English 'Do you understand what I am saying?' This question is in a different way pointing to the specific wording of the speaker or to the language code, so to speak. This formatting was found to be interpreted and responded to by the other participants as specifically addressing potential language difficulties or problems of understanding the Danish language. If the professional is experiencing doubt about whether the level of language proficiency of the other speaker is sufficient for continuing the ongoing interaction in Danish or perhaps for undertaking the internship/job applied for, then this question is a good option. It quite explicitly invites a specific account of the other person's language abilities or level of understanding and it does so in a way that does not easily allow the interaction to go on before the question has been answered and dealt with.

- The downside of using this formatting is that it is very direct and not possible to embed in the ongoing topical development. Furthermore it creates a potentially awkward situation in which the non-nativeness or otherness of the other person is emphasized with the resulting increase in asymmetry between the participants. That considered, however, it has the advantage of giving the other person a proper chance to explicitly reject the assumed language problem, as we saw in Extract 29 (Do you understand what I'm saying?).

Raising the Issue of Cultural Difference Based on Nationality

As shown in Chapter 4, the way professionals interpret and evaluate the candidates' experiences, competences and abilities draws on interpretative repertoires involving national stereotypes and the conceptual linking of nationality or culture. This is nothing particular to the specific professionals in question but is rather a reflection of how professionals and laymen alike use a shared common sense as a resource in sensemaking practices when encountering and evaluating strangers that are different from themselves. While we, as argued earlier, need to be critical and cautious of such assumptions and stereotypes, we also need to accept them as sensemaking tools and reflect on how such tools can be used in the best way possible. We need, in other words, to use the insights gained from studying categorizations of nationality for developing strategies of addressing the assumptions they involve and making them objects of negotiation rather than conceptual barriers. Professionals working with people of diverse national or ethnic origin need guidelines on how to raise concerns about cultural difference in constructive ways rather than implicitly and unknowingly applying national stereotypes and assumptions about cultural differences in their interpretation, categorization and evaluation of other people's practices. This will allow the negotiation of such assumptions which will ensure that the concerns which professionals might have are properly addressed. The central findings from Chapter 4 are in other words: (a) professionals draw on assumptions and stereotypes about national/cultural difference when they interpret and evaluate candidates' experience and competences; and (b) such assumptions about national/cultural differences should be raised explicitly rather than be applied implicitly since they can otherwise lead to the rejection or acceptance of candidates based on faulty premises.

As stated it is not extraordinary that professionals draw on stereotypes and assumptions about national/cultural difference but given their power and responsibility as gatekeepers there is a need to be aware of how such assumptions play into evaluative processes and what their consequences are.

- Assumptions that are implicitly applied or raised as part of the ongoing discussion about professional experience or educational background are difficult for the candidate to negotiate or object to. We saw this in Extract 10 (Colombia) and Extract 12 (Danish) where the employers were merely stating assumptions about differences between Danish work-practices and work-practices in the home country of the candidate. This made it difficult for the candidate to engage in dialogue or negotiation of such assumptions without overtly refuting or challenging the knowledge of the professional. This is obviously not an easy task within an asymmetric situation such as an interview.
- Besides making assumptions explicit and giving the other a chance to challenge them, professionals also need to reflect on and challenge these themselves. As we saw clearly from the Colombia example, people's experiences, practices, attitudes and 'ways' are as much a product of their professional, educational and social background as they are reflections

of a particular national or cultural membership. Concerns and inquiries about the professional or social compatibility of the other person with a particular workplace or function should consider and inquire into this complex history of practice rather than assume that nationality overshadows all.

- Assumptions about national/cultural background are often as much barriers in themselves as they are barriers in reality if they are not raised and laid out for negotiation or questioning. It is important to remember in relation to this that it is not only professionals but also candidates who draw on national/cultural assumptions about the other as we saw from Extract 14 (The first encounter) and Extract 13 (A Danish workplace). As unquestioned fictions, both stand equally in the way of concrete discussions about the reality of the future internship. There is however a noticeable difference in the assumptions of the Danish professionals and the migrant candidates:
  - o Candidates tend to draw on positive assumptions and stereotypes about Danes and professionals tend to draw on negative assumptions and stereotypes about 'the other'. This again was very clear from Extract 10 (Colombia), Extract 14 (The first encounter) and Extract 11 (Tradition).
  - o The assumptions about national/cultural difference formulated by the professionals are often related to a positive characterization of the Danish ways and a negative characterization of the nationality or culture of the 'other', namely the candidate. Since the candidate represents this otherness, the negative characterization works to their disadvantage and becomes a barrier for presenting themselves in a positive way.

Most of these problems pointed out above can be solved by the latter point, namely (b) that assumptions and stereotypes used as implicit resources by professionals and candidates alike should be raised as explicit objects of negotiation. A few pointers can be derived from chapter four with respect to how this can be done in the best way possible:

- When assumptions are raised they should be raised as specifically and explicitly as possible in order for the other person to respond to, ratify or negotiate them.
- Rather than raising overall and general stereotypes and assumptions about national differences, the professional should translate their concerns into concrete questions related to the specific concerns they may have. We saw in Extract 10 (Colombia) how the overall and abstract

formulation of difference initiated by the employer was ambiguous and confusing and how it was the concrete descriptions of kindergarten practices that revealed the similarity between the two systems.

- When assumptions about particular national stereotypes or presumed cultural barriers are raised, professionals should be aware that the delicacy and sensitivity of such issues can easily result in hypersensitive behaviour from the professional. We saw this in Extract 10 (Colombia), and also in Chapter 6, Extract 21 (The scarf) and Extract 22 (Liquor and pork), where the employers were accounting, hesitating and hedging their utterances. While this is a perfectly ordinary way of coping with delicate or potentially problematic issues, it potentially prolongs and obscures issues that could have been quickly solved. Furthermore it seems to make it more difficult for the other person to engage with the issues being addressed in a concrete and efficient manner. In short:

  - Raising assumptions about national/cultural differences in a respectful way and laying them out for negotiation and challenge is much less of a problem than implicitly using them as a basis for interpretation and evaluation. However this does not mean that it does not have consequences for the interaction and the distribution of power, rights and knowledge between the participants.

  - Raising the issue of national/cultural difference does create social distance between the participants because it accentuates the otherness of the candidates.

  - While this is not something that can be avoided professionals can ensure that candidates are presented with national/cultural assumptions in an explicit and are given the opportunity to negotiate and challenge these by their own first-hand knowledge and experiences.

Raising Concerns about Religious Conflicts, Practices and Limitations

Engaging with the issue of religion, or rather religious differences, is a difficult and delicate task since it constitutes an imposition on what most people consider to be individual rights of faith and involves addressing practices and preferences that to many are private and personal. Furthermore religion has been the subject of discussion and debate politically and publically and for this reason it is a controversial and delicate matter. Since Denmark is officially Christian and many areas of public and institutional practices in Denmark are regulated by the Christian calendar, religious issues discussed most often involve non-Christian practices and more specifically Muslim practices. While the complex reasons for this shall remain unaddressed here, it is a reality that particular Muslim practices have been considered and discussed publically as conflicting with 'Danish ways' and this is obviously a concern to employers who either experience or anticipate such conflicts. Given that this is the reality which is manifested in the orientations towards religion found in the internship interviews, a few findings and suggestions can be derived from the previous analysis with respect to how such anticipated or experienced concerns could be addressed in ways that minimize the imposition and disruption.

While it is perfectly understandable and sympathetic that employers orient to the delicacy of raising the issue of religion by accounting for and legitimizing their imposition and demands, it is clear from the analysis in Chapter 6 that this can have a counterproductive effect. We saw in the first two examples how the practical issue of wearing a scarf and not buying alcohol and pork was prolonged much beyond the response and solution provided by the candidate. This contributed to reinforcing rather than diminishing the awkwardness of the situation and prolonged the defensive role of the candidate. Employers and job consultants should for this reason consider the following:

- Striking a proper balance between on the one hand showing politeness and respect and on the other solving the concrete issue as efficiently and swiftly as possible.
- The flexibility and readiness displayed by candidates with respect to adapting to the demands of the workplace suggests that while religious practices of Muslims may have become objects of public and political controversy they may in reality present more of a conceptual than an actual problem for employers and candidates alike.
- Focusing on presenting the rules and demands of the workplace rather than presenting assumptions about possible conflicts of religious practices and work-practices. As found in Extract 23 (A religious institution), this allows the candidate to respond without being immediately placed in a defensive position while simultaneously minimizing the imposition and delicacy of problematizing the religiousness of the candidate.
- Reflecting on assumptions of religious conflict and addressing them directly rather than indirectly in the form of accounting. This provides a

chance for the candidate to negotiate and potentially dismiss or confirm the assumptions more efficiently.
* While humour can be a tempting way of dealing with delicacy and can, as shown in Extract 23 (A religious institution) help to establish a friendly, casual tone, it can also contribute to prolonging and reinforcing an awkward situation. We saw this in Extract 22 (Liquor and pork).

The Role of the Job Consultants

There are various ways in which the job consultants can work as advocates for the candidate and work to alleviate, mediate or mitigate a potentially difficult situation for the candidate. They represent an authority in the interactions with respect to their knowledge of and experience with the candidates and their experiences with previous internships.

* They can provide formulations that clarify or support the utterances of the candidates and hereby work as pre-closings (i.e. Do you understand?, The scarf, Danish).
* They can check to make sure that the candidate is following what is going on in the interaction, not only with respect to language difficulty but also with respect to complexities and specificities of the subject matter. This however has the potential negative side-effect of bringing attention to problems of understanding that might not be there and increasing the asymmetry of the situation. The formatting of such checking should be done in a way that is as embedded as possible and permits ambiguity of whether the assumed problem is related to the subject raised or the language as such (see Extract 16, Do you understand?). In this way the candidate is allowed an opportunity to request clarification without necessarily making the category of second-language speaker relevant.
* They can speak on behalf of the candidate on matters that are perhaps difficult to explain or deal with general procedures regarding the internship. The problem with this strategy is, however, that it tends to pacify the intern and thereby increase the asymmetry between the participants.
* Even though the job consultant might successfully apply some of the various ways in which they can function as advocates for the candidates, in the end the effectiveness of these is constrained by the participation

framework (i.e. Extract 21, The scarf; Extract 8, So you both have to learn Danish?).

• The contributions of the job consultants can at times be counterproductive in that they prolong particular topics that should perhaps rather be solved and closed as quickly as possible (i.e. Extract 21, The scarf; Extract 22, Liquor and pork).

Language in Interaction as a Method for Change

It is important to end this chapter and the book as a whole by emphasizing that the analytical findings and not least the interactional suggestions made are preliminary in two senses of the word.

First of all the analysis deals with institutional and interactional changes that are constantly changing and adjusting to the challenges of the job market, the candidates and the counsellors; many things may have changed and will continue to change in the future. It is recognized that job counsellors, employers and candidates are all different and that their practices, experiences and meanings may differ from those described here. However, it is my hope and expectation that practitioners and laymen alike will be able to recognize and make use of some of the findings and suggestions made in this chapter and the book as a whole.

Second, I use the word preliminary to humbly recognize the fact that proposing interactional strategies can never imply guaranteeing a particular outcome. Even if the findings and suggestions seem useful to some readers, they should only be considered supplementary input to the individual interactional and interpretative toolboxes we each have at our disposal. While they can in this way not be used as a recipe for successful multilingual interactions, whatever that is, it is my hope that they can be used as a basis for a self-reflexive discussion amongst practitioners who find that they meet similar challenges in their daily work. For laymen who simply have an interest in issues related to migration and interculturality they can hopefully contribute to a critical interactional awareness – that is, an increased sensitivity towards our own contribution to sensemaking processes and a critical awareness of the interpretative frameworks that inform such processes.

I have emphasized throughout this book how common sense and ideology are resources that we employ unconsciously and often unwillingly because they are available to us on account of our individual histories of socialization and our contextual embedding, and the same obviously goes for our interactional resources. While it is possible to reflect on, and analyze, the interactional and interpretative resources applied in a particular speech situation and the consequences of these, it is far more difficult to change habitual ways of action and conceptualization. This is not to say, however, that there is nothing to gain from trying or that we are all trapped in our culturally socialized selves. The notion of identity, culture and ideology presented in this book is fundamentally social-constructionist in its emphasis on how our actions and our identities are simultaneously constitutive of and constituted in processes of language and culture. What this means is that we are able to negotiate and challenge not only our structured ways of conceptualizing ourselves and others but also our structured ways of applying linguistic and interactional resources. If we were not able to reflect on and adapt our ways of speaking and interacting with others we would be truly doomed as social beings in a dynamic and heterogeneous social reality. We do this all the time as we engage with strangers in new contexts and as we engage with a variety of different contexts every day.

The purpose of the suggestions and pointers above is in other words not to dictate a particular form of behaviour and promise a particular outcome – the complexity of interaction and the specificity of every encounter is far too great. Rather, the purpose is to facilitate a reflexive process on interactional resources and interactional outcomes, which is based on empirical findings. Others before me have already taken important steps in this direction and made similar arguments. A central contribution within the field described previously as gatekeeping studies is the work of Gumperz, Roberts and Jupp (Gumperz *et al.*, 1979) who developed training material on cross-cultural job interviews. This work has had enormous implications for role-play-based methods of second-language teaching (Sniad, 2007). Another important source of inspiration for the ideas presented in this chapter is Norman Fairclough's reflections on critical language awareness in education (Fairclough, 1995), where he argues that critical language awareness should not be about determining appropriate from non-appropriate language use. Rather, the purpose and potential of critical language awareness is to reflexively address the ideological consequences of the way we use language – that is, how language use contributes to either reproducing or challenging oppressive structures of meaning and unequal relations of power between people and groups. An interactional approach to language awareness is the very recent development of the method CARM (Conversation Analytic Role-play Method) by conversation analyst Elizabeth Stokoe, who, on the basis of analyzing phone calls to a mediation service, has developed training material based on authentic interactions that can be used to overcome and prevent some of the 'problems and roadblocks of institutional interaction' (Stokoe, 2014). While the ambition behind this method is less emancipatory and more practical in its emphasis on generating reflection and discussion of how interactants can be more or less efficient in 'getting the job done', the methodological anchoring of this method in conversation analysis and membership categorization analysis is very similar to this book. What is illuminated by CARM is the potential of enriching and improving role-play methods to language teaching and training in general by using authentic recordings and empirical findings rather than simulated reconstructions to create awareness and change.

Finally, I would like to finish this book by emphasizing the central idea, which I find recurrent in all of these previous attempts to address the potential of language awareness and which inspired me to write this chapter and in fact this whole book. Namely the notion that if we accept that social reality, social identity and social relations are constituted in and through our use of language in interaction with others (Gergen, 2001, 1991, 1994), then awareness of the nature of this process and the nature of what is produced from it provides the seeds for change. The emancipatory force of language in this way lies in the potential to liberate us from fixated conceptualizations of a complex reality and not least from stagnated and inflexible ways of handling difference, change and heterogeneity.

Appendix 1: Legal Extracts

Legal Extract 1: The Integration Act

Chapter 4

The Introduction Programme

§ 23. The local council may offer activation to aliens who qualify for the introduction allowance pursuant to Chapter 5. The activation period is planned in accordance with the alien's individual activity plan, cf. § 19.

Stk.2. The activation period may include one or more of the following types of activities:

(1) Short guidance and clarification programmes on work- and education options and with access to try occupational interests

(2) Internship, including individual job-training with private and public employers pursuant to §§ 22 and 24 in the Act on Active Employment Measures.

(3) Specifically adapted educational activities

(4) Specifically adapted guidance and internship programmes, upgrading courses or other similar programmes combining work and education.

(5) Voluntary and unpaid activities based on the alien's own wishes; the local council shall assess the activities in terms of their societal relevance, or educational and work-related relevance for the individual.

(6) Adult or supplementary education in accordance with the alien's own wishes, included in the regulations on educational programmes to which educational support and educational leave can be granted, determined by the Minister for Employment pursuant to § 27, stk. 1, in the Act on Active Labour Market Policy and § 3, stk. 2, in the Act on Leave.

Source: *Lov om integration af udlændinge i Danmark (Integrationslov)* (1998) Chapter 4, § 23 (author's translation).

Legal Extract 1: Lov om integration af udlændinge i Danmark

Kapitel 4

Introduktionsprogrammemet

§ 23. Udlændinge, der i medfør af kapitel 5 er berettiget til introduktionsydelse, skal af kommunalbestyrelsen tilbydes aktivering. Aktiveringen tilrettelægges i overensstemmelse med den enkelte udlændings handlingsplan, jf. § 19.

Stk. 2. Aktivering kan omfatte en eller flere af følgende typer aktiviteter:

(1) Kortvarige vejlednings- og introduktionsprogrammemer med vejledning om arbejds- og uddannelsesmuligheder og med adgang til at afprøve beskæftigelsesønsker.

(2) Virksomhedspraktik, herunder individuel jobtræning, jf. §§ 22 og 24 i lov om en aktiv arbejdsmarkedspolitik, hos private og offentlige arbejdsgivere.

(3) Særligt tilrettelagte uddannelsesaktiviteter.

(4) Særligt tilrettelagte aktiverende forløb i form af vejlednings- og praktikforløb, erhvervsmodnende kurser eller andre tilsvarende forløb med en kombination af arbejde og uddannelse.

(5) Frivillige og ulønnede aktiviteter efter udlændingens eget ønske, som kommunalbestyrelsen anser for at have samfundsmæssig betydning eller betydning for den pågældendes uddannelses- eller arbejdsmæssige situation.

(6) Voksen- eller efteruddannelse efter udlændingens eget ønske, som er omfattet af de regler om uddannelser, hvortil der kan opnås uddannelsesgodtgørelse og orlov til uddannelse (positivlisten), som arbejdsministeren fastsætter i medfør af § 27, stk. 1, i lov om en aktiv arbejdsmarkedspolitik og § 3, stk. 2, i lov om orlov.

Source: *Lov om integration af udlændinge i Danmark (Integrationslov* (1998) Chapter 4, § 23.

Legal Extract 2: Act on Active Employment Measures

Chapter 11

Internship

§ 42 The local council may offer an internship with a public or private enterprise to aliens who need clarification of their occupational goals, or who face difficulties in finding employment on ordinary pay and working conditions, or employment with a wage supplement, owing to lack of professional, linguistic or social competencies.

Stk. 2. Persons, included by § 2, nr. 7, who receive unemployment support or special allowances pursuant to §§ 74 and 74 in the Active Social Policy Act can be offered an internship with the intention of testing the person's availability for work pursuant to the Active Social Policy Act §§ 74 b, 74 c, 74 g and 74 i.

Stk. 3. The offer is given with the intention of determining or upgrading the person's professional, social or linguistic competences as well as clarifying the employment goals.

Source: *Lov om en aktiv beskæftigelsesindsats* (2003) Chapter 11, § 42.

Legal Extract 2: Lov om en aktiv beskæftigelsesindsats

Kapitel 11

Virksomhedspraktik

§ 42. Personer, der er omfattet af § 2, nr. 1-5, og som enten har behov for en afklaring af beskæftigelsesmål, eller som på grund af mangelfulde faglige, sproglige eller sociale kompetencer kun vanskeligt kan opnå beskæftigelse på normale løn- og arbejdsvilkår eller med løntilskud, kan få tilbud om virksomhedspraktik på en offentlig eller privat virksomhed.

Stk. 2. Personer, der er omfattet af § 2, nr. 7, og som modtager ledighedsydelse eller særlig ydelse efter §§ 74 og 74 i efter lov om aktiv socialpolitik, kan få tilbud om virksomhedspraktik med henblik på afprøvning af personens rådighed, jf. lov om aktiv socialpolitik §§ 74 b, 74 c, 74 g og 74 i.

Stk. 3. Tilbuddet gives med henblik på at afdække eller optræne personens faglige, sociale eller sproglige kompetencer samt at afklare beskæftigelsesmål.

Source: *Lov om en aktiv beskæftigelsesindsats* (2003) Chapter 11, § 42.

Legal Extract 3: Declaration of the Aliens Act

> (2) have held permanent employment or been self-employed here in this country during the last 3 years prior to the announcement of permanent residency,
> (3) have not received any other financial assistance under the terms of the Active Social Policy Act or the Integration Act than negligible single-payment grants that are not directly related to subsistence or payments that replace or are comparable to salary or pension, and welfare
> (4) have achieved a significant connection and relation to Danish society.

Source: *Bekendtgørelse af Udlændingeloven* (2008) Chapter 1, § 11, Stk. 4.

Legal Extract 3: Bekendtgørelse af Udlændingeloven

> (2) i de sidste 3 år forud for meddelelsen af tidsubegrænset opholdstilladelse har været fast tilknyttet arbejdsmarkedet som lønmodtager eller selvstændig erhvervsdrivende her i landet og må antages fortsat at være dette,
> (3) i de sidste 3 år forud for meddelelsen af tidsubegrænset opholdstilladelse ikke har modtaget anden hjælp efter lov om aktiv socialpolitik eller integrationsloven end hjælp bestående af enkeltstående ydelser af mindre beløbsmæssig størrelse, der ikke er direkte relateret til forsørgelse, eller ydelser, der må sidestilles med løn eller pension eller træder i stedet herfor, og
> (4) har opnået en væsentlig tilknytning til det danske samfund.

Source: *Bekendtgørelse af Udlændingeloven* (2008) Chapter 1, § 11, Stk. 4.

Legal Extract 4: Declaration of the Aliens Act

Stk. 9. Unless specific reasons speak against it, the grant of permanent residency is conditioned by the alien

(1) having completed the introduction programme pursuant to the Integration Act, or if that is not the case, has completed another comparable programme, cf. stk. 11,
(2) having completed specific activities pursuant to § 31 a in the Act on Active Employment Measures, i.e. stk. 11,
(3) having passed a Danish test approved by the Minister for Refugee, Immigration and Integration Affairs, cf. stk. 11, and
(4) not having due debts to the government, cf. stk. 11.

Source: *Bekendtgørelse af Udlændingeloven* (2008) Chapter 1, § 11, Stk. 9.

Legal Extract 4: Bekendtgørelse af Udlændingeloven

Stk. 9. Medmindre særlige grunde taler derimod, er meddelelse af tidsubegrænset opholdstilladelse betinget af, at udlændingen

(1) har gennemført et tilbudt introduktionsprogramme efter integrationsloven eller, hvis det ikke er tilfældet, har gennemført et andet forløb, der kan sidestilles hermed, jf. stk. 11,
(2) har gennemført fastlagte aktiviteter i henhold til § 31 a i lov om en aktiv beskæftigelsesindsats, jf. stk. 11,
(3) har bestået en af ministeren for flygtninge, indvandrere og integration godkendt danskprøve, jf. stk. 11, og
(4) ikke har forfalden gæld til det offentlige, jf. stk. 11.

Source: *Bekendtgørelse af Udlændingeloven* (2008) Chapter 1, § 11, Stk. 9.

Legal Extract 5: Act on Danish Courses for Adult Aliens

§ 1. The object of courses in Danish as a second language (Danish courses) is to assist adult aliens, on the basis of their individual backgrounds and integrational goals, in acquiring the necessary Danish language proficiency and knowledge of Danish culture and society so as to make them participating and contributory citizens on equal terms with other citizens of society.

Stk. 2. The Danish courses must assist adult aliens in acquiring skills in comprehending and using the Danish language and obtaining knowledge of it so as to enable them to get employment and support themselves.

Stk. 3. The Danish courses must also further adult aliens' active use of the Danish language and assist them in obtaining common skills and knowledge which are relevant in relation to working life and education and life as citizens of a democratic society.

Source: *Lov om danskuddannelse til voksne udlændinge m.fl.* (2003).

Legal Extract 5: Lov om Danskuddannelse til Voksne Udlændinge m.fl.

§ 1. Formålet med uddannelse i dansk som andetsprog (danskuddannelse) er at bidrage til, at voksne udlændinge med udgangspunkt i deres individuelle forudsætninger og integrationsmål opnår nødvendige dansksproglige kompetencer og viden om kultur- og samfundsforhold i Danmark, så de kan blive deltagende og ydende medborgere på lige fod med samfundets øvrige borgere.

Stk. 2. Danskuddannelse skal bidrage til, at voksne udlændinge så hurtigt som muligt efter at have fået opholdstilladelse i Danmark tilegner sig færdigheder i at forstå og anvende det danske sprog og opnå kendskab til det danske arbejdsmarked, så de herved får mulighed for at komme i beskæftigelse og bliver i stand til at forsørge sig selv.

Stk. 3. Danskuddannelse skal endvidere fremme voksne udlændinges aktive brug af det danske sprog samt bidrage til, at de opnår almene kundskaber og færdigheder, som er relevante i forhold til arbejde og uddannelse samt livet som medborger i et demokratisk samfund.

Source: *Lov om danskuddannelse til voksne udlændinge m.fl.* (2003).

Appendix 2: Transcription Notations[1]

(.)	Just noticeable pause or micro-pause (less than 0.2 seconds)
(2.6)	Pauses timed in seconds
[ja] ok	Square brackets aligned across adjacent lines denote overlapping talk
[nå]	Denotes overlapping talk
hh.	In-breath
hh	Out-breath
ja-	Dash denotes sharp cut-off
wha:t	Colon denotes extension or stretching of the preceding sound
(word)	Brackets around words denote a guess at what might have been said if unclear
ja=	Equal sign denotes that there is no discernible pause between two
=nå	speakers' turns or, if put between two sounds within a single speaker's turns, shows that they run together
word	Underlined sounds are stressed
WORD	Words or sounds in capitals are spoken in loud voice
owordo	Material between 'degree signs' is spoken in low voice
>word<	Inwards arrows show faster speech
<word>	Outwards arrows show slower speech
£word£	Material between pound signs are spoken in 'smile' voice
word?	Question mark denotes an upward 'question' intonation
word.	The full stop indicates a 'sentence-ending' intonation
word,	The comma denotes a 'continuing' trajectory that indicates that the person has more to say
↑word	Upwards arrow denotes a rising intonation

Appendix 3: Overview of Data

The table below presents an overview of the internship interviews recorded and supplies some basic information about the participants and the circumstances of each individual interview. More specifically, the table lists the *type* of interview, the *gender* and *country* of birth of the internship candidates, the *workplaces* involved and the different *job consultants* arranging and participating in the internship interviews.[2]

Table 3 Introductory interviews

Job programme	Gender	Country	Workplace	Consultant
MHT-consult	F	Colombia	School	1
Kofoeds Skole	F	Bosnia	Kindergarten	2
Væksthuset	M	Somalia	Orchard	3
Væksthuset	F	Morocco	Homeless project	3
Væksthuset	F	Iran	Residential home	4
Væksthuset	F	Afghanistan	Home help company	4

Table 4 Follow-up interviews

Væksthuset	F	Iraq	Kindergarten	5
UCI	F	Lebanon	Residential home	6
UCI	F	Turkey	Residential home	7
UCI	F	Bosnia	Residential home	7
UCI	F	Iran	Residential home	8
UCI	F	Turkey	Residential home	8
UCI	F	Somalia	Residential home	8
UCI	F	Somalia	Residential home	8
UCI	F	Iraq	Residential home	8
UCI	F	Bosnia	Residential home	7

As indicated in the table, most of the internship interviews recorded were follow-up interviews. This is related to the fact that these interviews were planned well in advance, which often made it easier to arrange the recording of the interviews.

The internship candidates were all female except for one. The distribution of gender does not represent a deliberate or intentional choice on my part; it is simply representative of the distribution in the job-counselling programmes involved. The overrepresentation of women was, in part, related to the fact that most of the recorded candidates were participating in the UCI programme, which focused on residential home caretakers and mainly had female participants.

The candidates were all born outside Denmark and all of them spoke Danish as a second language. Three were from Somalia, three from Bosnia, two from Turkey, two from Iran, two from Iraq and one from Colombia, Morocco, Afghanistan and Lebanon. Again the distribution with regards to country of origin was randomly determined by the job-counselling programmes and the practicalities of arranging the recordings. With respect to the job consultants, the majority were born in Denmark and spoke Danish as a mother tongue, but two of them were born abroad and spoke Danish as a second language with Finnish and Persian as their respective first languages. The employers and the employees were all, except for one, born in Denmark.

The workplaces were different in all of the internship interviews, but because of the aforementioned UCI programme, which focused on residential home caretaking, there was an overrepresentation of interviews at residential home programmes. Although attempts were made to establish contact with, and obtain recordings from, some of the other programmes at UCI that focused on different employment sectors, this was not possible.

There was great variation in the job consultants arranging and participating in the internship interviews, even between different interviews with participants from the same job-counselling programmes. The individual consultants have been assigned a number each. The total number of job consultants involved was eight, with three different job consultants from Væksthuset, and three from UCI, one from Kofods Skole and one from MHTConsult. Four of the job consultants only participated in one interview, two of them participated in two interviews, one of them in three interviews and one of them participated in five interviews.

Appendix 4: Distribution of Cases Across Interviews

The following three tables provide an overview of the number and distribution of interviews in which nationality, language, and religion are made relevant.

Table 5 Cases where nationality or culture is made relevant[3]

	Employer	Employee	Job consultant	Candidate	Total interviews[4]	Total cases[5]
Initiating interview	7	1		6	8	20
Follow-up interview	4		2	2	6	11
Total interviews	11	1	2	7	**14**	31
Total cases	16	1	5	9		31

Table 6 Cases where language is made relevant

	Employer	Employee	Job consultant	Candidate	Total interviews	Total cases
Initiating interview	6	4	1	3	9	23
Follow-up interview	4		4	4	7	17
Total interviews	10	4	5	7	**16**	40
Total cases	19	5	9	7		40

Table 7 Cases where religion is made relevant

	Employer	Employee	Job consultant	Candidate	Total interviews	Total cases
Initiating Interview	4	1			4	5
Follow-up interview					0	0
Total interviews	3	1		1	**4**	5
Total cases	3	1		1		5

The tables displaying the three ways in which the otherness of the candidate is made relevant show that language is the most predominant way. It is made relevant in all of the interviews at one point or another, and often more than once during the interviews, which gives a total of 40 cases. Nationality is almost as predominant, since it is topicalized and made relevant in 14 of the interviews, which corresponds to about 81% of the total number of interviews. Again, there are several interviews in which it is made relevant more than once, which gives a total of 31 cases in which culture or nationality is explicitly topicalized. Finally, religion is a markedly less predominant topic in the interviews, with a total of 5 cases of religion being made relevant, distributed over 4 different interviews. As opposed to the topicalization of language, culture and nationality, which occur in both initiating and follow-up interviews, the topicalization of religion only occurs in the initiating interviews, and in none of these cases is it introduced by the job consultant.

Notes

(1) The following transcription notations are a simplified and selective version of the transcription conventions developed by Gail Jefferson as described by Atkinson and Heritage, and Hutchby and Wooffitt (Atkinson & Heritage, 1984; Hutchby & Wooffitt, 1998).

(2) The range of information presented in this overview was selected with a view to include some of the many categories and communities of meaning potentially relevant for the reader to create an impression of the corpus of data as a whole. They are not necessarily relevant to the participants, to the structure of the internship interview as presented in Chapter 2 or to the analysis as presented in Chapter 5.

(3) The present table includes orientations towards culture and nationality, although the latter cases do not always seem to involve the former and vice versa. They are combined based on the observation that one was often implying the other.

(4) Duplicate cases from the same interviews have been left out in this figure, which means that the number in this column may be smaller than the sum of the numbers appearing in the columns to the left of it.

(5) Some of the interviews figuring to the left of this column had more than one case of nationality, language, religion or culture being made relevant, which means that the number figuring in this column may exceed the sum of the numbers to the left of it.

References

Adelswärd, V. (1988) *Styles of Succes: On Impression Management as Collaborative Action in Job Interviews*. Vol. 23, *Linköping Studies in Arts and Science*. Linköping: University of Linköping.

Adelswärd, V. (1992) Interviewer styles – on interactive strategies in professional interviews. In J. Wagner and A. Grindsted (eds) *Communication for specific purposes. Fachsprachliche Kommunikation*. Tübingen: Gunter Narr.

Ahearn, L. (2012) *Living Language: An Introduction to Linguistic Anthropology*. Malden: Wiley-Blackwell.

Ahmed, S. (2012) *On Being Included – Racism and Diversity in Institutional Life*. Durham: Duke University Press.

Akinnaso, F.N. and Seabrook Ajirotutu, C. (1982) Performance and ethnic style in job interviews. In J. Gumperz (ed.) *Language and Social Identity*. Cambridge: Cambridge University Press.

Alexander, B.K. (2004) Passing, cultural performance, and individual agency: Performative reflections on black masculine identity. *Cultural Studies <=> Critical Methodologies* 4, 377–404.

Anderson, B. (1991) *Imagined Communities: Reflections on the Origin and Spread of Nationalism*. London: Verso. Original edition, 1983.

Antaki, C. (1994) *Explaining and Arguing: The Social Organization of Accounts*. London: Sage.

Antaki, C. and Wetherell, M. (1999) Show concessions. *Discourse Studies* 1, 7–27.

Antaki, C., Barnes, R. and Leudar, I. (2005) Diagnostic formulations in psychotherapy. *Discourse Studies* 7 (6), 627–47.

Atkinson, J. M. and Heritage, J. (1984) *The Structure of Social Action: Studies in Conversation Analysis*. Cambridge: Cambridge University Press.

Auer, P. (1998) Learning how to play the game: An investigation of role-played job interviews in East Germany. *Text* 18, 7–38.

Auer, P. and Kern, F. (2001) Three ways of analysing communication between East and West Germans as intercultural communication. In A.D. Luzio, S. Günthner and F. Orletti (eds) *Culture in Communication: Analyses of Intercultural Situations*. Amsterdam, Philadelphia: John Benjamins.

Bakhtin, M.M. (1981) Discourse in the novel. In M. Holquist (ed.) *The Dialogic Imagination: Four Essays by M.M. Bakhtin*. Austin: University of Texas Press.

Baptiste, M.C. and Seig, M.T. (2007) Training the guardians of America's gate: Discourse-based lessons from naturalization interviews. *Journal of Pragmatics* 39 (11), 1919–1941.

Bekendtgørelse af lov om en aktiv beskæftigelsesindsats, 1074 (07/09/2007).

Bekendtgørelse af lov om en aktiv beskæftigelsesindsats, 439 (29/05/2008).

Bekendtgørelse af lov om en aktiv socialpolitik, 1009 (24/10/2005).

Bekendtgørelse af lov om integration af udlændinge i Danmark (integrationsloven), 902.

Bekendtgørelse af lov om integration af udlændinge i Danmark (integrationsloven), 1593 (14/12/2007).

Bekendtgørelse af Udlændingeloven, 808.

Billig, M. (1991) *Ideology and Opinions. Studies in Rhetorical Psychology*. London: Sage.

Billig, M. (1996) *Arguing and Thinking: A Rhetorical Approach to Social Psychology*. Cambridge: Cambridge University Press. Original edition, 1987.

Billig, M. (1999) Whose terms? Whose ordinariness? Rhetoric and ideology in conversation analysis. *Discourse & Society* 10 (4), 543–582.

Blackledge, A. (2005) *Discourse and Power in a Multilingual World*. Amsterdam: John Benjamins Publishing Company.

Blommaert, J. (2013) *Ethnography, Superdiversity and Linguistic Landscapes: Chronicles of Complexity*. Bristol: Multilingual Matters.

Blommaert, J. (ed.) (1999) *Language Ideological Debates*. Berlin: Mouton de Gruyter.

Blommaert, J. and Backus, A. (2013) Superdiverse repertoires and the individual. In I. de Saint-Georges and J.J. Weber (eds) *Multilingualism and Multimodality*. Rotterdam: Sense Publishers.

Bremer, K., Roberts, C., Vasseur, M.T., Simonot, M. and Broeder, P. (1996) *Achieving Understanding*. London: Longman.

Britzman, D.P., Santiago-Válles, K., Jiménez-Múños, G. and Lamash, L.M. (1993) Slips that show and tell: Fashioning multicultural as a problem of representation In C. McCarthy and W. Crichlow (eds) *Race, Identity and Representation in Education*. New York: Routledge.

Brouwer, C.E. (2003) Word searches in NNS-NS interaction: Opportunities for language learning? *The Modern Language Journal* 87 (4), 534–545.

Brown, A. (2003) Interviewer variation and the co-construction of speaking proficiency. *Language Testing* 20 (1), 1–25.

Campbell, S. and Roberts, C. (2007) Migration, ethnicity and competing discourses in the job interview: Synthesizing the institutional and personal. *Discourse & Society* 18 (3), 243–271.

Carbin, M. and Tornhill, S. (2004) Intersektionalitet – et oanvändbart begrepp? *Kvinnovetenskaplig Tidskrift* 3, 111–114.

Cirkulæreskrivelse om naturalisation, 9 (2006).

Collins, P.H. (1998) 'It's all in the family': Intersections of gender, race, and nation. *Hypatia* 13 (3), 62–82.

Danmarks Statistik (2007) Indvandreres beskæftigelse er øget. *NYT*.

Day, D. (1994) Tang's dilemma and other problems: Ethnification processes at some multicultural workplaces. *Pragmatics* 4, 315–336.

Day, D. (1998) Being ascribed, and resisting, membership of an ethnic group. In C. Antaki and S. Widdicombe (eds) *Identities in Talk*. London: Sage.

Day, D. (2006) Ethnic and social groups and their linguistic categorization. In K. Buehrig and J.D. ten Thie (eds) *Beyond Misunderstanding: The Linguistic Analysis of Intercultural Discourse*. The Hague: John Benjamins.

Derrida, J. (1972) *La Différance*. Paris: Les Éditions de Minuit.

Derrida, J. (1981) *Positions*. Chicago: The University of Chicago Press. Original edition, 1972.

Drew, P. (2003) Comparative analysis of talk-in-interaction in different institutional settings: A sketch. In P. Glen, C.D. LeBaron and J. Mandelbaum (eds) *Studies in Language and Social Interaction*. London: Lawrence Erlbaum Associates.

Drew, P. and Heritage, J. (1992) Analysing talk at work: An introduction. In P. Drew and J. Heritage (eds) *Talk at Work: Interaction in Institutional Settings* (pp. 3–65). Cambridge: Cambridge University Press.

Drew, P. and Heritage, J. (eds) (1992) *Talk at Work: Interaction in Institutional Settings*. Cambridge: Cambridge University Press.

Edwards, D. and Potter, J. (1992) *Discursive Psychology, Inquiries in Social Construction*. London: Sage Publications.

Erickson, F. and Shultz, J. (1982) *The Counselor as Gatekeeper: Social Interaction in Interviews*. New York: Academic Press.

Fairclough, N. (1995) *Critical Discourse Analysis: The Critical Study of Language*. London: Longman.

Fairclough, N. (2001) *Language and Power*. London: Longman.

Festinger, L. (1954) A theory of social comparison processes. *Human Relations 7*, 117–40.

Firth, A. (1996) The discursive accomplishment of normality: On 'lingua franca' English and conversation analysis. *Journal of Pragmatics 6*, 237–259.

Fosgerau, C. (2007) Samtaler med politiet, Department of Nordic Languages, Copenhagen University, Copenhagen.

Fosgerau, C.F. (2013) The co-construction of understanding in Danish naturalisation interviews. *International Journal of Bilingualism 17* (2), 221–236.

Foucault, M. (1977) *Discipline and Punish*. London: Tavistock.

Foucault, M. (1978) *The History of Sexuality*. Harmondsworth: Allen Lane, Penguin Books.

Foucault, M. (1980) *Power/Knowledge*. Translated by C. Gordon, L. Marshall, J. Mepham and K. Soper. Brighton: Harvester Wheatleaf.

Gardner, R. and Wagner, J. (2004) *Second Language Conversations: Studies of Communication in Everyday Settings*. London: Continuum.

Garfinkel, H. (1967) *Studies in Ethnomethodology*. Englewood Cliffs: Prentice-Hall.

Garfinkel, H. and Sacks, H. (1970) On formal structures of practical actions. In J.C. McKinney and E.A. Tiryakian (eds) *Theoretical Sociology*. New York: Appleton-Century-Crofts.

Gergen, K.J. (1991) *The Saturated Self: Dilemmas of Identity in Contemporary Life*. New York: Basic Books.

Gergen, K.J. (1994) *Realities and Relationships: Soundings in Social Construction*. Cambridge, MA: Harvard University Press.

Gergen, K.J. (2001) *Social Construction in Context*. London: Sage.

Goffman, E. (1963) *Stigma: Notes on the Management of Spoiled Identity*. New Jersey: Prentice-Hall Inc.

Goffman, E. (1981) *Forms of Talk*. Oxford: Blackwell.

Goodwin, C. and Duranti, A. (1994) Introduction. In A. Duranti and C. Goodwin (eds) *Rethinking Context: Language as an Interactive Phenomenon*. Cambridge: Cambridge University Press.

Gramsci, A. (1971) *Prison Notebooks*. London: Lawrence and Wishart.

Gumperz, J.J. (1964) Linguistic and social interaction in two communities. *American Anthropologist 66* (6), 137–153.

Gumperz, J.J. (1972) Introduction. In J. Gumperz and D. Hymes (eds) *Directions in Sociolinguistics: The Ethnography of Communication*. USA: Holt, Rinehart and Winston, Inc.

Gumperz, J.J. (1982a) *Discourse Strategies*. Cambridge: Cambridge University Press.

Gumperz, J.J. (ed.) (1982b) *Language and Social Identity. Studies in Interactional Sociolinguistics 2*. Cambridge: Cambridge University Press.

Gumperz, J.J. and Hymes, D. (eds) (1972) *Directions in Sociolinguistics*. USA: Holt, Rinehart and Winston, Inc.

Gumperz, J.J., Roberts, C. and Jupp, T.C. (1979) *Crosstalk: A Study of Cross-Cultural Communication*. London: National Centre for Industrial Language Training in association with BBC.

Hall, S. (1997a) *Representation: Cultural Representations and Signifying Practices. Culture, Media And Identities.* London: Sage in association with The Open University.

Hall, S. (1997b) The spectacle of the other. In M. Wetherell, S. Taylor and S.J. Yates (eds) *Discourse Theory and Practice – a Reader.* London: Sage Publications.

Hall, S. and Du Gay, P. (1996) *Questions of Cultural Identity.* London: Sage Publications.

Hastrup, K. (2004) *Kultur – det fleksible fællesskab.* Århus: Århus Universitetsforlag.

Henkel, H. (2010) Fundamentally Danish? The Muhammad cartoon crisis as transitional drama. *Human Architecture* 8 (2), 67–81.

Hepburn, A. and Wiggins, S. (2005) Developments in discursive psychology. *Discourse & Society* 16 (5), 595–601.

Heritage, J. (1984a) A change-of-state token and aspects of its sequential placement. In J. M. Atkinson and J. Heritage (eds) *Structures of Social Action: Studies in Conversation Analysis.* Cambridge: Cambridge University Press.

Heritage, J. (1984b) *Garfinkel and Ethnomethodology.* Cambridge: Polity Press.

Heritage, J. (2006) Oh-prefaced responses to inquiry. In P. Drew and J. Heritage (eds) *Conversation Analysis.* London: Sage.

Heritage, J. and Watson, D.R. (1979) Formulations as conversational objects. In G. Psathas (ed.) *Everyday Language: Studies in Ethnomethodology.* New York: Irvington. Original edition, 1979.

Hester, S. and Eglin, P. (1997a) Membership categorization analysis: An introduction. In S. Hester and P. Eglin (eds) *Culture in Action: Studies in Membership Categorization Analysis.* Washington, DC: International Institute for Ethnomethodology and Conversation Analysis & University Press of America.

Hester, S. and Eglin, P. (1997b) The reflexive constitution of category, predicate and context. In S. Hester and P. Eglin (eds) *Culture in Action. Studies in Membership Categorization Analysis.* Washington, DC: International Institute for Ethnomethodology and Conversation Analysis & University Press of America.

Hester, S. and Eglin, P. (eds) (1997c) *Culture in Action. Studies in Membership Categorisation Analysis.* Washington, DC: International Institute for Ethnomethodology and Conversation Analysis & University Press of America.

Hjarnø, J. (1990) Indvandrernes situation på det danske arbejdsmarked: Strukturændringernes og stereotypiernes onde cirkel. *Politica* 22, 320–331.

Holmes, J. (2007) Monitoring organisational boundaries: Diverse discourse strategies used in gatekeeping. *Journal of Pragmatics* 39 (11), 1993–2016.

Holquist, M. (ed.) (1981) *The Dialogic Imagination: Four Essays by M.M. Bakhtin.* Austin: University of Texas Press.

Hummelgaard, H., Husted, L., Skyt Nielsen, H., Rosholm, M. and Smith, N. (2002) *Uddannelse og arbejde for andengenerationsindvandrere.* København: Amternes og Kommunernes Forskningsinstitut.

Hutchby, I. and Wooffitt, R. (1998) *Conversation Analysis.* Cambridge: Polity.

Hymes, D. (1972) Models of the interaction of language and social life. In J. Gumperz and D. Hymes (eds) *Directions in Sociolinguistics: The Ethnography of Communication.* USA: Holt, Rinehart and Winston, Inc.

Hymes, D. (1974) *Foundations in Sociolinguistics: An Ethnographic Approach.* London: Tavistock.

Jameelah, M.X. (2011) Body politicking and the phenomenon of 'passing'. *Feminism & Psychology* 21 (1), 138–143.

Jupp, T.C, Roberts, C. and Cook-Gumperz, J. (1982) Language and disadvantage: The hidden process. In J.J. Gumperz (ed.) *Language and Social Identity*. Cambridge: Cambridge University Press.

Kasper, G. and Ross, S.J. (2007) Multiple questions in oral proficiency interviews. *Journal of Pragmatics* 39 (11), 2045–2070.

Kerekes, J. (2006) Winning an interviewer's trust in a gatekeeping encounter. *Language in Society* 35 (01), 27–57.

Kerekes, J. (2007) The co-construction of a gatekeeping encounter: An inventory of verbal actions. *Journal of Pragmatics* 39, 1942–1973.

Khanna, N. and Johnson, C. (2010) Passing as black: Racial identity work among biracial Americans. *Social Psychology Quarterly* 73 (4), 380–397.

Kirilova, M. (2012) All dressed up and nowhere to go: Linguistic, cultural and ideological aspects of job interviews with second language speakers of danish, University of Copenhagen.

Kjærbeck, S. (1998) En undersøgelse af diskursorganisation i danske og mexikanske forhandlinger: Turn-taking og struktur i diskursenheder. *Copenhagen Working Papers in LSP* 5, 1–222.

Kjærbeck, S. (2003) Hvad er en vellykket aktiveringssamtale?: En undersøgelse af myndiggørelse og umyndiggørelse i handleplanssamtaler. In B. Asmuss and J. Steensig (eds) *Samtalen på arbejde: konversationsanalyse og kompetenceudvikling*. Frederiksberg: Samfundslitteratur.

Lepper, G. (2000) *Categories in Text and Talk*. London: Sage Publications.

Levinson, S.C. (1992) Activity types and language. In P. Drew and J. Heritage (eds) *Talk at Work: Interaction in Institutional Settings*. Cambridge: Cambridge University Press.

Liep, J. and Fog Olwig, K. (1994) *Komplekse liv: Kulturel mangfoldighed i Danmark*. København: Akademisk Forlag.

Long, M.H. (1983) Native speaker/Non-native speaker conversation and the negotiation of input. *Applied Linguistics* 4, 126–141.

Lov om danskuddannelse til voksne udlændinge m.fl., 375 (28/05/2003).

Lov om en aktiv beskæftigelsesindsats. 419 (10/06/2003).

Lov om integration af udlændinge i Danmark (Integrationslov), 474 (01/07/1998).

Lykke, N. (2003) Intersektionalitet – ett användbart begrepp för genusforskningen. *Kvinnovetenskaplig Tidskrift* 1: 47–56.

Mazeland, H. and Berenst, J. (2006) Sorting pupils in a report-card meeting: Categorization in a situated activity system. *Text and Talk* 28 (1), 55–78.

Miles, R. (1989) *Racism*. London: Routledge.

Mondada, L. (2004) Ways of 'doing being plurilingual' in international work meetings. In R. Gardner and J. Wagner (eds) *Second Language Conversations*. London: Continuum.

Nekby, L. and Özcan, G. (2006) Utbildning och arbetsmarknad – är den svenska utbildningen lika för alla? Norrköping: Integrationsverket.

Nielsen, M.F. (2002) Nå! En skiftemarkør med mange funktioner. In K. Kristensen (ed.) *Studier i Nordisk 2000–2001. Selskab for Nordisk Filologi. Foredrag og årsberetning*. København: Selskab for Nordisk Filologi.

Nielsen, M.F., Steensig, J. and Wagner, J. (2005) Konversationsanalyse i Danmark *Nydanske Studier* 34–35:182–216.

Nielsen, S.B. and Nielsen, M.F. (2005) *Samtaleanalyse*. Fredriksberg: Forlaget Samfundslitteratur.

Pomerantz, A. (1984) Agreeing and disagreeing with assessments: Some features of preferred/dispreferred turn shapes. In J.M. Atkinson and J. Heritage (eds) *Structures of Social Action: Studies in Conversation Analysis*. Cambridge: Cambridge Univesity Press.

Pomerantz, A. (1986) Extreme case formulations: A way of legitimizing claims. *Human Studies* 9, 219–229.

Potter, J. (1996) *Representing Reality: Discourse, Rhetoric and Social Construction*. London: Sage.

Potter, J. (2005) Making psychology relevant. *Discourse & Society* 16 (5), 739–747.

Potter, J. and Wetherell, M. (1987) *Discourse and Social Psychology: Beyond Attitudes and Behaviour*. London: Sage Publications.

Rampton, B. (1999) Sociolinguistics and cultural studies: New ethnicities, liminality and interaction. *Social Semiotics* 9 (3), 355–374.

Rampton, B. (2003) Hegemony, social class and stylisation. *Pragmatics* 13 (1), 49–84.

Rampton, B. (2005) Late modernity and social class: The view from sociolinguistics. In B. Rampton (ed.) *Working Papers in Urban Language and Literacies*. London: Kings College London.

Rampton, B. (2006) *Language in Late Modernity: Interaction in an Urban School. Studies in Interactional Sociolinguistics 22*. Cambridge: Cambridge University Press.

Rampton, B., Harris, R. and Small, L. (2006) The meanings of ethnicity in discursive interaction: Some data and interpretations from ethnographic sociolinguistics. In *ESRC Identities and Social Action Programme*. London.

Rezaei, S. (2005) Det duale arbejdsmarked i et velfærdsstatsligt perspektiv – et studie af dilemmaet mellem uformel økonomisk praksis og indvandreres socioøkonomiske integration. Roskilde: Roskilde Universitet.

Risager, K. (2008) Nyankommen i Danmark. In M.S. Pedersen and H. Haberland (eds) *Sprogliv – Sprachleben. Festskrift – Festschrift. Karen Sonne Jakobsen 60 år*. Roskilde: Institut for Kultur og Identitet: Roskilde Universitetscenter.

Risager, K. (2011) Tolken i det interkulturelle forskningsinterview. *Kult* Vol. 9. pp.87–105.

Roberts, C. and Campbell, S. (2005) Fitting stories into boxes: Rhetorical and textual restraints on candidates' performances in British job-interviews. *Journal of Applied Linguistics* 2, 45–74.

Roberts, C. and Campbell, S. (2006) *Talk on Trial: Job-Interviews, Language and Ethnicity. Research Summary: Department for Work and Pension*. Leeds: Corporate Document Services.

Roberts, C. and Moss, B. (2004) Presentation of self and symptoms in primary care consultations involving patients from non-English speaking backgrounds. *Communication and Medicine* 11 (2), 159–170.

Roberts, C. and Sarangi, S. (eds) (1999) *Talk, Work and Institutional Order: Discourse in Medical, Mediation and Management Settings*. Berlin: Mouton de Gruyter.

Roberts, C. and Sarangi, S. (2005) Theme-oriented discourse analysis of medical encounters. *Medical Education* 39, 632–40.

Roberts, C., Davies, E. and Jupp, T. (1992) *Language and Discrimination: A Study of Communication in Multi-Ethnic Workplaces. Applied Linguistics and Language Study*. London: Longman.

Roberts, C., Moss, B., Wass, V., Sarangi, S. and Jones, R. (2003) Patients with limited English and doctors in general practice: Educational issues *Sir Siegmund Warburg Voluntary Settlement*. Kings College London: London.

Roberts, C., Moss, B., Wass, V., Sarangi, S. and Jones, R. (2005) Misunderstandings: A qualitative study of primary care consultations in multilingual settings, and educational implications. *Medical Education* 39, 465–475.

Rogstad, J. (2001) *Sist blant likemenn? Synlige minoriteter på arbeidsmarkedet..* Oslo: Unipax.

Rosdahl, A. (2006) Integration på arbejdsmarkedet af ikke-vestlige indvandrere og efterkommere: En analyse af chancen for at få vedvarende beskæftigelse blandt langvarige modtagere af kontanthjælp og introduktionsydelse. København: Socialforskningsinstituttet.

Sacks, H. (1972a) An initial investigation of the usability of conversational data for doing sociology. In D. Sudnow (ed.) *Studies in Social Interaction*. New York: The Free Press.

Sacks, H. (1972b) On the analyzability of stories by children. In J. Gumperz and D. Hymes (eds) *Directions in Sociolinguistics*. New York: Holt, Rinehart & Winston.

Sacks, H. (1992) In G. Jefferson (ed.) *Lectures on Conversation*. Malden: Blackwell.

Sacks, H. (1992a) Lecture 6: The MIR membership categorization device. In G. Jefferson (ed.) *Lectures on Conversation*. Cambridge: Blackwell

Sacks, H. (1992b) Lecture 8 'We': category-bound activities. In G. Jefferson (ed.) *Lectures on Conversation*. Cambridge: Blackwell.

Sacks, H., Schegloff, E.A. and Jefferson, G. (1974) A simplest systematics for the organization of turn-taking for conversation. *Language* 50 (4), 696–735.

Saft, S. and Ohara, Y. (2003) Using conversation analysis to track gender ideologies in social interaction: Toward a feminist analysis of a Japanese phone-in consultation TV program. *Discourse and Society* 14 (2), 153–172.

Sahin, G. and Schröder, L. (2007) Närmar sig och fjärmar sig. Uppföljning av indikatorerna för utrikes föddes sysselsättning. Norrköping: Integrationsverket.

Sarangi, S. and Roberts, C. (1999) The dynamics of interactional and institutional orders. In S. Sarangi and C. Roberts (eds) *Talk, Work and Institutional Order*. Berlin, New York: Mouton de Gruyter.

Schegloff, E.A. (1980) Preliminaries to preliminaries: 'Can I ask you a question'. *Sociological Inquiry* 50, 104–53.

Schegloff, E.A. (1982) Discourse as an interactional achievement: Some uses of 'uh huh' and other things that come between sentences. In D. Tannen (ed.) *Analyzing Text and Talk*. Washington D.C.: Georgetown University Press.

Schegloff, E.A. (1997) Whose text? Whose context? *Discourse & Society* 8 (2), 165–187.

Schegloff, E.A. (2007) A tutorial on membership categorization. *Journal of Pragmatics* 39 (3), 462–482.

Scheuer, J. (2001) Recontextualization and communicative styles in job interviews. *Discourse Studies* 3 (2), 223–248.

Schultz-Nielsen, M.L. (2002) Hvorfor er så mange indvandrere uden beskæftigelse? In G.V. Mogensen and P.C. Matthiessen (eds) *Indvandrere og arbejdsmarkedet: Mødet med det danske velfærdssamfund*. København: Rockwool Fondens Forskningsenhed. Spektrum.

Shotter, J. and Gergen, K.J. (1989) *Texts of Identity: Inquiries in Social Construction Series 2*. London: Sage.

Sniad, T. (2007) 'It's not necessarily the words you say…it's your presentation': Teaching the interactional text of the job interview. *Journal of Pragmatics* 39 (11), 1974–1992.

Speer, S.A. (2005) *Gender Talk: Feminism, Discourse and Conversation*. Hove and New York: Routledge.

Speer, S.A. (2009) Passing as a transsexual woman in the gender identity clinic. In M. Wetherell (ed.) *Theorizing Identities and Social Action*. Basingstoke: Palgrave Macmillan.

Speer, S.A. and Green, R. (2007) On passing: The interactional organization of appearance attributions in the psychiatric assessment of transsexual patients. In V. Clarke and E. Peel (eds) *Out in Psychology: Lesbian, Gay, Bisexual, Trans and Queer Perspectives*. Chichester: Wiley.

Speer, S.A. and Parsons, C. (2006) Gatekeeping gender: Some features of the use of hypothetical questions in the psychiatric assessment of transsexual patients. *Discourse and Society* 17 (6), 785–812.

Speer, S.A. and Parsons, C. (2007) 'Suppose you couldn't go any further with treatment, what would you do?' Hypothetical questions in interactions between psychiatrists and transsexual patients. In A. Hepburn and S. Wiggins (eds) *Discursive Research in Practice: New Approaches to Psychology and Interaction*. Cambridge: Cambridge University Press.

Staunæs, D. (2003) Where have all the subjects gone? Bringing together the concepts of intersectionality and subjectification. *NORA* 11, 101–110.

Stokoe, E. (2014) The conversation analytic role-play method (CARM): A method for training communication skills as an alternative to role-play. *Research on Language and Social Interaction* 47 (3), 255–265.

Stokoe, E. and Hepburn, A. (2005) 'You can hear a lot through the walls': Noise formulations in neighbour complaints. *Discourse & Society* 16, 647–73.

Stokoe, E. and Edwards, D. (2007) 'Black this, black that': Racial insults and reported speech in neighbour complaints and police interrogations. *Discourse & Society* 18, 337–72.

Sundberg, G. (2004) *Asymetrier og samförstånd i rekryteringssamtal med andraspråkstalare*. In S. Hellberg (ed.) *Stockholm Studies in Scandinavian Philology*. Stockholm: Almqvist & Wiksell International.

Svennevig, J. (2001) Institutional and conversational modes of talk in bureaucratic consultations. In A. Hvenekilde and J. Nortier (eds) *Meetings at the Crossroads: Studies of Multiculturalism and Multilingualism in Oslo and Utrecht*. Oslo: Novus.

Svennevig, J. (2004) Other-repetition as display of hearing, understanding and emotional stance. *Discourse Studies* 6 (4), 489–516.

Svennevig, J. (2005) Repetisjon og reformulering som forståelsesstrategier i andrespråkssamtaler. In S. Lie (ed.) *MONS 10 Utvalde artikler frå det tiande Møte om norsk språk I Kristiansand 2003*. Kristiansand: Høyskoleforlaget.

Svennevig, J. (2009) Forståelse og sociale relasjoner i håndtering av språkproblemer i andrespråkssamtaler. *Nordand – Nordisk tidsskrift for andrespråksforskning* 4 (2), 35–64.

Svennevig, J. (forthcoming) Reformulation of questions with candidate answers. *International Journal of Bilingualism*.

Tajfel, H. (1981) *Human Groups and Social Categories*. Cambridge: Cambridge University Press.

Trads, S.F. (2000) *Interpersonelle Relationer i Medarbejdersamtaler*. Aalborg: Aalborg Universitetsforlag.

Tranekjær, L. (2011) I praktik som dansker. *Nordand – Nordisk tidsskrift for andrespråksforskning* 6 (1), 7–35.

Tranekjær, L. (2014) Discursive ethnography – a microanalytical perspective on cultural performance and common sense in student counseling interviews. In F. Dervin and K. Risager (eds) *Identity and Interculturaliy – Reflexivity in Research Methodology.* New York: Routledge.

Tranekjær, L. (forthcoming) Laughables as an investigation of co-membership through the negotiation of epistemics. In D.V.D. Mieroop and S. Schnurr (eds) *Identity Struggles at Work.* Amsterdam: John Benjamins.

Turner, J. and Giles, H. (1981) *Intergroup Behaviour.* Oxford: Blackwell.

Vološinov, V.N. (1973) *Marxism and the Philosophy of Language.* Translated by L. Matejka and I.R.Titunik. Cambridge: Harvard University Press.

Wagner, J. (2006) Læring og Integration. *Nordisk Tidsskrift for Andrespråksforskning* 1, 89–104.

Watson, R. (1997) Some general reflections on 'categorization' and 'sequence' in the analysis of conversation. In S. Hester and P. Eglin (eds) *Culture in Action: Studies in Membership Categorization Analysis.* Washington, DC: International Institute for Ethnomethodology and Conversation Analysis & University Press of America.

Wenger, E. (1999) *Communities of Practice: Learning, Meaning and Identity.* Cambridge: Cambridge University Press.

Wetherell, M. (1998) Positioning and interpretative repertoires: Conversation analysis and post-structuralism in dialogue. *Discourse & Society* 9 (3), 387–412.

Wetherell, M. (2005) Methods for studying multiple identities: Intersectionality, practice and troubled and untroubled subject positions. In *Methods in Dialogue – ESRC Seminar Series.* Cambridge.

Wetherell, M. and Potter, J. (1988) Discourse analysis and the identification of interpretative repertoires. In C. Antaki (ed.) *Analysing Everyday Explanation.* London: Sage.

Wetherell, M. and Potter, J. (1992) *Mapping the Language of Racism.* Hertfordshire: Harvester Wheatleaf.

Wodak, R. (1989) *Language, Power and Ideology: Studies in Political Discourse.* Amsterdam: John Benjamins.

Wooffitt, R. (2005) *Conversation Analysis and Discourse Analysis: A Comparative and Critical Introduction.* London: Sage Publications.

Zimmerman, D.H. (1998) Identity, context and interaction. In C. Antaki and S. Widdicombe (eds) *Identities in Talk.* London: Sage.

Author Index

Subject Index